THE GOLDEN FLEECERS

To deceive is ever to enchant.
　　　　　　　—PLATO

WALTER WAGNER
THE GOLDEN FLEECERS

1966
DOUBLEDAY & COMPANY, INC.
GARDEN CITY, NEW YORK

A portion of Chapter Two is drawn from
"The Man Who Talked Riches Out of Rock"
by the author which originally appeared
in TRUE Magazine and is used by permission.

For my mother, Anne Wagner, with love

CONTENTS

THE GOLDEN FLEECERS

I

CALIFORNIA, HERE I CON

Southern Californians are not the most sophisticated of
Americans.

—NEIL MORGAN

*They came—traveling light—in the first sidewheeler to touch the
shores of San Francisco; they came by shanks' mare, straddling
jackass ponies a size too small, on leopard-spotted Appaloosas,
albinos and strutting Arabian stallions; in the wake of the forty-
niners they came, past the bleached bones of those who hadn't
the wit, the grit or the luck to make it; they came aboard Cones-
togas across the Rockies, some of them men to match the mountains.*

*They came on the Central Pacific with the hammer blows of
Promontory's golden spike still echoing, and they billowed in on
the howling tails of the Santa Anas.*

*They came wearing silk shirts and satin smiles, flashing leather
boots, lavender ties, diamond stickpins and velvet-collared suits.
Mostly, their fingernails were clean.*

*From bleeding Kansas they came, and cannon-shocked Geor-
gia, snowbirds down from the Montana peaks and eagles up from
the Panhandle prairies; they came from the tank towns and the
two-fisted towns that already had been tamed, following and
leading the salt-of-the-earth, backbone-of-America Iowans, Ohi-
oans, Minnesotans and all the other honest men making the glory
trek to California.*

*They moved south—still traveling light—after night-riding, day-
hanging vigilantes began to calm things down in San Francisco.
They knew it was time to move when their patron saints, Crocker,*

Huntington, Stanford and Hopkins, were tarred with the brush of respectability.

They came to El Pueblo de Nuestra Señora la Reina de los Angeles de Porciuncula, the toughest town west of Santa Fe, still a maidenhead of opportunity.

They came for a fast look, and stayed for a lifetime.

Thousands came, then uncounted thousands more—boomers, shakers, minnesingers, sharks, pitchmen, imposters and pretenders, thieves, swindlers, rogues, quacks, cultists, mountebanks and humbuggers.

They came with a lust larger than life, men of charisma, style, color and flamboyance. They charmed, lured, seduced, soothed, outwitted, conjured, hypnotized, fascinated, bewitched, enchanted and captivated. With glittering talk, they breathed new hope into the dreams of the thousands who didn't strike it rich.

They came, trading the credulous a lightning rod for an overcoat; they rented their New Orleans hustlers as Paris whores and got twice the price; they strung oranges on desert Joshua trees and sold them for citrus groves; and because the honest immigrants expected it, they salted the streets with gold and thousands dropped off the wagon trains; they came with McGuffey educations and passed out Ph.D.'s for a price; they built the cities and boulevards, healed the sick, buried the dead, gave the dis-spirited religion, wooed the widows, created a folklore of their own.

Impatient men all, they invented what they did not find—mountains of diamonds, rivers of oil and cities of milk and honey. Some endured and prospered. Some, because they knew no other way, tore down what they had built and started again for the sheer hell of it.

*They came, ever traveling light, and the best of them laughed themselves to riches because nobody had a dictionary and nobody understood the brazen code of their house—*Caveat Emptor!

"United Industries of Canada is going to make each of you gentlemen wealthy," said Harry Bell in an impeccable British accent. "The stock split expected within the next three months will definitely, as you Americans are fond of saying, put you all on Easy Street."

Lieutenant W. D. (Tex) White snapped off the tape recorder.

The gadgets and the times now are jet age, but the enemy is still the same.

A big, easygoing man, the lieutenant stood in a borrowed college classroom in East Los Angeles, giving a remarkable lesson to a remarkable group of students.

"Harry Bell was one of the shrewdest con artists we've had in southern California, and that's saying something," he told the class with a sigh. "Harry was born in Pasadena and picked up his accent from watching Ronald Colman movies. It took us twelve years to nail him. He probably sold more than a million shares in his imaginary corporation. What you've just heard is a recording of his standard pitch to investors a couple of years ago at one of our better country clubs. The night this was taped—by the only suspicious citizen in the crowd—Harry ran up a score of one hundred twenty thousand dollars in stock sales for his phony company."

The case history of con man Harry Bell, including the replay of his voice in mid-pitch, is part of the lesson plan of an unprecedented attempt to hold the line against the tide of bunco brigands washed up on the shores of Los Angeles since the end of World War II. Formally tagged "Fraud Investigation," it is a finger-in-the-dike operation of the Bureau of Investigation, the agency of the Los Angeles County District Attorney's Office charged with the responsibility of coping with major fraud.

The first course of its kind in the nation, it is taught by Lieutenant White and several other veterans of the bureau's bunco wars to picked lawmen from every one of the county's incorporated cities. A passing grade requires successful breasting of midterm and final examinations. On completion, it earns two units of college credit for each of the officers.

"In fraud cases, we usually know who our man is," Lieutenant White tells his students. "The problem is gathering evidence against him that will stand up in court. An even more basic problem is simply to be sure that a bunco crime has been committed."

During the semester the lesson plan touches on the whole imaginative repertoire of the modern confidence man—theft by trick and device, false pretenses, embezzlement, altering and falsifying corporate records, welfare frauds, false insurance claims, auto transactions, consumer and real-estate frauds, misrepresentation by building contractors, corporate securities law, investments in oil and mining ventures.

So aware is Los Angeles officialdom that the city is a happy hunting ground for con men that the issue spills over into local politics.

Recently one local candidate for public office charged that the incumbent "practically ignores" consumer fraud.

"If elected," he declared, "I would clamp down on bunco artists instead of allowing them to make this county their haven."

State Attorney General Thomas C. Lynch makes an even stronger case. "California is the con capital of the world, and southern California is the prime target for consumer frauds in the United States."

To help fight the con men, Lynch has established a unique statewide network to monitor their activities.

"We have fifty-eight district attorneys' offices, all of whom operate independently," he explains. "Ordinarily, in local crime—a murder or holdup—there's no necessity for coordination between offices. But to combat bunco we are now acting as a central clearinghouse to gather and disseminate information to prosecute these cases."

Nevertheless, the Argus-eyed men of the bureau and the attorney general's monitoring network are often powerless against the majority of scam men because less than 40 per cent of all bunco crime, according to official estimates, is reported to the authorities. A "scam" is any scheme to defraud.

Bunco is the iceberg of the criminal sea, the major portion of it unseen and unknown to any law enforcement agency. Most victims are too chagrined to admit they have been taken. Says Lynch: "The shame and humiliation and stupidity of what they've done has so appalled them that they simply do not tell us about it."

A sizable portion of the victims are unaware that they have been taken. They write off their losses as a legitimate business proposition that didn't pan out. Many exhibit a dogged, unshakable faith that their money would multiply faster than the birth rate of India if the law would stop its harassment of the "decent, honest businessmen" who have promised them a wedge of a pie-in-the-sky promotion.

An Imperial Valley vegetable grower who had pumped $90,000 into a series of nonexistent oil wells stubbornly refused to testify at the trial of the con man who had been successfully bleeding him for ten years. The grower's gullibility quotient set some sort of record since investigators showed him evidence that the southern California county in which the wells allegedly existed was a geographical impossibility. The county, mythical as the alleged oil wells, was not even on the map.

The district attorney's office of Los Angeles County is the largest prosecuting agency in the United States. It is also the busiest, handling more than 100,000 criminal cases a year. It has a reputation as one of the toughest in the country and is proud of its 90 per cent conviction rate.

Traditionally, its philosophy has been one of hard practicality. "We are not policemen, sheriffs, social workers or educators. We are prosecutors, lawyers for 'The People' and our job is to fight crime in the courts," according to former Chief Deputy District Attorney Manley J. Bowler.

To fuel that fight in the courts, the Bureau of Investigation was established in 1913. It is the detective arm of the D.A.'s office; its major function is to provide evidence for the prosecution in cases where local facilities are inadequate. In the fight against fraud, it has become the Chinese Wall seeking to hold back the hordes of con men.

The investigators, the backbone of the bureau, are a comparative handful of civil service field men, the professionals assigned to match wits with the canniest of all criminal adversaries.

A crackerjack elite among lawmen, investigators are carefully chosen for the bureau from the hundreds who apply each year for places in its ranks. Bright, energetic, talented, most are college-trained and have an average of five years' experience in police work before reaching the bureau.

The investigator's life is seldom in danger, even when, as often happens, he works under cover. He rarely uses his service revolver. His whole approach is cerebral. Routinely, he juggles more than a dozen cases at a time. Cruising the city in an unmarked car, he will, on a typical day, check leads on at least half a dozen cases in various stages of development.

Inch by inch, the investigator builds the meticulous case that is often followed line for line and word for word by the deputy district attorney assigned to prosecute in court.

But the investigator's ranks are numerically small, and the forces and circumstances arrayed against him and the citizenry he does his best to keep unconned, are awesomely beyond control.

Fraud is as old as the world—and to beleaguered Los Angeles it only seems as if the crime is a local monopoly. There was misrepresentation in the Garden of Eden. The architect of the treasury of Rameses III, according to Herodotus, built a secret passage to siphon the gold of his master. Crooked dice have been found in the tombs of Pharaohs.

"All through history we find the evil of fraud and man trying to protect himself against the swindler, the liar, and the cheat with negligible success," Inspector J. G. E. Murray of the Royal Canadian Mounted Police notes in the *The Journal of Criminal Law*. "Individuals practised fraud as a profession in ancient and medieval times. Throughout the ages men of glib tongue and lacking in moral sense have practised deception upon their fellows for their own personal advantage and gain."

But in southern California never have so many practiced so much deception upon so many of their fellow men for so much personal gain and advantage. No one knows how much they milk from the local economy. Official estimates range up to $100,000,-000 a year. But any figure is misleading because of those six victims in ten who prefer to mask their losses in dented bank balances rather than face the ego-shattering truth that they have been outsmarted.

Why the magic attraction of con men to Los Angeles?

The conditions are perfect—it offers chaos, cash, consumers, climate and cooperative courts.

The area has a highly mobile, restless population. Few householders know their neighbors. Few live in one place for very long. Los Angeles is a raging disarray of bulldozers, roaring freeways, shimmering acres of tracts, a diverse sprawling 4071 square mile county of 76 cities, 103 districts and 373 special districts.

"The bunco men are not going to go out and develop a new territory when they have one ready made in California," says Attorney General Lynch.

When it comes to cash, prosperity is not just around the corner. It is standing on every street corner and lounging at every bar, history's fattest paycheck in its jeans and capris, looking for action. The average annual income of Los Angeles families is almost $9000, a total package of $20,000,000,000 a year.

The fabled westward tilt that has made California the most populous state in the nation, with the growth of the southern part of the state outstripping the north almost two to one, has served to expand the market for hawkers of all goods and services, including those of the con men. The population of Los Angeles has tripled since 1950 to over six million, and before 1980 another three million will settle in, an unending herd of potential sheep ready to be shorn by the golden fleece men.

Southern California is the "place in the sun" of the American dream. Despite the smog, the climate is by far the most attractive feature of Los Angeles, perhaps the only feature the professional boosters and real-estate developers haven't oversold.

But the 328 rainless days a year and temperatures that average a comfortable 65 degrees provide an equally hospitable climate to the lawless. Southern California sun helps make Los Angeles "one of the most criminally active cities in the nation." So attests the local office of the FBI. "Crime and the fight against crime is basically the same everywhere. But the warm weather provides an added inducement to criminals fleeing Eastern cities."

Crime has increased five times faster than the population, and the citizens of Los Angeles understandably fret over the frightening upward curve of murder, rape, narcotics cases, robbery, juvenile delinquency and the hot-fingered lunatics who regularly try to burn the place down.

Even the most conscientious of citizens has little time to study the mounting curve of the fraud charts. Moreover, Los Angeles has been historically tolerant of the bizarre, and to the average citizen the con man is still something of an eccentric, a source of anecdote, a joke quickly told, enjoyed and forgotten.

Judge Roy Bean, the renowned Texas jurist ("The law west of the Pecos"), learned the trade of judicial con man in the 1850s while working in Los Angeles as a ranger. "The corpse is fined forty dollars for carrying a concealed weapon," is a classic bit of Bean's prairie justice that has amused generations of southern Californians.

Two members of the City Council were arrested in the 1920s for fraud at mid-point of a council meeting. Immediately after the offending officials were removed from chambers, the councilmen continued their august deliberations. The town laughed. No one wrote an angry letter to the editor. It never occurred to anyone to be shocked.

In late 1964, faculty gatherings in the city's universities were enlivened with the gay tale of a mortgage broker, audacious as the hoary con men who specialized in selling the Brooklyn Bridge. He had promoted himself into a rarefied scale of living that included a $250,000 mansion in Bel-Air and ten-dollar haircuts by the simple device of peddling a hallowed $400,000 hunk of the Westwood campus of U.C.L.A.

Aside from the tolerance of the man in the street, the most striking advantage the con man has going for him in Los Angeles is the tolerance of the courts and a body of Santa Claus statutes.

In California law, there is no such crime as fraud. Con men are generally prosecuted under provisions of the penal code which defines grand theft.

"Every person who shall feloniously steal, take, carry, lead, or drive away the personal property [of a value exceeding $200] . . . by any false or fraudulent representation or pretense, defraud any other person of money, labor or real or personal property, or who causes or procures others to report falsely of his wealth or mercantile character and . . . obtains credit and thereby fraudulently gets or obtains possession of money, property, or obtains the labor or services of another, is guilty of [grand] theft."

The quaint provisions of Penal Code 487 also define grand theft as stealing more than fifty dollars' worth of "domestic fowls, avocados, olives, citrus or deciduous fruits, nuts and artichokes." And a holdover from frontier days makes it a felony under state law to abscond with a "horse, mare, gelding, any bovine animal, any caprine animal, jack, jenny, sheep, lamb, hog, sow boar, gilt, barrow or pig."

Thus, the con man who appropriates a sow boar or several million dollars' worth of property faces an identical penalty. "Grand theft," according to Penal Code 489, "is punishable by imprisonment in the county jail for not more than one year or in the state prison for not more than ten years."

Multiple counts of grand theft must be proved in court to take the scam men out of action for any appreciable length of time. In practice, however, even on multiple-count convictions, sentences run concurrently rather than consecutively. Most con artists serve only the minimum jolt of their one to ten, carefully collecting the five days a month clipped off their sentences for good behavior. And their time-honored custom is to use the respite in prison to hatch new scams or perfect old ones.

"Judges and the people themselves look upon a crime against property as not being nearly so serious as a crime against a person," says one inspector in the bureau.

"An armed robber who walks into a liquor store and steals ten dollars will get San Quentin. But a bunco artist can steal $100,000 and get straight probation the first time. And this is very often the case because he hasn't committed a crime of violence."

The bureau men are understandably appalled by the psychology of lenience. "The bunco boys don't have a gun in their hands when they steal," the inspector says. "But I've seen the damage they do to some of their victims, people who've worked hard and lost their life savings. This gets us into the violin music and hearts and flowers, but God damn it, it's true.

"Like the car dealer or the furniture manufacturer, the professional bunk deals in volume. Most of them would prefer to take ten pigeons for $2000 each than one sucker for $20,000. But no one thinks of the harm done to the ten little guys, their families, kids and jobs."

Robert J. Bauer, president of the Los Angeles Better Business Bureau, adds that "penalties meted out by the courts in commercial fraud cases are so light that they represent only a small percentage of the money acquired through misrepresentation."

Ralph Wyatt, president of the Eagle Fabric Company, after being indicted for fraudulent use of the mails, was fined only

$1500, given a suspended jail sentence, and placed on two years probation. Seven of his associates received lesser fines and only one year of probation each.

The outfit lured people into buying knitting machines and promised to buy back the garments they produced. According to postal inspectors, the work-at-home scheme grossed $4,000,000. The machines, imported at a cost of $35, acquired by the company for $95, were sold at $300.

"Hasn't the time come when white-collar bandits should be recognized as such and sentenced accordingly?" Bauer asks. "A suspended sentence and a small fine represent only a tiny percentage of the amount stolen, and is not much of a penalty or a deterrent. In many instances investigation and trial costs the government more than the fine. For the most part, white-collar bandits are con men and the government should not permit them to con it out of imposing appropriate sentences."

Touching another facet of the battle against con men in Los Angeles, Judge Vincent S. Dalsimer says, "The average consumer in this county is subject to greater risks from bunco artistry than in almost any other county in the state, because such frauds are generally treated only as misdemeanors."

Another fact going for the con man is one that embarrasses officials. They are reluctant even to discuss it. It's an open secret, however, around the Los Angeles Civic Center that because the area has grown so rapidly and serious felonies have increased so alarmingly the penitentiaries are overcrowded. "We can't get them all in," one judge admits candidly. "The cells have to be saved for the murderers and the armed robbers. What else can we do?"

Because of the high intelligence of scam men, judges and penologists feel they are susceptible to rehabilitation. The courts and parole boards therefore habitually veer to lenience.

"But almost every bunk man we catch has a record," says a bureau man. "We have found that most of them do not rehabilitate themselves. A few do, but these are usually the ones who haven't been too successful. Generally, it doesn't happen. Usually, we find the hard pro, even during his trial or probation, is out on the street still operating his scam."

One promotor found guilty in 1957 of selling $12,350 in a paper mining venture was sentenced to five years' straight probation. He was nabbed again while still on probation for similar offenses and finally sentenced to two years and a $6000 fine.

"A confirmed con man," says the bureau official, "almost never changes."

The same loot the con man steals usually goes to provide the best defense money can buy. Their lawyers are always first class.

"It boils down to the fact that the Constitution isn't equal for everybody because money does talk," says a hard-bitten, high-ranking bureau officer. "The sharper attorneys know the weaknesses of individual judges. I'm not talking about pay-offs, but about the idiosyncrasies of individual judges. One might be death on wife beaters or drug addicts, but he isn't bothered much by con men. And these attorneys, more times than I care to think about, manage to get their clients into the right courtroom."

He cites the case of a stockbroker the bureau had been chasing down for three years. "He stole at least $2,000,000 and ruined scores of people who trusted him. He had six expensive lawyers, and not only got off, but the only night he spent in jail was the night I booked him!"

"The con man we have today is probably as smart or smarter than the deputy district attorneys who prosecute him," says James B. Morse, assistant chief and twenty-year veteran of the bureau. "We've got men who know the law, but they've got to know what the violations are on every type of bunco crime, every type of conspiracy. It's a Herculean job. The con man researches the law that applies only to his sphere of operations. Using his ability to manipulate people and his understanding of the weaker points of the law, he can make us look silly."

"A lawyer who defends himself has a fool for a client," is an ancient legal maxim that has been disproven in Los Angeles courts numberless times by con men acting as their own attorneys. The supreme con man revels in the give and take of the courtroom. He welcomes the duel of minds, and uses the lance of language to portray himself as a misunderstood white knight.

"Con men are at their best as defendants," says one deputy district attorney.

Many a makeshift lawyer-con man has fought cunningly and often victoriously in his own behalf.

After hearing eleven months of testimony against a real-estate sharpie, who defended himself against charges of bilking 119 homeowners of more than $700,000 by placing phony second mortages against their property, a jury brought in a "Not guilty" verdict.

The judge, still dazed, told the defendant, "I think you have done a remarkable job of conducting your defense."

"Thank you, your honor," he replied, tossing off an epigram worthy of Oscar Wilde, a moment before leaving the courtroom as a free man. "I would like to compliment the jury on the sagacity of its verdict, the prosecutor on the brilliance of his arguments and the bench on the wisdom of its last observation."

The personality and resourcefulness of the con man are ceaseless wonders, even to the lawmen charged with running him down.

"He isn't W. C. Fields any more. The old snake oil salesman has donned suede shoes and black silk suits," says Attorney General Lynch. "They are such affable Americans that they make our astronauts look slightly shifty-eyed and foreign.

"The con men of today are polished, high-pressure salesmen. They're experienced and have been in many lines. They are extremely capable and well-schooled in the psychology of selling. The profits are so enormous that it inspires them to work hard, work cleverly and work fast. There's no mark of the swindler about them. They're well-dressed, well-spoken, well-heeled. They stay at the best hotels and drive the most expensive cars.

"They are a new breed—no question about it."

Says Inspector Claudie D. Hawkins of the bureau: "As a group, they are sociable, good mixers, superb salesmen, well-educated and cultured. You can't take a wino and set him up as a bunco artist. He couldn't talk anyone out of anything. People are becoming smarter and it's getting harder and harder to fool them. That's why the bunk men and their scams have become more sophisticated."

Investigator Donald L. Lundquist views the con man in psychological terms. "Greed isn't their primary motivation. They have a quirk or twist in their ego that makes it absolutely mandatory that they put something over on the other guy in order to exist. The majority of them could make a very substantial legitimate living. They have the intelligence, the background and the ability to make money. But they can't pass up the opportunity to fleece a victim. I think they have to do this to get along each day just as you and I have to eat.

"Ego is their staff of life. They have to be recognized in the same way that a criminal from one of our minority groups will pull a job, walk four blocks to a bar and brag that he's just knocked over a gas station. This drive to show the world how clever or daring he is often leads to a con man's downfall."

One other weakness in the armor of a con man is his *modus operandi*. "The *m.o.* of a professional bunco artist is as distinctive as that of a safe-cracker," says Lundquist. "Once he gets a scam that works he will, as a rule, stick with it. He may have some flourishes, a little deviation, but basically it's always the same. Since nothing succeeds like success, he will retain that *m.o.* throughout his entire life of crime."

Big con, southern California style, has been customized. There is a scam to fit every type of victim, high or low income, urbanite and suburbanite, young or old, the dropout and the professor, the born suckers and the lifelong sophisticates.

"It's true that a great many victims are people of advanced years, some almost approaching senility," says Attorney General Lynch. "Others are ignorant, people from Mexico and Central America unaccustomed to the ways of America. But the con man takes a pretty good reading of the type of person with whom he's dealing. They're not only able to defraud the gullible, they are experts at defrauding hard-nosed businessmen. It happens every day.

"And the idea that an honest man can't be cheated is tragically untrue. Victims in most cases are honest. Unfortunately, people still hope to get something for nothing without stopping to think that they are trying to obtain a reward far in excess of the value given for the services rendered."

The modern practitioner of big con has kept pace with the times. He has woven himself deep into the fabric of life in southern California. He is in the suburbs, in the walnut-paneled offices along Wilshire Boulevard, he holds a front-row pew, if not the altar, in church. He is in the high-powered pressure palaces of Hollywood. He is selling real estate and automobiles, cure-alls and diplomas. He is everywhere there is a buck to be made and a sucker to be had.

From three-for-a-dime Mexican jumping beans sold along Olvera Street (which somehow never jump when the tourists get them home) to the multimillion-dollar swindles concocted and operated in Beverly Hills, the con men of Los Angeles spin, toil and reap.

Past and present, California and con have been heart and artery, a collective outpouring of imaginative guile the like of which has not been seen anywhere else in all history.

2

GOLD

The Odyssey of Homer Mills . . . and a Few Others

Q. When does gold fall out of the sky?
A. When a dust storm contains particles of gold. A dust
storm which hit Los Angeles in 1933 dumped over 1½
tons of gold and silver particles on the city but it wasn't
feasible to recover it.
—Item from Los Angeles *Herald-Examiner*

He had ridden most of the morning, chasing down a couple of
stray horses. As the blazing noon sun peaked, he reined up for
cover under a grove of trees. Rounding up the strays would take
longer than planned. Disgustedly, he stabbed his knife into a wild
onion root. The blade came up tinged with gold—the first strike in
California history.

His name was Don Francisco Lopez, not James W. Marshall; it
was June, 1841, not January, 1848, and the place was southern
California's Placerita Canyon, not Sutter's Mill.

"The news of this discovery soon spread among the inhabitants,
from Santa Barbara to Los Angeles, and in a few weeks hundreds
of people were engaged in washing and winnowing the sands of
these gold fields," runs a contemporary account.

Gold settled northern California and made it rich. But strikes in
the south, never as extravagant as the mother lode upstate, occurred often and tantalizingly enough to keep the spark of a
bonanza alive. Enough millions were tilled from southern California gold fields to give the feel if not the substance of a full-
scale rush.

The first recorded con artist to work a gold swindle among the
locals was Barney Cummings, a patient, bewhiskered miner in his

early forties who appeared in Los Angeles along with ten thousand other prospectors after fresh strikes were made in 1857 in Placerita, Bouquet and Mint canyons.

Barney was a loner, stumbling into town from the hills every few months to sulk moodily behind a shot glass. But when he showed up one Saturday evening with a poke of gold and crossed the plaza to the Mexican whorehouse behind the fire station to buy up the establishment's goods and services for the entire evening, word of his sudden wealth—and prowess—spread quickly.

The next day Barney disappeared into the fastness of the canyons, leaving behind a lot of tired girls. He already was something of a legend.

A week later he was back to repeat his expensive and formidable indulgence at the crib. This time Barney lingered in town for a few days. His gruffness began to melt under the relaxing influence of striking it rich, not to mention the full-scale release of his tensions among the dark-eyed *señoritas*. He appeared in a new suit, complete with nugget stickpin. He was shaved and perfumed and almost friendly. But when the talk turned to the location of his mine, he was silent as the desert night. Saying he trusted no one, Barney wasn't even going to register his ground.

Dozens of would-be claim-jumpers tried to follow Barney each time he returned to his mine to replenish his nuggets. But he always moved at night and lost them easily.

After some two months of the ostentatious show of wealth, a syndicate headed by Charles Fifield, a prominent feed merchant, offered Barney $100,000 for all rights to his claim.

Barney had to be coaxed a bit—but he gave in. He wrote out exact instructions to the mine and signed away all his rights.

Fifield and his cronies spent the rest of their lives looking unsuccessfully for gold on Barney's diggings.

They also spent the rest of their lives unsuccessfully looking for Barney.

Seth Endicott made no pretense of being a miner. He dressed in quiet black and appeared to be exactly what he said he was, a New England businessman looking for sound, conservative investments.

He took up residence at a Los Angeles saloon frequented by free-spending miners. While they crowded up to the bar, Seth occupied a lonely corner table. He nursed his single whiskey like a Vermont farmer seeing the long winter through with a solitary piece of firewood. His drawn-out guzzling quickly won him the reputation of a miser and the ragging of the miners.

"They'll dump Boston into the Pacific before he buys a round," was one of the kindest jabs that Seth heard.

When a stubby, derby-wearing stranger wandered in, declaring he had a solid gold brick for sale, the miners jeered. Every man jack of them knew gold, and they only trusted it in nuggets or dust. They also knew all about the hoax of coating a lead brick and passing it off as gold.

"Talk to Seth—he'll buy your brick," one of the miners suggested with a wink.

The stranger sat down and told Seth in a loud, pleading voice, "It's solid gold, I swear it. I'll sell it for only a thousand dollars."

"Not interested," Seth said, looking from the brick to the bottom of his empty whiskey glass.

The stranger bought a couple of rounds. Somehow the more Seth drank the more fascinated he became with that gleaming brick.

"You can have it for seven hundred fifty dollars. I've got to get back East and tend to my dying sister," the stranger said.

None of the miners believed the slicker had a dying sister any more than they believed his brick was genuine. If it was, he could sell it in a minute at the bank for five times the price he was asking.

But the miners wanted to see skinflint Seth taken. "Buy 'er— she's a bargain," one grizzled codger urged.

The liquor by now had overtaken Seth's normally good judgment. "I'll give you five hundred dollars for your brick."

"A deal," the stranger said.

After Seth had passed him the money, the stranger bought a round for the house, and whispered sly confidences in the ears of several miners. Then he tipped his derby and left.

"News for you, skinflint," one miner jeered. "You've been skinned!"

Seth had had enough. Righteous anger shooting sparks from his dark eyes, he shoved his chair back and stood up. He weaved slightly as he addressed the assemblage. "I'll trust my business judgment against that of any man's. I'll wager five thousand dollars that this is a genuine gold brick."

One of the miners who had been privy to the whispered confidences of the derbied stranger threw his poke on the table. "You're covered."

"Got any more to bet?" said another prospector thirsting for easy money.

Seth extracted $10,000, and placed it on the table. The miners passed the hat and in a few moments the table held $30,000 in cash and gold and the disputed brick.

Seth was in the vanguard of the swirling mob that shouldered its way through the batwings and down the street to the assayer's office.

Assayer Malcolm Fenton adjusted his spectacles and inspected the brick. He hefted it. He took up a knife and carved at the edges. The procedure took several minutes.

The assayer's verdict sent a chill through the quiet, intense crowd. "No doubt about it, she's genuine!"

Seth was out of town an hour later.

He and his derby-hatted confederate worked the swindle for twenty years in every gold camp in California.

Using a solid gold brick as bait is an ageless gimmick among con men. With various flourishes, it still is being worked in Los Angeles today.

"The most intriguing thing to me about the old-time swindles," says Attorney General Thomas C. Lynch, "is how long the same one can be used, how faithfully the people involved will follow the traditional pattern with almost no variation at all."

One of the most durable of the solid gold brick swindles is the "Mexican treasury," a scam that veteran bunco investigator Kenneth Scarce says "was being worked a hundred years ago, and will be taking people a hundred years from now." A wealthy businessman is approached by a pair of con men and handed a gold bar that checks out as genuine. The mark is then told by the bunk men that they need $10,000 to pay off Mexican treasury officials to recover another $100,000 in bullion they have stashed away. When the mark pays, the con men disappear.

Another variant is to approach the sucker with a story that a fortune in gold bricks is locked in a trunk in El Paso, Texas, the property of a once-rich Mexican family forced to smuggle it out because of government restrictions. In exchange for several thousand dollars, the sucker is given the keys to a nonexistent trunk.

A trunk filled with gold was also used as a lure to swindle a wealthy Oregon farmer and three of his friends at Los Angeles International Airport in 1963. The foursome was approached by a six-foot, two-hundred-pound man dressed in cowboy regalia. He sold them a trunk supposedly containing 1032 ounces of gold dust, worth $36,000, for $25,000. In return for their money, the farmer and his friends received the keys to a locker and the trunk. When they opened the trunk, instead of gold dust, they found it filled with sand, rocks, nails, metal shavings and a lead bar.

The con man was picked up the following day in Chicago with $24,990 still in his possession. Tried in Los Angeles, he claimed he intended to turn the money over to the government and report the four men to the Secret Service for violating federal laws restricting the possession of gold.

"Fantastic," said Superior Court Judge Robert Clifton, agreeing with the jury that found him guilty of grand theft. He gave him one to ten for working the venerable scam.

For more than a century and a half, the elders of several villages in Mexico, casting covetous eyes at gringo riches in southern California, have sent their con men to Los Angeles to work the "Spanish prisoner" bunk, a scheme passed down from father to son along with the family Bible.

When village funds run low, two young men are chosen for the solemn responsibility of going north and returning with a rich gringo.

In Los Angeles, they canvass the better night clubs and bars. When a suitable victim is found, he is approached and offered half a map to a gold mine.

The con men explain that the other half is in the possession of a friend who, unfortunately, is in a Mexican prison. If his way can be bought out for $10,000 the prisoner will be grateful enough to put his half of the map together with theirs and they can divide the millions from the mine.

The trip to Mexico follows, and things happen fast. The first $10,000 isn't quite enough to bribe the guards and free the prisoner. The mark is induced to send home for another $10,000. After that's delivered, he is slugged and wakes up one morning on the U. S. side of the border—grateful to be alive.

"We suspect dozens of our wealthier citizens have been victimized by this racket," says Investigator Scarce. "But they don't want anyone to know they've been made fools of, so they take their losses and don't complain."

But the victims of Preacher Thomas Underwood, who hit Los Angeles in 1946, did a lot of complaining. They complained that their good preacher, singing the glories of speculation from the pulpit, had stripped the flock of more than $200,000 for phony shares in a British Columbia gold mine.

Oklahoma-born, Underwood mixed swindles and sermons for years. Involved in several bogus insurance schemes in Texas, he was defrocked when his Los Angeles gold swindle was exposed.

The preacher had induced dozens of parishioners, other ministers and seventeen members of the local fire department, to invest in the Canadian mine in an elaborate swindle he worked with two confederates.

Shorn of every nickel they invested, the parishioners told their stories to bureau investigators. Underwood, meantime, had fled back to Texas, but was nabbed there on the insurance charges. After he completed a penitentiary term, Los Angeles petitioned for his extradition, which the governor of Texas refused.

Investigator Donald L. Lundquist says, "I'll never forget for as long as I live a poor little old woman with an invalid husband who lived in a house that sat back of another house, a one-bedroom affair. When I asked her why she had invested her life's savings of two thousand dollars in the gold mine she told me, 'Mister, in this day and age, with all the trials and tribulations we face, if I can't believe in my minister, who can I believe in?'"

Many in southern California, to their everlasting regret, chose to believe in another swindler, the all-time king of the gold mine promoters.

"The Blossom Mine is richer than the streets of heaven," the chunky speaker told his fashionable audience of two dozen mesmerized ladies, the full membership of the Los Angeles Women's Club. It was a sultry August afternoon in 1948. Homer Cecil Mills, a legendary mining magnate in the West and a man with the reputation of consistently finding precious metals in places where others had failed, sketched a boundless future for his listeners.

"You might as well get used to the idea—everyone in this room is going to be rich as a maharaja. And not some time in the distant future—the first dividend will be declared in three months!"

There was a burst of spontaneous applause.

The well-tanned tycoon rolled his hand back over his long, flowing white hair, adjusted his string tie, eased his 180-pound frame forward on alligator-encased boots and stabbed his big white Stetson into the air. "You've heard of Sutter's Mill, the Comstock Lode and the Anaconda? All of them put together are small change in comparison to the Blossom!"

A collective gasp went up from the ladies. The madam chairman of the club's entertainment committee, who had luckily snagged the distinguished entrepreneur as a guest after meeting him through a mutual acquaintance, was inwardly congratulating herself.

"Now, whether or not you decide to invest in the Blossom," the speaker continued, picking up a bulky black satchel, "I have a present for everyone here. It arrived only a few hours ago, brought from the mine by special messenger."

He opened the satchel, dipped his hand in, and casually littered the table with a shower of glittering gold nuggets!

The room erupted into chaos as the women forgot their manners and grabbed at the nuggets.

An hour later the club had pledged a total of $65,000 for shares in the Blossom Mine. . . .

Summer faded into fall and winter and still no dividends arrived. The worried madam chairman, after fruitless and repeated inquiries at Mr. Mills's office, concluded she must tell her club members that they had been swindled out of every dollar they'd invested in the Blossom.

For the disappointed ladies, there was a long period of austerity in household budgets. For Homer Mills, the razzle-dazzle performance before the women's club was but another score in a masterful and flamboyant career as a con man in the lively world of penny mining stocks.

Homer had all the classic qualifications of the supreme bunco artist, plus one. He had flair, showmanship and iron nerve. He was canny, smooth-talking and his kindly brown eyes and affable manner helped inspire confidence among the suckers.

Even a hardened police officer, who knew him intimately for years, said it was hard to believe he wasn't the most honest man who ever lived. "After listening to that silken spiel of his," the cop admitted, "I had to pinch myself to keep from handing him my pension money."

Homer's biggest plus, however, was his knowledge of the law. He spent more than half his adult life as a prosperous and respected attorney in two states until he was disbarred in 1936—though he never permitted that technicality to keep him from indulging his love of the courtroom. After his disbarment, he was involved in almost as much legal action as Oliver Wendell Holmes, all of it *in propria persona,* defending himself, and adroitly so, in a long series of litigation right up to the Supreme Court.

Homer's two great, lifelong enthusiasms were law and mining. The law allowed him to indulge the practical side of his personality and mining permitted his considerable imagination to run at full throttle.

To hear Homer tell it, never in all the history of American mining had there been as fabulous a treasure as that lodged in the bowels of the Blossom, located a poker chip's throw outside Searchlight, Nevada.

To various suckers at various times, he claimed its mineral wealth contained (in alphabetical order) copper, gold, lead, nickel, platinum, radium, silver, tin, tungsten, uranium and zinc, all of them nudging each other in titanic proportions.

The only potential asset of the Blossom that he never sold or promised was the air rights. In his sales pitch, he let it be known that the Blossom's 180 desert acres held an independent fortune in deep water springs; oil enough to fuel the nation waited to gush forth at the touch of a bit; the mine's mineral rights extended into Searchlight itself, under every house and store; the value of the very ground, once a housing project, hotel and gambling casino were built, would be more precious, foot by foot, than Ft. Knox.

Every one of Homer's self-proclaimed assets in the Blossom was pure myth. Though thousands sought their fortune with him, only one fortune was amassed—his own. His take from peddling shares in the Blossom and a batch of other pie-in-the-sky mining ventures is conservatively estimated by investigators at an average $500,000 per annum for each of twenty years—a respectable $10,000,000 score for a Missouri-born poor farmer's son who left school after the tenth grade.

Homer's odyssey really began when as a young man he drifted to the Snake River country of Idaho and settled in Twin Falls. After meeting a friendly local lawyer who saw promise in him, he read law and proved a gifted apprentice. At twenty-three, he was admitted to the bar in both Idaho and California.

Some folks thought he could go all the way to the State House; he rose from U. S. Attorney for the District of Idaho to prosecuting attorney at the county seat of Rupert in 1915.

Folks in the southern part of the state were talking about Homer. They also liked to talk about the wild stampede of 1884 up north in Coeur d'Alene country where one of the world's richest strikes of silver and lead was still booming the state's population and prosperity.

Homer listened to the old-timers' tales of striking it rich and got his first taste of mineral fever. He cast aside thoughts of politics and decided his future was elsewhere. He moved to Los Angeles, opened a law office, and through a client he was representing in a mine suit, got his second taste of mineral fever. It was enough to make him a lifelong addict.

He began speculating on a grand scale, investing in a couple of dry oil wells on a thirty-thousand-acre lease in New Mexico. He bought California copper and gold mines at Neenach, Goff and the Old Woman Mountains. To support his enterprises, he mortgaged and lost his house and sold his $12,000 law library.

Completely strapped for cash by 1930, Homer was reduced to pocketing a fee without troubling to perform any legal services for his client. It led to his first trouble on the wrong side of the law. A charge of grand theft was finally dismissed, but it was still serious enough for the fussy California State Bar to suspend his license for a year.

Over the next few years, Homer's mining losses continued. In 1936, he was hauled back before the State Bar on new charges of "habitual misuse of clients' funds," "moral turpitude" and "violation of professional duty." His name was stricken from the rolls of California attorneys.

He turned hopefully to his mining properties, but fortune still eluded him. Cash, in the depression thirties, was hard to come by, so he used checks—which bounced. Since he was an ex-lawyer gone wrong, the court's sympathies were with him and he probably would have been released on probation had not a new violation reached the judge's ears.

Homer had played jailhouse lawyer and promised a cellmate he could spring him for fifty dollars. The judge, adding a scorching lecture on what he now thought of turncoat lawyers, put Homer away for a one to ten term at San Quentin.

He was out in eighteen months, a changed man. His prison respite had given him time to think about what he wanted to do with the rest of his life. He was fifty-one years old. As a disbarred lawyer and ex-con, his profession was closed to him. But he still had a lawyer's inside knowledge of the law which if used wisely from now on could help him. The geology books he had read in prison strengthened Homer's belief that there was a fortune to be made in mining. His mistake was that he had tried to acquire the fortune by honest speculation. The way to make a fortune was to let others take the risks.

That line of logic almost immediately catapulted Homer into the ranks of self-made millionaires.

Over the next twenty years, he created and relentlessly sold shares in a watered armada of mining properties, a tangled fleet of half-factual, half-fictional corporate entities without peer for brazen ingenuity. He collected corporations with the ferocity of a housewife accumulating trading stamps. Some existed only in his mind, some only on paper, some were played-out claims he picked up for peanuts.

Homer named each of his companies with the delicacy of a prospector separating rock from gold. It was important that his properties have a certain romantic yet solid ring.

Buried still in a thousand attics are shares in Homer's semantically enticing but nonexistent American Gold Mines, Inc., and the Golden Dawn Mining and Milling Co. Homer also believed in richness by association, coining another of his mythical properties the Homestake Mining Co. The mere mention of Homestake, the 1874 South Dakota bonanza that developed into the largest gold mine in the Western Hemisphere, sent shivers of delight down the spines of investors.

Homer even sold shares in the Dutch Oven Mining Co.; this was especially ingenious since that storied southwestern claim was lost three years before his birth and not rediscovered until three years after his death.

But the flagship of Homer's corporate navy was the Blossom, an honest-to-goodness but played-out claim. Considering that he paid only $3500 for the lease, his return on the investment rivals that of plungers who bought AT&T thirty years ago.

He sold the Blossom's stock under a cover of half a dozen parent companies, notably the Searchlight Uranium Corp., which, with exacting coincidence, came into being in the earliest stages of the postwar frenzy for that atomic mineral.

He liked nothing better than to back up his claims to the Blossom's versatile wealth (its gold alone he estimated at various times to investors at anywhere from $2,000,000 to $25,000,000) by inviting would-be shareholders to see for themselves.

A pair of southern Californians who came to see for themselves on a memorable weekend trip to Searchlight in November, 1951, were real-estate broker John Tucker and Fred Adamowski, an executive for a business machines company. Each had several thousand dollars to invest and each had been passed on to Homer through friends.

When they arrived at the Blossom in Homer's snappy new car, Tucker and Adamowski were whisked down the 325-foot shaft. The first impressive thing they saw was a group of ham-handed miners drilling like there was no tomorrow.

Shouting above the din to make himself heard, Homer pointed out the splendid treasures. "That's a gold vein over there and right here's the richest lead deposit I've ever seen."

Homer now raised his hand with a dramatic flourish, the signal for his miners to stop drilling. He picked up a handy Geiger

counter, motioned for Tucker and Adamowski to move in closer
so all hands could listen to the rich beat of radioactive uranium.

"The Atomic Energy Commission wants all we can produce,"
Homer said dramatically.

"Incredible," Tucker declared.

"There must be a king's ransom down here," added Adamowski.

Homer raised his hand again and his conscientious crew went
back to its drilling.

Just before they stepped into the elevator for the trip up,
Homer stooped and retrieved, seemingly at random, a couple of
pieces of ore. Handing them to his companions, he observed,
"This ought to pay you for your trouble in coming up here today."
(When Tucker and Adamowski later had the samples assayed,
the stuff priced out at $600 a ton.)

Aboveground, Homer pointed to his two busy hoist men, who
were raising the ore to the surface. They strolled over to two
giant bins where, Homer explained, the ore was stored before
shipment to the smelter.

Homer now dropped casual references to the oil waiting to
surge from the bottomless booty of the Blossom. He indicated a
point in the distance where a New York syndicate planned to
build the casino, hotel and air-conditioned housing tract with a
swimming pool in every back yard, water to be supplied, of
course, from beneath the Blossom's surface.

"The former owners took hundreds of millions out of this mine,"
Homer told Tucker and Adamowski. "Then they abandoned it
when they thought it was played out. But I gambled and sunk a
shaft a hundred feet deeper than the old one and hit it big!"

He now confided he was letting his two friends in on the deal
because he needed more capital to turn the Blossom's present
boomlet into a full-scale boom with three shifts clawing out the
millions as in days of old.

By now manipulating them as he would a pair of puppets,
Homer drove his two marks over to an eight-room house he main-
tained near the Blossom. "You fellows could probably use a drink.
Besides, I want to show you the smelting receipts."

Meantime, as soon as the dust from Homer's car had settled,
all activity at the Blossom ceased. Homer's hired hands now gave
themselves up to their real vocation—boozing. Homer had not

only salted the mine with ore, but his "miners" were imported winos from Los Angeles, up for a healthy day in the desert to play their roles in his drama. Homer believed in putting on a good show.

From Homer's house, Tucker and Adamowski, by now drowned in dreams of golden wealth and gasping to invest in the Blossom, were moved on by their generous host to the nearby pleasure palaces of Las Vegas. Homer volunteered to supply wine, women and song.

As colorful and convincing as was Homer's stage-managed drama at the Blossom, most investors never got the chance to view the spectacle—they were willing to take Homer's word for how rich he was going to make them.

Homer rounded up clients with bulging pockets by taking inexpensive ads in newspaper classified sections in various parts of the country. He also used a couple of professional steerers to feed him other clients. But more important, other stockholders told their friends. One woman, a fashion designer and innocent Judas goat, fed him more than $100,000 through her acquaintances. A doctor in Watsonville, California, told his friends and over a sixteen-year period personally contributed more than $70,000 to Homer's enterprises on a no-questions-asked basis. (Even at Homer's later trials the doctor refused to believe the charges against him.)

The con man's victims ranged from the naïve to financial supersophisticates. He took file clerks and stockbrokers, widows and bankers, parking lot attendants and professional speculators.

For the ego-oriented, he had another flawlessly executed dodge. If a mark was doubtful about investing, Homer invited him to a "board of directors" meeting, as artfully staged as the inspection trips to the Blossom. Homer rigged the phony board meetings to elect suckers to high office. His logic was appealing.

"Once you're a board member," Homer would reason, "you'll really be on the inside. You'll know exactly what's going on before we release the news to outsiders."

It worked every time. As soon as the investor bought in, the "board" (either some of Homer's steerers or other previously duped investors) voted him into office. Singlehandedly, Homer created almost as many vice-presidents as Madison Avenue.

The price of Homer's shares was always fluid. He sold at anywhere from a penny to one dollar. But he packaged a deal more artfully than the House of Rothschild. He added "guaranteed returns" within thirty to ninety days. When the dividends failed to materialize, he often used this "temporary" situation as a wedge to go back to his investors to ask for more money. There were always unanticipated expenses—payroll, taxes, retimbering, shipping charges to the smelter, blasting powder to dislodge a newly discovered vein.

He kept a huge ledger book labeled "Prospects," a list of more than five hundred of his shareholders who were good for more than one score. In a six-year period, according to her own testimony, one retired Los Angeles schoolteacher gave Homer $14,000 in five separate transactions. "His excuse for needing the money each time always seemed so logical," she testified.

Homer not only sold his shares and promises of quick dividends, but he always threw in a percentage of the mine. He was habitually vague about how many outstanding shares there were in any of his properties, but in his contracts Homer blithely gave away any percentage his instinct told him it would take to part a sucker from his cash. In the Blossom alone, Homer probably sold in excess of 30,000 per cent.

In the late forties, with his Los Angeles operation flourishing, Homer left for Chicago. He'd already done thousands of dollars' worth of business through the mails with Windy City customers. He'd also had encouraging correspondence from a Chicago broker who was ready to float an issue of 400,000 shares at fifty cents per share in the Blossom.

Homer proved as persuasive in Chicago as elsewhere. His sales soared. But the sleuths of the Securities and Exchange Commission, who had been following his activities for some time with great interest, suddenly descended. An eight-count indictment, including mail fraud and violation of SEC regulations, was returned against him in federal court. The SEC said Homer had picked the pockets of thirty-nine investors who had sunk a total of $277,000 in five of his properties.

Homer promptly denied the charges, reassured his investors, prepared to do battle in court in his own defense, and went right on selling shares in the self-same mining properties that were labeled phony in his indictment.

The government's witnesses were fascinating.

An engineer testified he had bought 1150 shares at ten cents each, in Homer's five mines. After his purchase, he had been unable to pin Homer down on the promised dividends from his investment. An attractive widow said that a few days after she delivered $5000 to Homer he appeared in a new car. She had advanced him a total of $36,000 in cash and securities. On one occasion, she gave him the deeds to three lots, which he used as collateral for bank loans. He failed to repay the loans and it cost her $7625 to get back her deeds. On another occasion, she placed the title to her home in escrow to permit Homer to borrow $6000 on the property. That time, it cost her $5523 to get back her home.

A wholesale businessman testified he'd decided to invest after Homer assured him that a fresh uranium strike at the Blossom was worth, conservatively, $4,000,000.

The sheepish stockbroker came forth and admitted the pending underwriting of the Blossom.

Mining and geology experts discredited Homer's claim of a new uranium strike at the Blossom. They ridiculed his multimineral mirage of copper, gold, lead, nickel, etc. They stated flatly that there were no commercial ore reserves on any of Homer's properties.

Summing up, the government contended that Homer's mines were worked out, that some were caved-in and flooded at the time of the stock sales and that Homer lied when he claimed he had invested $75,000 of his own money in the properties.

Sitting grandly and imperturbably through it all as the government built its impressive case against him, Homer seemed not at all troubled. He called no witnesses on his own behalf, but charged four of the prosecution's witnesses had perjured themselves. He declared that his operations were legitimate and people had a right to invest with him if they chose to—a "free enterprise" defense that he was to use again and again.

The jury of six men and six women, free-enterprisers all, believed Homer. He was acquitted on all charges. In the jubilation after the verdict, the jury crowded around Homer to congratulate him. So jubilant were most of the jurors that to prove the faith and justice of their verdict, several pressed checks and cash on him for stock!

Back in Los Angeles, Homer waxed fatter and richer. He gave himself up to the good life. He had divorced two wives, but kept an attractive secretary in constant attendance at a year-round suite he maintained in a downtown hotel. He also took to traveling several months a year in the company of young and attractive ladies. He was a familiar figure at the Vegas gaming tables for years, making a great show of dropping thousands of an evening. He lost money like a man who had his own money machine.

His losses, of course, were easily replenished. He went right on selling stock to all comers. True, not all of his investors were completely happy with his management. Complaints drifted into the FBI, the Los Angeles Bunco Squad, the district attorney's office and the SEC. But the wily Homer was untouchable. He continued to operate brazenly in the open.

By 1954, Homer had won a reputation as an elder statesman of business. Clients now were coming to him, seeking his advice on how to handle their investments. One of them was William C. Hull, a wealthy Seattle plastics manufacturer, who had just sold his business and was looking for a new location in the Los Angeles vicinity. Friends had recommended that he look up Homer when he arrived in town.

Hull went to Homer's hotel, got him on the house phone and explained his problem. Could Homer find him a new factory? Homer said he was a mining man himself. He didn't know much about the plastics business but he'd see what he could do.

Before Homer ran down to the lobby to meet Hull, he'd put through a phone call to Seattle and found that Hull's references checked out. Homer and Hull hit it off at once. In a few moments, Homer was on the phone, trying to run down—without success— a contact in plastics for Hull.

"Have you ever thought about investing in mining stocks?" Homer asked.

"No," said Hull firmly, "I want to stick to a business I know."

Homer suggested that Hull accompany him on an exploratory

trip to the Blossom. "No obligation, of course. But I want you to see this property with your own eyes."

By the time Hull had been given Homer's first-class tour, including the playlet at the Blossom, he had changed his mind. Hull decided to get his feet wet with a $3000 flyer in the Blossom.

From Hull's point of view, the terms were heady. Homer gave him thirty thousand shares in Searchlight Uranium and a guarantee of 10 per cent of the smelting receipts from the Blossom's ore until a total of $6000 was returned to him within a year. Homer told him that in a few months his thirty thousand shares would be worth over $100,000. He also gave Hull a sixty-day option to increase his holdings on the same basis for an additional investment of $5000.

"The deal's too good to pass up," Hull admitted.

On the day the agreement was to be made final, Hull brought along his wife, Georgia, and a cashier's check made out in his name. Homer bowed in courtly fashion to the pretty Mrs. Hull as he accepted the check and turned over the contract and stock certificates. He examined the check with a practiced eye and told Hull he'd apparently forgotten to endorse it.

Hull, as he endorsed, told Homer it was a pleasure to do business with a man of his financial acumen.

"You'll never be sorry," he assured the Hulls, blowing the ink dry on the signature.

"By the way," Hull added, almost as an afterthought, "I'd like to give you one of my business cards."

Homer smiled and glanced down at the card. It read, "Lieut. William C. Hull, Bunco Squad, Los Angeles Police Department."

"I knew there was something funny about you," Homer said, his composure quickly regained.

Hull walked to the door and opened it. In walked six officials, a pair of SEC men, a couple of patrolmen and two police photographers. Hull ordered a thorough search of the suite. In forty-five minutes of examining Homer's files and records, over one thousand incriminating documents were found and bundled off to headquarters.

Hull's undercover work (with the aid of the policewoman who had posed as his wife) resulted in a fourteen-count indictment against Homer—twelve for grand theft, one attempted grand

theft and one for selling stock without a permit, a violation of the
California Corporate Securities Law. In addition, the district attorney's office had witnesses who would testify they had lost more
than $100,000 to Homer over a nine-year period.

The law, the law thought, had finally nailed Homer Mills. Two
extremely able deputy district attorneys, Fred N. Whichello and
Herman Arterberry, were assigned to prepare the massive case
against him. The D.A.'s men painstakingly sifted through the
documents that Hull had commandeered. They drew large cardboard charts, matching the two hundred exhibits they planned to
introduce at Homer's trial against each of the counts.

Out on bail, Homer kept right on peddling stock in the Blossom. A mere fourteen-count indictment was not going to deter
him. Homer, always congenial, took to dropping by the D.A.'s
office as Whichello, Arterberry and Hull burned the midnight oil,
putting the case in shape.

He'd take off his big Stetson, put his feet on the desk and light
a cigar. He was cordiality itself and everything between the con-
tenders was soon on a pleasant, first-name basis.

"Fred, you fellows are wasting your time. They tried to do
this to me in Chicago. I'm afraid I'm going to beat you same as
I did them."

"Now, Homer," Whichello said, "you have to admit we really
have you this time."

Homer didn't for a moment agree. "Why don't you boys forget
about trying me and buy some shares in the Blossom?"

"If we did, we'd use it as evidence," Whichello smiled.

Now glancing at Hull, Homer persevered. "Bill, you hold onto
that stock I sold you. It'll make you a rich man. We're only two
feet away from a vein of gold four feet thick."

The incongruity of pushing his stock at the men charged with
putting him out of business apparently never occurred to Homer.
Right up to his trial, he kept dropping by for friendly chats. Only
when he couldn't wheedle a stock sale did he turn casually to the
mounting series of charts the lawmen were building on him.

He would inspect the charts and blandly suggest ways of
strengthening the state's case against him. He was still proud of
his knowledge of the law and confident he would beat the rap
in court.

Homer's preliminary hearing drew crowds of fascinated spectators. His distinguished long white locks combed down to his neck, his natty dress, his deference to the court gave him the aura of the persecuted underdog come to battle all the power of the state of California.

Homer's defense was brilliantly simple. He claimed Hull entered his suite without a search warrant and the ransacking of his quarters constituted illegal search and seizure. All the evidence against him therefore was inadmissible.

Thus armed, Homer took the hearing in municipal court in easy strides as Whichello paraded his phalanx of swindled investors, the crucial testimony of Hull and assorted assay and geology experts who removed any doubt of the quality of Homer's mines.

Homer again called no witnesses, though he had a legion of ever faithful supporters who would at a mere nod troop eagerly into court to testify to his character and honesty.

Homer kept the proceedings humming. From behind his defense counsel's vantage, he gently badgered witnesses during his cross-examination. He even scolded a city payroll clerk—a woman who had lost $4000 to him—for failing to pay an additional $1000 he claimed she owed on their last transaction.

Homer was not above making witnesses appear ridiculous. Questioning one of his smaller investors, an aircraft inspector, he asked:

Q. Now, what did I tell you about the Blossom?

A. You said it was a rich mine, would make me a millionaire, and to get in on the ground floor.

Q. Make you a millionaire on a two-thousand-dollar investment?

A. That is what you said.

Q. Are you positive?

A. Yes, I am.

Even the judge smiled.

As the case dragged on through Superior Court, Homer spent what were probably the happiest days of his life, a heaven-sent opportunity to indulge both his law and mining enthusiasms. He'd thrust and parry with the prosecution through the morning and part of the afternoon. After court, he'd return to his hotel and close more deals for stock.

As would any sensible lawyer, Homer used every delaying tactic allowed him by the law. He filed a flurry of writs, petitions, motions and demurrers and caviled at the minutest details of the official reporter's transcript of the proceedings.

His trial finally ended in April, 1956. He was convicted on thirteen counts. Through it all, Homer held stoutly to his defense of illegal search and seizure and that he was offering investors an opportunity to reap the benefits of the free enterprise system. Despite the conviction, Homer was far from through.

In applying for bail at the conclusion of the trial, Homer drew an arch observation from Judge Bayard Rhone:

"The matter of bail gives me considerable concern because I don't want the defendant to be in a position where he raises the money by the sale of mining stock for which no permit has been issued."

Nevertheless, Homer got out on bail while his case went up for review before the State Appellate Court. The judge's worst fears were realized—Homer kept moving his stock. Thousands more poured into his pockets, assuring him of an adequate defense even if he wasn't saving money representing himself.

Once the Appellate Court began its review of Homer's conviction, the legal battle moved to the loftiest levels of jurisprudence. And Homer's faith in his illegal search and seizure defense was vindicated with the help of a landmark case the Appellate had decided a year earlier in which the conviction of accused bookmaker Charles H. Cahan had been set aside because evidence against him was obtained by police without a search warrant and with the aid of a hidden microphone. Up to that time, the federal rule that admissible evidence must be obtained without violating Constitutional guarantees against unreasonable search and seizure did not apply in California courts.

But in ruling on Homer's conviction, the appeals court carried the Cahan precedent even further:

"It will be noted that Hull had in his possession all the knowledge and evidence he needed to make a case on the sale of the stock to him. He knew there was no corporate permit; he had the written contract of sale, the stock certificate and the check; he had a witness. . . .

"So with respect to the crime for which Mills was arrested, Hull had no occasion to make any search whatever. He had no search warrant and it was not claimed Mills consented to the search.

"So all charges in counts 1–12 were gotten on illegal search and seizure. If the search and seizure were unlawful, the heart of the proof upon each count other than 14 was a fruit of the poisonous tree."

Homer had won a tremendous legal victory. He had pioneered and sustained the "fruit of the poisonous tree" doctrine in California. He had also forced the state to spell out and reaffirm the federal rule on admissible evidence.

Homer came out of his legal jousting with the appeals court convicted on only one count, the minor violation of selling stock without a permit. And only by an eyelash did the court uphold even this one conviction. Homer claimed that his transaction with Hull fell within the exemption of the State Corporations Code, which allows a private sale of stock.

"Defendant's own testimony would have sustained a finding in his behalf on this issue, but it was disbelieved by the trial judge," the Appellate said.

To clear himself entirely, Homer immediately sent his case up to the U. S. Supreme Court, now turning all his legal ammunition against the police.

In his supporting brief to the highest court in the land, Homer thundered: "It is not amiss to observe that it is just such conduct of these snooping, zealous, narrow-minded and interfering officers, with their supporting bureaus and commissions, which have made ghost towns of the West.

"To such an extent men have ceased to be free and independent. Have we reached the stage in this nation when free and independent men must get permission of someone in the police state before we can transact any private, innocent business?"

The Appellate's reversal, meantime, had rocked the D.A.'s office. There had been a dozen unsuccessful attempts in thirteen years to nab Homer, and it now seemed that his legal talents would again help him slip through the net. The D.A.'s men half believed that the Supreme Court would uphold Homer. Moreover, even as they waited for the court ruling from Washington, D. C., a fresh flood of complaints flowed in, indicating Homer was back in business bigger than ever.

Wearily, Investigator Robert H. Meng was assigned an undercover mission similar to Hull's. It took Meng two months to win Homer's confidence. He was joined by another investigator, Edwin A. Shrader, on the appointed day in a Hollywood restaurant to witness Meng's transfer of $2500 to Homer for shares in the Clemantine Mine, a Barstow, California, claim Homer was pushing at the moment.

Homer was rearrested, tried again on grand theft and corporate securities violation.

"Business is based on confidence," declared Homer, by now outraged at the law's harassment. His statement to the court bristled with indignation.

"The vice of entrapment, practiced by officers sworn to uphold and defend the law, lies in the ugly and vicious efforts on their part to induce an otherwise innocent person to do something upon which officers can make an arrest and proceed to prosecute him. This is a series of events of such gravity as to shock and offend civilized standards of decency and fairness."

Despite his eloquence, Homer was convicted in his second trial. And the U. S. Supreme Court ended his legal recourse by refusing to review his first conviction.

The state finally got him into a prison cell. After its costly, elaborate campaign to put him there, Homer spent less than nine months behind bars. He died in 1958, without regrets, perhaps the last man of the twentieth century to advocate pure laissez faire.

Of his seventy-one years, a shade more than two were spent in jail. To the time of his death, Homer was still selling shares in the Blossom—to fellow cons!

3

OIL

Gold in Los Angeles—Color It Black

"We're All Out Here In California Where The Gushers Are . . . And We Just Ought To Clean Up. . . . Come On, Folks, Get Aboard For The Big Ride. . . ."
—C. C. JULIAN

The oil rig rolled to a stop on the quiet Long Beach street with a great squealing of brakes. The driver tumbled out and moved up the walk to the pleasant two-bedroom home of Mr. and Mrs. Percy Stump.

"Just wanted to warn you, Mrs. Stump, to park your car on the street for the time being. Our rig will be blocking your driveway," the man said matter-of-factly.

"Are you from the city, is it some kind of street improvement?"

"No, ma'am, we're going to drill for oil, sink a well on your front lawn first thing in the morning. We'll try not to bother you much."

The man tipped his hard hat and left, leaving his monstrous rig parked in the street overnight.

The Stumps looked on in frozen horror as a crew of three arrived at seven-thirty the next morning and reparked the rig on their lawn. Mr. Stump, a retired schoolteacher, shook himself and marched outside.

He demanded that the equipment and men be removed at once. The man in the hard hat told him, "Sorry, we've got a permit from the city to drill."

"But," Mr. Stump sputtered, "this is our house. It's private property."

"You own the house, sure enough, but I own what's under it.

If you'll look at your deed you'll find the subdivider kept the mineral rights to every house he built on this street."

Panic-stricken, Mr. Stump grabbed at the one out that the man offered. In exchange for having the crew and equipment removed, he purchased the mineral rights to his home for $2700.

The con was worked all over southern California for years. Sharp operators bought up oil option rights from subdividers for next to nothing. They had no idea if there was oil on any of the homesites and cared less. They had no intention of drilling. Their rigs were rented and successfully served the purpose of intimidating and terrifying homeowners into signing the expensive contracts for the mineral rights.

Oil is an inescapable fact of life in southern California. A spindly forest of derricks thrust up from back yards, shopping centers, hillsides and sidewalks. A $275,000 exploration well, sunk a few blocks from Civic Center, came in with a three-hundred-barrel-a-day production, touching off an oil boom in the heart of the city.

"The Los Angeles basin is one of the most attractive areas for exploration in California," said a spokesman for Standard Oil. "Downtown Los Angeles and West Los Angeles may contain oil reserves of one hundred million barrels."

The oil-oriented atmosphere provides a bull market for con men. Roy Ipson was sentenced to three years in prison in 1964 for selling over $250,000 worth of stock in twenty-two "producing" wells to dozens of investors. Ipson sold interests for $4000 each that were supposed to bring in revenues of $700 a month until the Bureau of Investigation discovered that the wells existed only in the fertile imagination of the swindler. A few months earlier, a promoter with a similar m.o. was taken into custody in a Hollywood motel room, charged with fleecing a Los Angeles woman of $117,000 for another batch of nonexistent oil wells.

One of the most ingenious of the oil con men was a dynamic little sharpshooter named Casey Stearns, five feet two of Barnum showman. Casey raced throughout the state in the 1950s signing up knots of investors for his wells. He had an affectionate feeling for each of his groups, referring to them as his "families." Dozens of his families were stashed in different parts of the state, in San

Francisco, San Jose, Long Beach and Los Angeles. None of the families, of course, knew of the existence of the others.

Casey wasn't crude enough to sell his interest in nonexistent wells. He owned title to thirty-two legitimate wells. The only problem was that his biggest producer brought in a snappy three barrels a day. The others were worn-out gravel pits. Still, Casey had the knack of bringing in a modest flow of oil at any time he cared to take the trouble.

When his funds ran low, he invited a family member to one of his wells. Casey and the mark would go out to the site where a big derrick and an adjacent tank sat impressively. A ladder ran up to the lip of the tank to a small platform. Climbing up to the platform, the mark could watch as Casey turned a valve near the derrick. Oil would come gushing out immediately.

After watching that flow of black gold, the mark couldn't reach for his checkbook fast enough. Later, Casey, to prepare for the next victim, would return to the site and hook up a small pump to a line that no one had noticed before. He would then pump the oil from the tank the mark had seen back up the hill to another tank where it had come from in the first place.

He used the gimmick time and again, always successfully. His victims included a superior court judge and a number of prestigious lawyers in San Francisco.

When some of the family members finally began to doubt Casey, the bureau moved him into San Quentin after discovering he had earned close to $500,000 on his operations. Casey had sold 151 per cent in one of his wells and in another he had peddled 168 one-sixty-fourth participations!

But the pie was cut even thinner in the 1930s by a pair of promoters who invited everyone in Los Angeles to a 115-acre parcel of land in the Saugus-Newhall area for a beer and spareribs picnic. Two giant derricks dominated the site as the promoters gave glowing accounts of the oil riches that would soon be pouring in. Several hundred people shelled out for a $1/640$ interest in the field, and found out later, after the pair had disappeared with their cash, that there wasn't any oil and that the derricks had been tossed up only for the day of the picnic as gingerbread.

Petroleum seepage was spotted in the Los Angeles area as early as 1860, only eleven years after the fabled invasion of the forty-niners to San Francisco and the Sacramento Valley. But oil wealth in the south eventually dwarfed the gold riches of the north. "In California, gold was the whore, but the madam was oil," says one historian.

The first real boom was touched off by Edward L. Doheny, an ex-Colorado miner who dug a hole in a vacant lot on Second Street in downtown Los Angeles in 1893. Using a hand windlass to pull up the dirt, he hit a small ten-barrel-a-day well. But it was enough to start the stampede and start Doheny on a stormy, controversial career as an oil baron.

Wells began to explode in every farmer's field. The farmers forgot about barley and corn and listened to the propositions of the oily speculators who flooded in for the easy money. Hundreds of them were sweet-talked into selling their fields outright. Prices of $1000 an acre looked good, but the few who had the presence of mind to hold out and lease their land became millionaires.

The oil produced a no-holds-barred, wild and wooly atmosphere. In the 1890s, the same laws that governed gold mines ruled the oil strikes. There had to be a discovery before a claim could be filed. When small operators, patiently drilling in sand, finally brought up a bucket that indicated oil, agents of the larger companies, tipped by hired spies, moved their derricks alongside and began drilling. They had the legal if not the moral right to come in and drill cheek by jowl with the outfits that had done the hard preliminary work. There were gun fights and pitched battles to protect the claims, and competing crews, guarded by riflemen, raced around the clock to spud in first. Many a deserving wildcatter, until the statutes were changed to outlaw this brand of larceny, saw his riches stolen from under his feet.

In the 1920s southern California provided the operating base for three of the most incredible oil swindles in American history. One helped to kill a president, another shook an industrial empire, and the third produced the most exotic petroleum pirate of them all.

On a speaking tour to the West Coast aboard a special train in June, 1923, Warren Gamaliel Harding, twenty-ninth President of the United States, received a long coded message from an aide in Washington with the first shocking details of a Senate investigation of oil leases at Teapot Dome, Wyoming, and Elk Hills, California. After reading the message, Harding went into a mood of deep depression. Newsmen aboard his train reported his despondency was caused by the betrayal of his friends. Harding fell ill, supposedly of food poisoning. He died on August 2. The shock of Teapot Dome, said members of the presidential entourage, hastened his death. The full story of the scandal also shocked the nation.

Harding's close friend, Secretary of the Interior Albert Fall, had been bribed by two oilmen to hand over government oil leases. Harry Sinclair had given Fall $300,000 for the Teapot Dome concession, and Ed Doheny, the ex-Colorado miner who had grubbed in the Los Angeles earth to trigger his fortune, had paid $100,000 for southern California's naval oil reserves at Elk Hills.

Fall and Doheny were indicted for bribery and conspiracy. Fall went to prison and Doheny was acquitted. Sinclair was found innocent of fraud, but served a brief term for contempt of Congress.

The big Richfield Oil Company was thrown into receivership in 1931 after auditors discovered an operating loss of $54,000,000! Top company men, to the tune of $50,000 a month, had been charging off lavish personal expenses to the firm. A $50,000 suite in a Los Angeles hotel was maintained for the private pleasures of executives, pleasures that had little to do with the oil business. Some executives had blithely borrowed up to $500,000 in personal loans from the company till. On one occasion, a chartered airplane flew over a chartered company yacht as it sailed on a party cruise to Catalina Island. The plane wafted gardenias on the deck amid the golden-skinned Hollywood actresses who were guests of the businessmen.

But the Teapot Dome–Elk Hills and Richfield scandals were eclipsed in southern California by the high jinks of another oil highbinder whose impact on the local scene was far more thunderous.

He watched the derrick quiver—like the shaking of the Eiffel Tower. "Damn, that's beautiful," the lanky, anonymous driller said aloud as the gusher exploded in an oil field outside Beaumont, Texas.

It wasn't the aesthetics of the black gold pouring skyward in a thrilling rush that he admired. He'd seen dozens of gushers, and helped bring them in during six years of back-breaking labor in Texas and California oil plays. What he found really beautiful was the fact that the onyx liquid could be turned into an endless river of green at the bank.

But this gusher, like all the others, was another man's fortune, and all that interested the forlorn, envious Canadian oil-field hand, standing on the rich prairie on a night in 1921, was his own fortune.

Courtney C. Julian sighed in resignation. Then he heard a booming Texas voice call his name. The voice materialized into Big Dan MacKenzie, a square-jawed, cigar-chomping promoter with a local reputation for selling leases in wildcat wells that invariably turned out dry as Death Valley.

"I hear your tongue's slicker than a rattler's," MacKenzie said.

Julian wiped his grimy fingers on his work clothes and stuck his hand out. "Didn't think you'd bother looking me up after I passed the word that I wanted to work for you."

MacKenzie smiled through yellow teeth. "Anyone with brass enough to send for Big Dan is a man I want to meet. So you'd rather sell oil than drill for it?"

"That's about it," said Julian.

MacKenzie had nothing to lose by hiring Julian. For his part, Julian jumped at the chance to peddle Big Dan's leases on a straight commission basis. A roughneck and tool dresser before he'd worked up to driller, Julian had discovered the enduring truth that oil-field laborers seldom made a fortune. A promoter like Big Dan, who took in hard cash in exchange for easy ethics and didn't have to break his back, was his idea of a successful man. And, more than anything else, Julian hungered for success.

For a man of thirty-six, he hadn't much to show for his life thus far. Nearly six feet tall, with an oval, not quite handsome face, he sported a country boy haircut and a frayed suit as he boarded the train for Los Angeles the morning after meeting Big Dan. The promoter's leases were tucked securely in his pocket.

Julian was born on a Manitoba farm in 1885. He sold newspapers, drove a milk wagon, clerked in a clothing store, worked as a plumber's assistant and a $1.50-a-day pick-and-shovel laborer to help support his widowed mother.

In his twenties, he floated into Regina, Saskatchewan, and got a job as a real-estate salesman, discovering he had a knack for getting people to like and trust him. Trading in lots, he ran up a stake of $6000, began speculating in raw land and lost his capital. He moved to California, got his first laborer's job in an oil field outside Bakersfield. Disgusted at seeing all those gushers come in for someone else, he went back to Canada. He sold jewelry and building supplies and ran up another stake for real-estate speculation. He failed again, and drifted to Texas for work in the oil fields.

That record didn't presage much of a future for Julian. But he was brimming with hope that his hour had finally struck. This time he had to make it. As unlikely as it seemed at the moment, he did—and big.

He had a meteoric rise and fall as one of the brainiest, breeziest and brazenest con men in California history, a sensational, super-charged, hell-raising promoter, a financial swashbuckler in the grand tradition.

He did everything flamboyantly, becoming the gaudiest of all the playboys of the razzmatazz jazz age of the twenties. He lived like a sheik, complete with harem. The money he tossed around with fantastic generosity made Diamond Jim Brady look like a cheapskate.

In only thirteen years, he amassed and lost four million-dollar fortunes. His tangled financial dealings eventually engulfed most of the top Los Angeles bankers and businessmen in scandal and led to the jailing of the district attorney.

He emerged as one of the most skillful copywriters and radio demagogues in the nation, and used those skills to victimize thousands of suckers and then convince them they had been swindled by others.

Once he got rolling, Julian's life was one bizarre episode after another. He created his own style, and even in death that style proved matchless.

Fortunately for him, Julian hit Los Angeles in the midst of a gigantic oil boom. More than ten thousand newcomers a month were pouring in, most of them gasping for an interest in an oil well. Though still obscure, he had no trouble selling Big Dan's doubtful leases. Predictably, the wells that Big Dan drilled back in Texas turned out to be dry holes.

Rather than return to hard labor in the oil fields, Julian hung on, living by his wits. He managed to put together a small private syndicate and acquire a lease in the Huntington Beach field outside Los Angeles. But that venture also failed.

In 1922, the oil boom hit its peak. The Santa Fe Springs field, its gushers spouting five thousand to eight thousand barrels a day, had just been opened up. Julian fast-talked himself into a four-acre lease on a piece of the precious ground. He got it by offering the owners $30,000 in cash and a 30 per cent bonus on every barrel.

But he had bought the lease with nerve only. He didn't have the money, and when he tried to raise it among plungers who had gone along with him on previous deals, he came up empty-handed. His small circle of investors was by now completely disenchanted.

To find the money, he devised a simple plan. He decided to advertise. But the ads he wrote were unique. Nothing like them had been seen before on the staid financial pages of newspapers. They were shrewdly and adroitly shaped to appeal to the mass mind of the time. His slogans were easily understood, direct and candid, and he had his headlines set in big black type.

"Come On In, Folks, The Water's Just Fine . . . I'll Tell You, Folks, You'll Never Make A Thin Dime Just Lookin' On . . . I've Got A Sure-Fire Winner . . . We Just Can't Lose . . . We're All Out Here In California Where The Gushers Are And We Just Ought To Clean Up . . . Come On, Folks, Get Aboard For The Big Ride. . . ."

The citizens loved the straight-from-the-hip approach. Julian talked in the language of the man in the street. They "got aboard" all right, for $175,000 in only sixteen days. Julian was on his way at last. He immediately launched four more syndicates on the wings of the same type of unsophisticated advertising.

Then Julian had a stroke of wildcatter's luck, the turning point of his career. Every one of the five wells came in and doubled the money of investors. His reputation was made, and

the man in the street at last had a champion, someone who would
cut him in on all those oil riches that previously, according to
Julian, the big operators had hoarded for themselves.

C.C., as he asked everyone to call him now, became the hero of
the underdog. He gloated about his successes in new ads, and
though he advised widows and orphans that the "oil game" was
not for them, he nevertheless set up an installment payment plan
for small investors who kept pressing money on him. He swiftly
organized eight more syndicates, luring investors with the success
of his first five. Only one of this batch made money. But to the
average small investor, it didn't matter; he trusted C.C. to bring
the rest of those gushers in at any moment.

With money arriving by the sackful, C.C. decided to form the
Julian Petroleum Company with an authorized capital of 400,000
shares, to be sold in $100 units of two preferred shares plus one
share of common.

To sell the stock, he wrote more of his florid ads: "When We
Get This Julian Corporation Under Way We'll Make That
Standard Oil Crowd Turn Flipflops . . . I'm Not Kiddin', Folks,
You're Lookin' Opportunity Right In The Eye."

More than forty thousand of the folks believed him, and the
stock sold out in record time.

C.C. put some of the new capital to work. He rented almost an
entire floor of the Loew's State Building on Broadway, hired a
staff and furnished the offices lavishly. He bought leases, wells,
pipelines, tanks and a chain of thirty-five service stations. The
idea was to have a completely integrated oil operation, from
the well to the consumer's gas tank.

But C.C. didn't put all the money into the company. He remembered the hard days in the oil fields, and now that he had a
gusher of his own he was going to make sure he got a healthy
piece of it. He didn't stint in ladling out the loot for himself.

He dumped the thirteen syndicates he had formed into the
new company. For putting those together, he took over $500,000
in commissions. He also kept 30 per cent as his own share in all
the producing wells, but rather than risk the uncertainties of a
continued flow of oil, he transferred the risk by capitalizing his
rights, dividing them into small shares and selling them to the
public. This brought him another million dollars. From the shares

in the company, he raked off twenty dollars a unit in cash, good for $2,300,000. Then he also gave himself a bonus of one share of common stock for each unit he sold. This provided $1,000,000 more.

By December, 1924, less than three years out of his driller's work clothes, C.C. had made more than $5,000,000. For the moment, nobody seemed to notice that Julian Pete wasn't earning a dime in profits or dividends. As for C.C., now that he had his hands on some real money, he was too busy elsewhere to take time out to run the company.

With his affluence, he turned himself out in a dude's wardrobe. He had a weakness for candy-striped silk shirts and polka-dot ties. He wore a derby pitched at a rakish angle. White spats and a magnificent gold-headed cane added to his sartorial splendor.

Immersing himself in the good life, he turned up in all the class speakeasies, a different flapper on his arm each evening. Invariably, he bought champagne for the house; then from a horse-choking roll he peeled off thousand-dollar bills to cover everyone's tab for the evening. One night he got into a fist fight with Charlie Chaplin, battling him to a draw.

He tipped in hundred-dollar bills. He bought a fleet of Rolls Royces and Pierce-Arrows, and gave most of them away to casual acquaintances.

He got himself a valet, and the parties he threw were legendary. He would stay drunk for days, his nerves so shaky he had to raise a glass to his lips with both hands. His valet would oversee his safe arrival at one of a score of hideaway apartments and hotel suites he maintained for his various girl friends. He was especially lavish in his spending on women. He showered cars, diamonds, furs and costly apartments on his favorites. He spent $200,000 alone on one love nest, then didn't trouble to visit the blond love-bird roosting there more than a half-dozen times a year.

The wife he had married in Canada in 1910 when he was a plumber's assistant he installed, along with his two daughters, in an opulent $250,000 English-style mansion. He spent $100,000 on the furnishings, including a gold bathtub, but seldom got around to spending an evening at home.

He also bought a radio station, and thought seriously of buying one or two of the largest newspapers in Los Angeles. When complaints began to drift back to him that some of his stockholders were getting edgy because the huge dividends he had promised weren't materializing, C.C. ran down to the station and blasted the "oil trust" and the "big fellows" who were trying to ruin him and all his small investors.

What was killing profits in Julian Pete wasn't only C.C.'s lavish spending of company money, but the law of the market place. The supply of oil simply exceeded the demand. The gushers were so bountiful that none of the companies could sell all the oil they produced. To reduce the supply, Julian's competitors began limiting production by shutting down many of their wells. But while the competition could afford to cut back production, C.C. found many of his own wells drying up. He was taking less than $15,000 worth of oil a month out of his dwindling wells. And even for this, he could find no market. Moreover, new drilling on his leases had failed to bring in a single gusher.

A couple of additional weaknesses in Julian Pete began to bob up. In organizing the company on a well-to-consumer basis, C.C. had omitted one vital installation—a refinery. He had been leasing this facility, but his attacks against the other oil companies angered them to the point that they refused to let him use their refineries to extract the gasoline from his crude.

Julian Pete shares began a steady decline on the Los Angeles Stock Exchange, from fifty dollars to thirty-five dollars.

His troubles now were compounded by the government. The Collector of Internal Revenue slapped a suit on him to recover $792,565.50 in personal taxes on unreported income. Cash and securities worth between $250,000 and $300,000 were seized.

He was also having a battle with the state of California. The Commissioner of Corporations charged him with violation of the blue-sky laws—illegal sale of stock, deception and manipulation. His books were seized and so was $1,800,000 in cash.

The price of Julian Pete tobogganed to nine dollars a share.

Julian pleaded with bankers for new loans. They refused. The five Los Angeles dailies also closed their columns to his advertising. His company was losing money hand over fist. He was digging into his own pocket to meet his payroll. In all, he poured $500,000 from the funds he had earmarked for himself back into Julian Pete to keep it from collapsing entirely.

Checkmated at every turn, Julian publicly cried foul against the bankers and competing oilmen. His now misbegotten company was a liability, and C.C. wanted out.

Magically, an anxious buyer materialized, an ambitious nobody named Sheridan C. Lewis, a thickset, broad-shouldered Texas lawyer living in a cheap boardinghouse and having trouble paying his bill. Lewis traveled with a bosom buddy, Jacob Berman alias Jack Bennett, only twenty-seven years old, but a whiz at financial manipulation. Lewis fronted for the partnership while Berman stayed in the background.

Lewis was Julian's peer as a con man. A meeting to discuss the sale of the company was set up at the Biltmore Hotel. When C.C. arrived, he was confronted by Lewis and some very impressive legal talent, led by Senator William H. King of Utah, whom Lewis had somehow managed to retain.

The haggling began and figures in the millions were tossed around the room like cigar ashes. But the two principals were bargaining with sheer gall. Julian was almost broke and Lewis had skipped into Los Angeles a few months before barely a step ahead of an army of Texas creditors.

Still it was a perfect match. Julian was desperate to sell and Lewis, though no one knew why at the moment, was even more desperate to buy.

Lewis claimed he had arranged $2,000,000 in new loans from banks and private investors to refinance Julian Pete. C.C. nodded, but before coming to a final agreement, he insisted on one proviso—he wanted that last $500,000 that he had poured into the company returned. The condition was acceptable.

Without a nickel changing hands, C.C. signed over to Lewis what was left of the assets and the hopes of more than forty thousand stockholders in Julian Pete.

Thus freed of his albatross, C.C. resumed the good life. He had salvaged less than $75,000 in cash from Julian Pete. And since the good life required enormous overhead and enormous amounts of loose cash, C.C. looked around diligently for a fresh transfusion of capital.

In less than a year he was back in action with a fresh promotion. Since the newspapers were still closed to him, he went on the air with a series of teaser announcements. Writing or talking, C.C. shucked out the same old highly effective corn: "I've got a wonder coming up, and folks, she's not only warm, she's red-hot —right off the coals. How big? Oh, I don't know—she looks like a hundred million dollars."

A few days later, the softening-up continued: "I have a project on hand that from a money-making standpoint should make the biggest oil project look like a punched-out meal ticket. So just save your dimes and dollars, because even one dollar invested in this new wonder of mine should make you a nice piece of change."

The "new wonder" that C.C. unfurled was the Western Lead Mining Co., a lead and silver property that he claimed had been discovered by a "death defying desert rat." Two million shares were offered and the stock was accepted for trading on the Los Angeles Exchange. It opened at $1.50, sold handily, and at the end of the first day of trading closed at $1.57.

To assure a steady rise, C.C. kept up a drumfire of radio bulletins: "Out of forty assays, the lowest value I got was thirty dollars ten cents to a ton, and some ran as high as ninety dollars a ton. Our mining, milling, transportation to railroad and smelter should not exceed eight dollars a ton. So you can see how high the profits are going to be."

The price of Western Lead soared to $2.00.

Next C.C. announced that the world had been unexpectedly overtaken by a shortage of lead (a "shortage" no one but C.C. had uncovered). "This should drive the price of lead to fourteen or fifteen cents a pound this year, the doubled price more than doubling the Western Lead profits."

Now it took $2.50 to buy a share.

Only six weeks after he had formed the company, he was able to make another enthusiastic announcement: "Folks, the constant daily telegrams from the mine of new ore bodies being opened up at Western Lead would positively knock your eye out."

The price went to $3.00.

Soon Julian was able to add the boundless enthusiasm of his mine superintendent to his own: "C.C., you can tell the world for me that I believe we are sitting on top of the greatest silver-lead deposit on earth, that within ninety days from today I will have trainloads of high-grade ore on their way to the smelter."

That jumped Western Lead to $3.50.

But the corporation commissioner began to get suspicious of the "greatest silver-lead deposit on earth" and an investigation was launched.

Western Lead immediately nose-dived to $1.80, more than 125,-000 shares being traded in one day. The next day it was down to $1.50. A week later the price was ninety cents. To save the stock from wholesale unloading, C.C. grabbed a microphone and frantically announced that a "new vein" had been uncovered. That held the line for a time.

But when the results of the commissioner's investigation were made public, Western Lead was suspended from trading. And there was panic in the streets. Thousands of confused, cursing investors flooded the floor of the exchange. The overflow tied up traffic for hours. Hasty barricades were thrown up and police called out to keep the crowd in line. Hundreds of people streamed into C.C.'s office, begging for an explanation.

He had a lulu. He told the clerks and pensioners who had been shafted that Western Lead's demise was the fault of the brokers and bankers. He took to the air and denounced the "men who rob the public of its savings through dishonest stock selling and manipulation. Black-hearted tricksters preying and feasting on unprotected widows, ulcers of humanity."

He wasn't the first to discover that the best defense was a strong offense.

The commissioner's investigation had disclosed that Julian's Western Lead Co. was pure "blue sky." There wasn't any mine. There wasn't any lead or silver. There wasn't even a mine superintendent. Western Lead was a collection of fourteen undeveloped claims on which a total of only $7000 had been spent before Julian took them over.

Still—when the smoke cleared—C.C. had a $1,200,000 profit, investors had worthless stock certificates. Lax laws covering sale of securities gave authorities no power to prosecute.

It had taken C.C. only four months to whipsaw his way to a new fortune. With the nest egg, he plunged onward to new piracy. He took $1,000,000 of his profits and bought a silver and copper mine in Arizona, paying cash. This became the Monte Cristo Mining Co., and C.C. began selling shares at once. But the corporation commissioner was on to him now, and moved fast. C.C. was forbidden to sell the stock in California. So he rechartered the company in Nevada, and called it the New Monte Cristo Mining Co. But that was battered down too. He reorganized again, this time calling the property the Julian Merger & Mines Co., but the commissioner stepped in to put him out of business once more. Nevertheless, C.C. sold enough shares in the three companies to raise another $1,500,000.

By any name, the Monte Cristo was another washout. Its lower levels were filled with water and it was eventually sold for $14,-857 to satisfy two receivership judgments.

"I learned a lot about mining," said C.C., explaining the lack of profit-bearing ores. So had his stockholders. Dozens of lawsuits for recovery were filed against him.

The collapse of Western Lead followed by the debacle of the Monte Cristo companies hardly had time to register when an even more stunning financial bomb exploded. On May 5, 1927, Julian Pete was suspended from trading and declared bankrupt!

Again there was panic along Spring Street. One stockbroker committed suicide in a taxicab. Another broker was murdered in cold blood by a stockholder. Several presidents and vice-presidents of Los Angeles banks resigned and scheduled hasty trips to Europe. Pathetic streams of desperate investors again flooded into C.C.'s office begging him to bail them out.

The story behind the Julian Pete bankruptcy was fantastic. Under the stewardship of Lewis and Berman, the company had undergone an unbelievable financial castration. They had issued and sold more than four million bogus shares in a company that had only 400,000 authorized shares. The oversubscribed stock had brought $150,000,000!

To work the colossal fraud, Lewis had bought control of a respected brokerage firm and put Berman in charge of running it. Berman issued the phony stock as fast as he could get it off the printing presses, using the telephone directory to find names to fill in on the unauthorized stock certificates.

Though C.C. was not directly involved in the overissue, he was getting $5000 a week in secret from Berman against the $500,000

Lewis had promised him. C.C. along with the other insiders in the Los Angeles financial community had heard rumors of an overissue months before Julian Pete's collapse. But it was in his interest to keep the company afloat, so he ignored the rumors. A lot of other powerful men were also interested in keeping Julian Pete afloat, though they too suspected the overissue. The banks had given huge loans to Lewis, there were lucrative commissions at stake for the brokers, and outside millionaires were able to demand usurious interest rates to support the investment pools and syndicates that had been formed to speculate in the company's stock.

The day after Julian Pete fell C.C. announced that he would broadcast the names of the culprits who were responsible. The bilked investors were screaming for whipping boys and blood, and C.C. said he would give them what they wanted—and more. For C.C., this was a heaven-sent opportunity to make everyone forget about Western Lead and the Monte Cristo.

The night of the broadcast thousands turned out. The streets were blocked for half a mile in every direction outside C.C.'s radio station. Loudspeakers were set up for the majority who couldn't get into the studio. Over the airwaves, millions heard what became one of the most remarkable and famous broadcasts in radio history.

"Folks," he began, "I've been offered one million dollars in thousand-dollar bills to keep quiet. But the bankers aren't going to muzzle me. They couldn't shut me up for fifty millions. I have 'em where I want 'em. For six years I've been waiting for this chance. They don't have money enough to buy me off.

"Julian Pete has been wrecked by the greed of these Los Angeles bankers and their friends. They bled the concern white through loans at usurious rates of interest, through bonuses, commissions and extorted gifts."

He paused dramatically. Then he not only named the names of the men he said were responsible for the collapse, but he spelled out each name and called each a thief, a crook or a liar.

The broadcast sent the Los Angeles temperature up to the bursting point. The grand jury rushed to question witnesses. And the first witness was C.C. himself, dewy-eyed, righteous and innocent. He repeated the charges he'd made on the radio.

The grand jury eventually returned conspiracy and usury indictments against Lewis and fifty-five of the city's mightiest bankers and businessmen, including movie titans Louis B. Mayer and Cecil B. De Mille. Berman, also under indictment, had skipped to Paris, supposedly with $630,000 strapped in a money belt around his waist and with another $3,000,000 stashed in European banks.

To the consternation of many, C.C. wasn't indicted for anything. But the greatest shock was yet to come. In a long series of subsequent trials, many of them tainted with the smell of jury tampering, all the defendants, Lewis included, were acquitted! Only Berman, who had returned voluntarily from Europe, was convicted on three counts of forgery.

Superior Court Judge Schauer declared angrily, "The net result of justice in the Julian cases has been the conviction of one lone defendant. Justice has failed!"

The reason it failed (in addition to the unproved charges that jurors had been reached) became apparent when the Los Angeles *Times* printed the damning diary of a mild little tailor named Milton Pike. It did no less than accuse District Attorney Asa Keyes of accepting bribes from go-betweens for the defendants at the Spring Street shop where the meticulous and observant Pike stitched away.

Keyes was brought to trial, and the major witness against him was Berman, who had his conviction set aside in exchange for his testimony. Berman said that Keyes had received over $175,-000 plus gifts for "letting up" in court. The D.A. got one to fourteen years at San Quentin.

Berman's millions were never found. But he and Lewis were later convicted in another oil swindle and the government sent them to Leavenworth for seven-year jolts.

From this titanic mess, C.C. emerged completely unscathed. He had solidly managed to identify himself with the victims. He began to travel widely with his girl friends, to Cuba, Mexico and Europe. But financial troubles were plaguing him once more. Hundreds of thousands of dollars in judgments and lawsuits on the Western Lead and Monte Cristo promotions were successfully filed against him. It became increasingly obvious to C.C. that he needed still another transfusion of capital.

Figuring he'd about had it in Los Angeles, he looked around for a new base of operations. He decided on Oklahoma City, turning up there with a bodyguard, his valet and a claim that he had only $400 in cash.

Swinging his gold-headed cane, he declared: "I've come to Oklahoma City to stage a comeback. I believe this is the only place under the shining canopy of heaven where such profits as I am so firmly determined to make for the good people here, can quickly be made."

C.C. obviously hadn't lost his touch. He rented offices in the Cotton Exchange Building and had no difficulty finding backers for his new enterprise, the C.C. Julian Oil & Royalties Co. This time he sold his shares through the mails, mostly to old customers in Los Angeles who still had unflagging faith in their aging champion.

In less than a year, he bloomed again as a millionaire. He had raised $2,250,000 in the new oil promotion. "Just like picking money up off the street," he boasted.

He bought a $25,000 airplane and hired a private pilot. There were more new cars and more new girls. The opulent parties began again. When Oklahoma City got dull, he loaded the plane with friends and ducked below the border to enliven the night life of Nuevo Laredo.

But the tide was beginning to turn. Back in Los Angeles he was thrown into involuntary bankruptcy and in 1931 his wife sued for divorce, filing sensational charges. Pretty, titian-haired Mary Olive Julian named four corespondents—a Texas girl who, she said, had accompanied her husband to Europe, a Cherokee Indian girl in Oklahoma City and two girls in Los Angeles "of tender years" who had been with him on the trips to Mexico and Cuba.

"It's tragic that so sweet a woman as my wife should permit herself to be influenced by my archenemies and other persons having ulterior motives," said C.C.

The divorce was granted and the ex-Mrs. Julian put her mansion and its furnishings up for auction. The nineteen-room home with heart-shaped swimming pool on four acres of ground went for $65,000. The auction turned into a carnival. Tourists trooped through the house to admire the gold bathtub, a vendor sold pop from the hood of one of C.C.'s used Rolls Royces, and a Greek Orthodox priest, speaking to few listeners, railed against the "wages of sin."

And the "wages of sin" did seem to be piling up for C.C. Oklahoma investigators discovered that he had put only $150,000 of the money he'd raised into the new company. The other $2,100,-000, it was assumed, went for his personal amusements. He was charged with violation of mail-fraud statutes and arrested.

But even in jail C.C. lived well. His valet appeared outside his cell each morning and handed him a fresh change of clothes. From behind bars, to a group of reporters who dropped by for an interview, he said, "I'm not finished yet, boys. I'll be back. Hell, the easiest thing in the world to do is to make a million dollars."

A few days later, C.C. was released on $25,000 bail. Then a stockholder with a $200,000 judgment against him forced him into court to reveal his assets.

With his flair for showmanship, C.C. gave a heart-rending performance. He emptied the contents of his pockets, which contained nine keys, a pocketknife and a small amount of money.

"I have no property of any description in this state, country or world," he announced as he piously tossed his "assets" before the judge.

He was declared a bankrupt, with liabilities of $3,057,436.53. And he still had to face the mail-fraud charges and a possible prison term.

That was unthinkable. So C.C. jumped bail, traveled to Canada by train under the alias of T. R. King. Afraid that the police might be waiting for him at the Vancouver docks, he hired a speedboat, had himself run out beyond the twelve-mile limit, and climbed aboard a vessel heading for the Orient.

He settled in Shanghai, the Brazil of its time. The international settlement of the city was a colorful haven for White Russian refugees, defrocked priests, cashiered officers from a dozen armies, and men on the run from the police from all over the world. Best of all, the city, under British influence, had no extradition treaty with the United States.

C.C. was soon a familiar figure, striding around in his garish dude's wardrobe and swinging his ever present cane. He was

fifty years old now, but still doing what came naturally, hiring a
lovely nineteen-year-old secretary and opening a small office to
organize Chinese capital into oil syndicates.

But somehow it wasn't the same. The Chinese weren't as gullible as Americans. C.C. went heavily into debt after failing to
swing a single major deal. He was evicted from the Hotel Metro-
pole and his elaborate wardrobe (and cane) seized to cover
two months of unpaid bills. Then from the States came word that
President Franklin Roosevelt was about to sign a new extradition
treaty, written to snare another fugitive, Samuel Insull, who had
fled to Greece after his $2,000,000,000 utilities empire crashed
amid charges of fraud. The law would give U. S. consular officials
the right to arrest American fugitives in a number of nations,
China included, outside the territorial limits of the United States.
Oklahoma Governor William H. Murray planned to use the new
international agreement to bring Julian back.

On the Sunday evening of March 25, 1935, C.C. appeared to
be in a jovial mood, despite all his troubles. Dressed in his one
remaining suit, he called for his secretary and they went to the
fashionable Astor House for dinner.

C.C. ordered the most expensive meal on the menu. With the
brandy, he had the waiter bring cigars. He smoked one lovingly,
smiled and waved to acquaintances at nearby tables. He let the
gay music of the hotel orchestra wash over him.

A few minutes after midnight, C.C. excused himself, and went
upstairs to a room he had rented for the evening. He took a small
pouch from his pocket, mixed its contents in a glass of water and
drank. The poison killed him six hours later.

Though he had averaged almost $1,000,000 a year since the
day he left the oil fields, he was buried in a pauper's grave. His
ex-wife cabled forty dollars for a pine box.

Of all the epitaphs, one of his lawyers in Los Angeles perhaps
said it best: "The bastard knew how to live and knew how to
die."

4

REAL ESTATE

Bunco, Boomers and Ten-Percenters

Under all is the land. Upon its wise utilization and widely
allocated ownership depend the survival and growth of
free institutions and of our civilization.
—From Code of Ethics,
National Association of Real Estate Boards
(*California Real Estate Magazine*)

In a burst of rare national generosity, the United States in July,
1963, formally ceded 437 acres of El Paso, Texas, to the government of Mexico. Presidents John F. Kennedy and Adolfo Lopez
Mateos agreed the grant was "a victory of law and reason."

But unsatiated ultranationalists in Mexico City used the occasion to renew their clamor for the redress of what they considered
an old and unforgivable swindle, the loss to the U. S. of Catalina
and several other offshore southern California islands.

The Catalinans promptly dismissed the claim as "preposterous"
and "impossible to sustain." From his redoubt in Avalon, Catalina's touristy capital, the city manager, jaw set firmly seaward,
declaimed: "We stand ready to repel any invasion that might be
forthcoming and will fight to the last man."

Despite the shaft of sarcasm, the Mexican diehards had an intriguing theoretical case. The 1848 Treaty of Guadalupe Hidalgo
ended a bitter, angry real-estate war between the United States
and Mexico. The peace settlement ceded Arizona, New Mexico,
Texas and California to the victorious Americans. But after all the
Hidalgo papers had been shuffled and signed (under Major
General Winfield Scott's artillery), some small-print purist discovered that mention of Catalina and a few other specks off the

coast of southern California had been entirely omitted. The extremist Mexicans have tenaciously clung to the omission as the basis of their claim.

But the Hidalgo Treaty did more in southern California than cloud the ownership of some dirt-chip islands in a comic-opera controversy.

It paved the way for the first American real-estate sharks to steal from the Spaniards what they in turn had stolen from the Indians—who were on hand in 1542 to meet the boat of California's discoverer, Juan Rodríguez Cabrillo. Father Junípero Serra and his Franciscan priests arrived 227 years later and built the storied twenty-one missions along the California coast. But the missions, despite the picturesque, sanctified place they have in current local folklore, were little more than a blind behind which the holy fathers pulled off the first land grab in southern California.

The fathers gobbled up the land in the name of the Church. They baptized and converted the Indians and paid them off in cheap wine for back-breaking dawn-to-sundown labor. By 1834, the San Gabriel Mission alone was worth nearly $80,000,000. It was a baronial complex of seventeen huge ranchos stocked with gigantic herds of cattle, horses, sheep and three thousand Indians who had built the adobe plantation under the same serflike conditions Negroes had suffered in building the plantations of the Southern aristocracy.

Under Spanish rule, Indians often were held against their will at the missions as "slave laborers and serfs . . . and were seldom permitted to live as families. Those who tried to escape felt the full force of raiding parties which brought them back dead or alive," said a report submitted to the California State Board of Education in 1965 by the American Indian Historical Society.

The Society asked for revision of school textbooks to depict a better image of the Indian even though it meant tarnishing the image of the mission padres. It was especially critical of a fourth-grade state-approved text that describes the "busy" and "happy" life of the Indians at the old Spanish missions: "This is either ignorance or deliberate falsification." The texts now in use, the report added, treat the Indian superficially and contain misinformation, misinterpretations and misconceptions. It also charged that California teachers were "largely uninformed" on the subject of Indian history.

The Board of Education endorsed the report as "responsible" and said textbook publishers would be expected in the future to heed its contents and suggestions.

The original idea behind the missions was that they were to be the forerunners of civilian-controlled cities. After an initial ten years of virgin colonization the Franciscans were supposed to turn them back to civil authorities. But the worldly fathers had too great a proprietary interest in what they had wrought.

Mexico, after winning its independence from Spain in 1821, chafed under the power of the Spanish priests. In 1836 the Mexican government broke that power by issuing a series of decrees that secularized the missions. Half the land was supposed to revert to the Indians and the other half was given in grants to high-caste Spanish and Mexican soldiers and civilians.

The secularization decrees broke up the power complex of the padres. But the good fathers, rather than bow to authority in Mexico City, revengefully refused the orderly transfer of their missions. Instead, they threw the land and stock up for grabs on a first-come, first-served basis. When the dust had settled, the long-suffering Indians had managed to grab off only a few scruffy cows and sheep and the most fearless of the dons had grabbed off horizon-hurdling empires.

The grandees ruled their plundered estates with the arrogance of divine-right kings. One of them, brandishing an exquisite pistol, had a habit of conducting trials and executions from his saddle.

To the outbreak of the U. S.–Mexican War in 1846, the dons lived high, wide and handsome. It proved to be the briefest of golden ages. Drought and falling prices killed their cattle business. Whoring, gambling and borrowing money at spectacular interest rates from rapacious American loan sharks killed their future in California.

In 1850, two years after the American-dictated peace of Hidalgo, California achieved statehood. The grandees were forced into U. S. courts to prove they had clear title to their ranchos. The dons, by now unbelievably poor in everything but land, spun off large tracts from their holdings to shrewd Yankee lawyers to defend their claims. But the lawyers got richer, the dons poorer; the average land grant case took seventeen years to adjudicate. Ultimately, the U. S. upheld only seventy of the more than five hundred original Spanish and Mexican grants. It didn't matter, however, since virtually all of the ranchos had passed to Americans in some of the most shockingly flagrant land steals in history.

The 26,000-acre Rancho de los Alamitos sold for $152 in delinquent taxes. A $2.50 unpaid tax bill lost a chunk of ground that was sold in 1864 for $2,000,000. The Rancho Santa Gertrudes, easily worth $1,000,000, was lost for want of $5000. The 17,000 acres which became the city of Downey was lost to loan sharks who compounded interest at 5 per cent a month. The original debt had grown out of a fifty-dollar Christmas loan and the former owner killed himself at the sheriff's sale. The Rancho Rodeo de las Aguas was perhaps the most stunning bargain of all. It went for $500 in cash and $800 in notes. The name subsequently was changed to Beverly Hills.

The lusty Spanish dons were all but obliterated from southern California. A descendant of the fierce old grandee, Don Julio Verdugo, ended up as a tamale peddler on a backwater Los Angeles street.

The age of the ranchos had ended. So had the Civil War, and in St. Louis, St. Joe, Chicago and Philadelphia conniving wagon masters and their agents spread word of the gleaming paradise awaiting in California. An incredible trade in route maps, gold claims and farm sites developed among Easterners who didn't know California from Calcutta. Early memoirs of immigrants are filled with pathetic, bitter stories of gold mines that turned out to be nonexistent, of farms that turned out to be hard rock and scrub, and worse, much worse, than the land they had sold east of the Missouri in exchange for a mirage in California. Those who weathered the rugged wagon journey were foxed and fleeced on arrival in Los Angeles by storekeepers, land promoters and bankers.

The greatest of the con men arrived in the guise of railroad tycoons. The Southern Pacific rammed its rails into Los Angeles in 1876, touching off a minor boom. When the Santa Fe bulled into town some ten years later, the competition got rough. Now the call of the con men in southern California began to be heard round the world.

To fill their barren acres and keep the cars loaded, the two railroads stopped at nothing. A ferocious rate war broke out. The Santa Fe began hauling Midwesterners to Los Angeles for one dollar per passenger. The Southern Pacific met the rate. Six Santa Fe passenger trains arrived in Los Angeles daily, and in 1887 the Southern Pacific brought in more than 120,000 people.

"It was the greatest mass movement in history of good, plain, middle class God-fearing men and women," said one enthusiastic newspaper.

No one caviled with the ethics of the railroads and how they were bringing the God-fearing into southern California. Anything went.

The two roads opened offices all over the Midwest and the East, making outrageous claims for the opportunities in southern California. The railroad agents even fanned through the villages of half a dozen European countries, notably Ireland, and sold lots in southern California before the immigrants booked passage.

Whole Midwestern communities were enticed to pack up lock, stock and population for the glory ride to California. In Michigan and Iowa brass bands played them down to the train. But along with the naïve corn-shuckers, the trains also carried the townsite sharks who had already carved up, swindled and created phony booms in Wichita, Kansas City, Chicago, Minneapolis and Seattle.

When these real-estate shell men hit Los Angeles, they found a paradise. The whole town was on a land binge.

Ministers with deeds nestled in the pages of their Bibles cajoled parishioners after Sunday services to purchase lots. Bellboys offered a piece of a tract first, a woman second. It took two hours to get a haircut, most of the time spent bargaining over a lot owned by the barber.

"Two-thirds of our population were, in a sense, more insane than sane," wrote Harris Newmark, an early-day businessman. "Syndicates, subdivisions and tracts: these were the most popular terms of the day. There were enough subdivisions to accommodate ten million people and enough syndicates to handle the affairs of a nation."

The suckers camped in lines outside the tents of the real-estate men for two or three days for the privilege of buying a slice of a newly announced subdivision. Most of them hoped to turn around immediately and resell at a profit. Even the places in line became valuable, going for up to $100.

The shell men, packed a dozen to a tent, established values that had no relationship to reason. Prices often went up by no other yardstick than the clock, a promoter arbitrarily announcing that "after 1 P.M. tomorrow the price advances $100."

Some tracts were sold by lottery, spiced by the promoter's never-fulfilled promise that cottages would be built on the land of the first dozen winners.

Dry creeks and lots buried underwater were sold as land with "water privileges." Lots with "scenic attractions" proved to be located on the incline of a mountain or at the bottom of a chasm.

Colonel Bartlett's 7th Infantry Band blared a river of suckers down to the site of "Magnificent Monte Vista, the Gem of the Mountains, the Queen of the Valley." Block-long parades, led by freaks, elephants and tigers made a circus of land selling. The suckers were also shuttled into subdivisions by private railroad cars and signed up at barbecues and picnics.

Outrageously exaggerated advertising, the pure bunkum style of copy writing that survives in southern California real-estate ads to this day, flowered in the eighties.

"Boom! Boom! Boom! Boom! in Arcadia!" "Whittier! Whittier! Whittier!—Queen of the Foothills and Crown of the San Gabriel Valley." "Peerless Long Beach." "Tustin the Beautiful." "Santa Ana . . . The Metropolis of Southern California's Fairest Valley! Beautiful! Busy! Bustling! Booming!" "Ho, for the Beach! To-morrow, To-morrow! Marvelous Grand Auction Sale at Santa Monica. 350—Acres—350." "Glendale—Veni, Vidi, Vici."

One awestruck resident who returned from a two-month trip to the East counted more than a dozen new townsites laid out along the Santa Fe tracks between San Bernardino and Los Angeles.

In four years, more than one hundred towns, most of them pipe dreams, were platted. At the height of the insanity, in July, 1887, over $500,000 changed hands daily in real-estate deals.

"The crime of the age," one editor declared when it all fell flat in 1889. Sixty-two of the paper cities collapsed, never to rise from the carnage of speculation.

"The inevitable collapse came and values tumbled fully as rapidly as they had advanced," wrote Newmark. "Many found themselves with overwhelming debts and mortgages quite impossible of liquidation. Readjustment took years and years. Many of our greatest boomers and speculators lost all hope; and more than one poor suicide so paid the price of his inordinate craving for wealth."

The spoils had gone to the shrewdest of the con men, who made their fast killings and got out. "The good, plain, middle class God-fearing men and women" stayed, and because there was no alternative, patiently tended their inflated lots, waiting generations for values to again approximate the prices they had paid.

Things picked up in 1906 in a flash beach boom, but it too was phony and ephemeral. Hysteria and mob-bidding broke out at Redondo Beach. Women pledged their jewels to speculate in lots at ten times their intrinsic value. The Los Angeles *Times* reported, "Businessmen went crazy for the time being, and took checks which never could be cashed, and thus tied up property which might have sold at high figures. Contracts flew from hand to hand so fast that no one knew where the title ran."

By 1914, the indefatigable boomers had organized a feisty chamber of commerce. Los Angeles was drowsing temporarily, lots were a glut on the market. So the boomers went out to drum up trade.

"With a steam siren whistle on its locomotive screaming a noisy farewell," ran the Los Angeles *Herald-Express* account, "a Chamber of Commerce excursion of Los Angeles gladhanders left for the Imperial Valley and Arizona to cement business friendship. The Long Beach brass band will lead the 125 Los Angeles businessmen as a parade through each city. The band will play 'I Love You, California' in every city on the road. The trip will take in Calexico, El Centro, Holtville, Imperial, Brawley, Nyland, Yuma, Douglas, Bisbee, Tucson and Phoenix."

Not until the 1920s did Los Angeles see a population influx to eclipse the surge of the eighties. Lured by oil, motion pictures and the climate, more than 1,300,000 settled in Los Angeles

County. The real-estate promoters were waiting again, and shortly eight new cities were established. They hired barkers, herded prospects into buses for a "free lunch and ride" to the subdivisions. The heat was turned up inside the buses and no one was allowed to move out of the sweatboxes until five to ten dollars was deposited on a lot.

By the end of World War II, the population flood that has yet to subside began rolling into southern California, and the ethics of the real-estate salesmen seeking to house the new migrants are still in the grand tradition.

Currently, one of every five real-estate salesmen in the United States is in California, the ranks swollen by vague widow ladies from the Midwest, part-time housewives, barbers, movie extras and car salesmen—undereducated dabblers who will sell anything to anyone with the cash for a down payment.

"Real Estate Promoter Gets Jail" is a standing headline in the Los Angeles press. Hundreds of salesmen and brokers are stripped of their licenses each year by the real-estate commissioner in Sacramento for a variety of shady practices. So thick are the con men in the real-estate offices that the state legislature has passed a bill to compensate buyers defrauded by brokers.

"A unique concept in state regulation," said Governor Edmund G. Brown when he signed the legislation. "It provides a new degree of confidence for the public when dealing with real-estate brokers."

The measure provides that a buyer who obtains a final judgment against a real-estate licensee on grounds of fraud may recover up to $10,000 from a special fund created by broker contributions and administered by the real-estate commissioner.

The law spurred the California Real Estate Association into a remarkable justification of the shaky ethics or ignorance of its own members. "A broker can be held responsible for the acts of his salesmen. Increasingly, he can be held responsible for his own mistakes," said an article in the Association's magazine, urging its 45,000 members to sign up for fraud insurance.

"Here is an actual case reported to our insurance people and covered by insurance. A salesman in a . . . broker's office showed the wrong piece of property [a vacant lot] to a client. The client retained an architect to design a home on the property. When the purchase of the lot went on record, it was discovered to be the wrong lot. The correct lot was much more difficult on which to build. The Realtor was sued for $5,000."

Without a word of censure for the outrageous stupidity of the salesman, the Association points out the advantages of having the insurance to "protect the broker against his liability of even intentional fraud of his salesmen" and "liability for errors and omissions."

Though Sacramento has toughened requirements for obtaining a broker's license, putting applicants through a grueling all-day examination, hundreds of salesmen and brokers continue to run roughshod over the ethics of their own code.

The new tracts, meantime, multiply at a staggering rate, and the lush prose that brings the buyers in is familiar to the student of southern California real-estate advertising. The copy hasn't changed much.

"Special Showing 'Til Midnight at Canoga Park . . . Suburb of Destiny." "You'll Love Living in Costa Mesa, Nature's Penthouse." "Come Fly With Us to Apple Valley." "Homes For Children With Families." "This Is It. Seascape. Sunset. Champagne." "Don't Settle For Less Than Paradise in the Burbank Hills." "A World Apart—Think of Newport Bay." "Fantastic—Buy, Look-Look!!!—Pay More, What For." "Live Here—Speculate."

The frantic pace of life in southern California is also reflected in the ads: "VA Or FHA Repossessions—Take Your Choice," "Gone To East," "Gone To Colorado," "San Francisco Transfer," "Must Sell Fast—Bought Another," "Oregon Transfer," "Chicago Transfer," "Portugal Bound," "Husband Gone, Wife Deserted," "South Pacific Transfer," "Phoenix Transfer," "Nevada Transfer," "Moving To Senior Citizen City," "Job Transfer."

The spirit of the boomer is everlasting. In 1964, Mayor Samuel W. Yorty proposed that $100,000 be earmarked to establish a promotion office in New York City "to tell the Los Angeles story." This was in addition to the $3,000,000–4,000,000 already spent in such promotion by private industry, banks, utilities, land developers and chambers of commerce.

Where once agents roamed through European villages to ferret out immigrant buyers, southern California land promoters these days jet to London, Frankfurt and Zurich seeking big-money investors for get-rich-quick speculation. One outfit has combed over $6,000,000 from investors in Britain, West Germany, and Switzerland.

Real estate is one of the quickest ways to make or lose a fortune in southern California. Virtually everyone has a story to tell about a missed chance to pick up a valuable piece of property when it was selling for next to nothing.

Southern Californians are possibly the most real-estate-conscious people in the world. They are also the world's ranking suckers for real-estate cons. Since 1956, the local Better Business Bureau has warned against new rackets in phony appraisal and listing fees, desert land, free lots and guaranteed valuations of property. But the fleecing continues, and the roll call of bizarre and brazen cons is endless.

Ettie Lee, the seventy-seven-year-old aunt of Secretary of the Interior Stewart L. Udall, charged she was taken by a couple of fast-talking real-estate people when she agreed to pay $200,000 for Death Valley Junction, an abandoned ghost town she purchased in 1960.

Miss Lee, a retired schoolteacher who planned to turn the site into a senior citizens' community, testified in Superior Court that one of the brokers had whisked her through an inspection of the town's facilities—hotel, coffee shop, barber shop, gasoline station, bank, curio store, laundry and ten homes. She was assured that everything was in working order.

But it didn't take long to discover that she had actually purchased a desert relic.

Judge Brodie Ahlport declared: "The town was obviously a ruin beyond recall. Notwithstanding its romantic past, it was not an operating community as represented.

"The service station had one working pump and the general store had some stock on its shelves, but the rest of the shops were only idle places in an idle village whose adobe walls bulged and leaned.

"Sagging roofs gaped to let in both the starlight and the desert wind. The smell of decay and ruin was everywhere. To have repaired and restored the town would have cost far more than it was worth."

During the trial it was established that the brokers had paid only $40,000 for the town, made only superficial repairs and set up false fronts for businesses which did not exist.

In scaling down Miss Lee's obligation on the property to $75,000, the judge concluded, "The defendants have reaped enough."

By simply promising he had an in with the Teamsters Pension Fund, a Beverly Hills broker racked up a score of $107,250 in fees. He had convinced his clients, including a syndicate of investors planning to build a private hospital, that he could arrange millions in favorable construction loans by simply picking up the phone and calling union officers. He was convicted on five counts of grand theft when witnesses for the union testified they had never heard of him.

A real-estate trader, who operated under more than thirty aliases, was flayed by a Los Angeles judge for stealing from "the poorest segment of our population without pity." In a twelve-day trial, it was found that his *m.o.* consisted of renting cheap houses at high rents and exorbitant interest to elderly couples with false promises that rent would apply to the cost of the house under an option to buy. His victims numbered in the hundreds.

"I always took care of myself without any help and thought others should do the same," he declared in his own defense. "I sold hard and was often carried away with my sales pitch."

In ordering him to adopt only one name and use no others, the judge added: "All the names you assumed were to give people the impression they were dealing with a very important corporation, second only to General Motors and United States Steel instead of a cheap little outfit designed to cheat the poor and helpless."

In 1962, a ring of seven men was convicted of bilking more than $2,000,000 from two hundred homeowners in a complex scheme that depended on issuing trust deeds or mortgages. The ring sent letters to householders with clear titles, offering them top-heavy prices for their property. If they accepted the deal and signed away their titles, they were given a 25 per cent down payment in cash and told they would receive a trust deed for the balance. Then the hustlers would borrow as much as possible on the titles from banks or savings and loan institutions and pocket the money. The homeowners later discovered that the

lenders held first mortgages on their homes and that the real-
estate firm was without funds to pay them the 75 per cent still
due.

The seven men had drained off about $1,500,000 in net profit
from the swindle in a little over two years of operation. In putting
away the ringleader, the judge declared: "In all my years on the
bench all the armed robbers who have come before me have not
created as much havoc in the community as this defendant has
with his pen."

By 1963, a kindly little old lady broker who could double for
Whistler's mother had conned over $1,000,000 by buying and
selling houses condemned by the state for freeways. She raised
the money to buy the houses by issuing fictitious notes and trust
deeds on the property as security for the borrowed funds. Then,
without knowledge of the persons who loaned the funds, she
would sell the houses, pay off the loans and begin the cycle again.
The scheme snared her in a vicious circle of borrowing and repaying loans. It also sent her to prison on a conviction for grand
theft and forgery.

Ninety-nine per cent of California's homes are financed by trust
deeds issued by savings and loan firms, banks or private lenders.
Similar to the traditional mortgage, the trust deed offers several
advantages to the lender, particularly the privilege of selling de-
faulted property after 111 days without going into court.

The trust deed was designed by legitimate California financial
men to attract capital from the East to underwrite the state's real-
estate development. With its advantageous provisions for lenders,
the money flowed in readily.

But in the mid-1950s a new type of local trust deed firm came
into prominence. Dozens of others soon flowered and bloomed,
aping the assembly-line selling methods of the man who became
the Henry Ford of the trust deed industry.

Dapper David Farrell was a businessman in search of an idea.
An elder in the Mormon Church and a veteran who had served
two years as a prisoner of the Germans in World War II, he had
drifted through a series of jobs and investments with indifferent
success for nearly ten years after his discharge.

Then in July, 1954, he hit upon a brilliant idea, an idea that ultimately developed into a $43,000,000 swindle!

With three employees, Farrell opened the Los Angeles Trust Deed & Mortgage Exchange at 626 South Spring Street, next door to the Los Angeles Stock Exchange.

His company, capitalized at $10,000, functioned much like a stock exchange, except that trust deeds instead of stocks were listed on its "big board." Farrell's exchange, for the first time, was to provide a vast liquid market on a local, regional and national scale for fast cash out of trust deeds at a fair market price, offering sellers a market of thousands of prospective buyers.

It would now be possible to buy and sell trust deeds as easily as stocks. Investors who had been burned in the stock market and who felt uneasy that the destiny of their money depended on changing economic conditions and remote corporation officers in executive suites, could understand and appreciate the novelty of Farrell's idea. Their money, after all, would be protected by the cornerstone of American prosperity—land!

But for all its seeming advantages, Farrell's idea was slow to catch on in a big way. He discovered that investors still feared the inevitable ups and downs of the market place and shied away from risk, even in so tangible an investment as California property.

To overcome such reluctance, he shopped around for a refinement, a way to remove the risk of fluctuations. Small investors, who collectively provided the billions that financed all large American enterprises, wanted a good return on their money, but they also wanted security. That was why most people put their money in banks.

Farrell almost immediately came up with an ingenious new wrinkle that apparently would guarantee security with high profits. He took large ads in the Los Angeles press and printed expensive slick-paper brochures to inform the public of his gee-whiz scheme.

He advertised "guaranteed returns on secured trust deeds." He not only guaranteed the investment, but he would pay a striking 10 per cent interest every month on every dollar invested! The interest-bearing trust deeds would provide investors with an income for life!

That was pretty heady stuff. Farrell's 10 per cent interest rate more than tripled the going 3 per cent the banks were paying and it more than doubled the 4 per cent return from savings and loan institutions.

Predictably, Farrell's business boomed. He had built a better mousetrap and the world began to beat a path to his door. He had also founded Los Angeles' 10 per cent industry.

By 1959, five years after his modest beginning, Farrell was a whopping success. He had expanded from what he told investors was "just an idea" back in 1954 to a volume of $25,000,000 in purchase orders. He had twelve branch offices scattered all over California, planned to open another in Denver. Farrell also installed his brother, Oliver, as an executive in the firm.

While competing bankers and savings and loan men looked on with jaundiced eye at Farrell's operation, investors were gleeful. The 10 per cent interest rolled in month after month.

"We owe our success to our nearly seven thousand customers who fully appreciate the necessity for a higher yield during these times of increasing inflation and higher taxes," Farrell said. "People who live on fixed incomes particularly need the greater return made possible by carefully selected trust deed investments."

Farrell was living under a halo of public trust. People continued to invest in growing numbers and the 10 per cent interest checks continued to arrive on time. The financial community marveled at his business acumen.

Frank E. Kennamer, Jr., the chief enforcement attorney for the Securities and Exchange Commission, also marveled at Farrell's acumen—but for a different reason. Having watched Farrell's rise with decided suspicion, he called the trust deed king in for a meeting and raised a number of objections to his operation, particularly his advertising of guaranteed returns. Kennamer felt that investors were not being told of the risks.

Farrell wanted to cooperate with the SEC. He asked Kennamer how his firm could meet the objections of the watchdog agency.

"The best way you can comply with the law," the SEC sleuth said, "is to go back to your office and lock it up."

"I'll be happy to do anything except lock my door," he replied indignantly. "I don't think your advice is very American and I didn't spend two years in a German prison camp to be told I couldn't operate my business."

Farrell stayed in business. But he hired a former SEC lawyer to handle a mounting volume of litigation being drummed up against him by various state and federal agencies.

His ads continued to promise 10 per cent guaranteed returns. From all over the world, money poured in. His volume zoomed to over $40,000,000.

Then the earthquake hit! Farrell, his brother Oliver and his controller, Stanley Marks, were arrested by federal investigators and charged with thirty-one counts of violating mail-fraud statutes and the Securities Act of 1933. Bankruptcy proceedings against Farrell's company were also initiated.

Investors screamed for an explanation. They had taken a financial ride into the utopian valley of guaranteed returns and wanted to know what had gone wrong. How could a $40,000,000 company tumble overnight? Wasn't the firm backed by good, solid property worth many times $40,000,000? Why weren't they going to receive those sweet 10 per cent interest checks any longer?

Contending explanations raged on the front pages of the press. A government spokesman declared Farrell's operation was the "biggest fraud case in the history of the SEC." It was "a conspiracy to defraud on a massive scale."

Farrell called a press conference and announced, "We'll sue them for a million dollars." Denying all the charges, he said that since a private citizen cannot sue the government, he had instructed his attorneys to level his million-dollar suit for libel against the SEC officials responsible for the indictment.

He charged the government agency with attempting "to create public distrust in his company with untrue and irresponsible statements to the press." He said such statements were deliberately phrased to put his firm out of the trust deed business.

"Our business this year will be, we estimate, somewhere around $8,000,000. In July we received about $1,500,000 in new money from trust deed investors." He said no customer had ever suffered a loss or failed to receive his full 10 per cent interest or complained of treatment by his firm.

"I want an opportunity to clear these matters up once and for all, so that the public will have confidence in the type of business we are operating."

Farrell's opportunity would come in court. For the moment, he was out of business. His firm was thrown into bankruptcy.

Along with the indictment, Thomas E. Sheridan, chief of the criminal division of the United States Attorney's Office, announced that Farrell had obtained a visa the previous August, causing the government to believe he intended to leave the country. The government also had information, Sheridan added, causing investigators to believe Farrell had placed certain funds in foreign countries. His bail was set at $200,000.

The trial, billed as the anatomy of a swindle, opened in an atmosphere of quiet drama. It would last for five weeks. The government would question forty-seven witnesses, introduce 2100 exhibits and attempt to unravel a $40,000,000 puzzle that some investigators thought was the economic crime of the century.

Assistant U. S. Attorney Edward Medvene was charged with the prosecution. The federal lawyer pulled no punches in his opening statement.

"These defendants deliberately and with premeditation schemed to defraud investors. The company was guilty of misstating material facts and also failed to advise investors of the speculative nature of the investment firm.

"More than ten thousand people have invested funds, including their blind aid and social security pension monies.

"The money was coming in too fast for the firm to find adequate and secure property for trust deeds. As the money kept pouring in and with LATD promising to pay ten per cent on it, it was necessary to get more and more trust deeds with less and less security."

Medvene charged that many of the trust deeds were created on raw and unimproved land, that LATD did not have enough financial capital behind it to stay liquid and that money was misappropriated.

"The evidence will show that it was consistently necessary to apply funds of investor 'A' to meet the obligations of investor 'B.' As long as the money was coming in and exceeding the money going out, the firm could operate. But once the funds stopped coming in fast enough, the house of cards collapsed. And they knew it had to collapse."

Farrell's attorney, Lloyd F. Dunn, denied it all in his opening remarks. "The defense revolves on the basis that the officers were acting in good faith. David Farrell planned to devote his life to this business and make available to the public trust deeds on a basis that was not previously available." The defense attorney added that there is no evidence of conspiracy, misrepresentation or fraud and that while a "sales pitch" might have been made, no one was intentionally misled.

The first government witness was one of Farrell's assistants. He testified that he was ordered by Farrell to create a "bank-like" atmosphere in the firm's dealings with customers. He also said that all advertising brochures about the operation were prepared by Farrell.

A major item of curiosity was the extent to which Farrell had personally profited from the firm's operation. The government estimated that he had received a total of $750,000 in commissions and fees and an additional $200,000 in earnings in the last two and a half years the company operated—that he had become wealthy while running the firm at the expense of investors.

Oliver D. Brock, controller for the trustees of Farrell's bankrupt firm, spelled out the details. He testified that in 1958, 1959 and the first five months of 1960, Farrell received $239,802, not including any income he might have received from various side participation agreements with developers of subdivisions. Brock said that $600,000 was spent on advertising from January, 1958, to June 6, 1960, through a firm controlled by Farrell. In addition, $542,960 was transferred via check from the general funds of the firm to one of its wholly owned subsidiaries for "coordinating expenses or fees." Oliver Farrell had also done well. In the same period, he had drawn a total of $267,329.

Spectators gasped—but they were to be shocked into disbelief when they learned that at the time the Farrells were drawing enormous salaries and commissions, there were only pennies in the cashbox.

John M. Modglin, assistant cashier of the Security First National Bank, said that between April 17 and November 18, 1958, the bank returned seventy-three checks to LATD because of insufficient funds. At one time, he noted, the balance in the firm's checking account was $1.28.

Medvene next put a former LATD accountant on the stand to show the behind-the-scenes machinations required to juggle the huge operation. The witness ticked off these points:

1. LATD's general policy was to introduce a trust deed into an investor's account that was worth more than the total amount the investor had put into the company.

2. The firm's method of computing the cost of trust deeds so that they would earn 10 per cent for an investor generally resulted in overcharges to investors and was not based on accepted accounting practices.

3. Internal records of the company often showed less money in an investor's account than the records which the company sent to the investor showed.

4. The policy of paying 10 per cent on an investment changed during the course of his employment so that effective March 1, 1959, an investor would be required to leave his money in the company at least six months to draw any interest.

5. On at least one occasion during a "crash program" to sell all trust deeds in the firm's inventory, delinquent trust deeds were placed in investors' accounts.

6. When the firm had a growing demand for trust deeds but a small supply on hand, earnings for investors were taken from company funds.

7. At times, the company had more assets listed on its books than it actually owned.

The accountant explained the latter point occurred when an investor sought to liquidate his account. If there wasn't a trust deed under his name, LATD's policy was to pull one out of inventory and introduce it into the investor's account "for a couple of minutes." The investor was paid on the basis of that trust deed, then the company would repurchase it and return it to inventory for resale to another investor later. But this forced the firm to repurchase at a higher cost with the result that the value of the trust deed often would be inflated.

The accountant concluded that LATD operated in such a way that investors, not the company, took all the risks.

That conclusion was buttressed by another witness, one-time

head of LATD's San Francisco office. He said that buyers of trust deeds on two tracts in the San Francisco area were not given all the facts about the property. "Prior liens" were not listed when customers received their trust deeds. As the firm grew and demand increased, more and more deeds were sold on unimproved lands.

Next on the stand was a Marin County attorney, who explained how trust deeds totaling about $1,100,000 were created by Farrell on four occasions to help finance Reedlands, one of the San Francisco tracts.

He said LATD advanced money to the developer to buy the land and make improvements. David Farrell was to receive up to half the profits in the development for securing the necessary financing. Eventually about $800,000 worth of trust deeds were placed on parts of the development, but additional financing was still needed. So trust deeds worth another $228,000 were created on still another section of the development, making a total of more than $1,100,000 in encumbrances against the project.

Then a San Mateo developer, Charles F. Foster, told of Farrell's "riskless" investment policy in a Sacramento land deal. He outlined involved financial transactions in which trust deeds valued at almost $2,000,000 were "manufactured" on four hundred acres of unimproved land to be known as Capital Park Estates. Farrell financed the project by selling the trust deeds to his investors, but he retained a personal 50 per cent interest in the fifteen-hundred-lot tract without putting up a nickel of his own money.

If the financial details were getting somewhat involved, the stories of victims were simplicity itself, a testament to Farrell's adroit advertising.

Mrs. Dora Franks, seventy-two, told the jury she invested $1000 in LATD because she was convinced her money would be secured by the American home. The Los Angeles woman said she had made no previous investments and admitted she was not schooled in finance.

An eighty-seven-year-old San Franciscan, Oscar Johnson, said he invested his life savings of $1067 and lost every cent. "I had been saving for an emergency. And within sixty days of investing I had a big one. My wife broke her hip. We had no money and I had to send her to the county hospital." He said he had been assured at the time he invested that his money could be withdrawn any time he wanted it.

Manfred Danner, sixty-nine, of Oakland, whose only income came from a pension and social security, told how he cashed insurance policies and invested $10,100 just a few weeks before the firm collapsed. Danner said he asked to have his money returned after reading about litigation between the SEC and the company. "I thought that the sooner I got out the better off I would be. But the salesman talked me into leaving my money in. I never got anything back."

Fred F. Collins, fifty-three, of Huntington Park, said he invested $5000 because he was told his money would be "safe as money in the bank. I never received a dime of it."

A retired Oakland resident, seventy-two-year-old Richard White, said he put in $9000 and was given trust deeds to land which he thought was improved. "I checked the property on maps in Marin County and found it was covered by brush. I could see no improvements of any kind."

Language instructor Herman Hartmann invested more than $10,000. "I found out later I was buying trust deeds, but I didn't want to deal in those. I thought I was investing the money like putting it into a bank and would just collect interest."

Bostonian Lyle S. Cummings, sixty-six, said he invested $26,-000 because of the "guarantee" of 10 per cent interest. He told of reading about the company in the papers. "I wrote them and they sent me a brochure outlining the plan. The brochure had several interesting points including statements like the home is the best investment and the money was guaranteed. I thought I was investing in a home."

A big loser was a Hollywood television writer who invested his total wealth of $49,000. Bertram Castle said he and his wife wanted to retire to write a book and that they planned to live on the 10 per cent interest of their life savings.

"I was impressed by the bank-like appearance of the building, offices, and equipment," the writer said. "And equally impressed by David Farrell, who looked at ease, competent and capable."

Not all the victims had taken their losses philosophically. Wearing a yellow raincoat and an embittered expression, a fifty-four-year-old ex-farm laborer, who had invested $2100 in LATD, robbed a Los Angeles bank after reading of the firm's failure. The holdup man blamed the government for his loss. He told arresting officers, "I only wanted to get back the money Uncle Sam owes me."

The government's last witness was an accountant who testified that there was a shortage of more than $8,000,000 on the company's books the day LATD went into receivership. Shortages, he said, included delinquencies in investors' accounts, and similar shortages existed in hundreds of trust deeds.

The United States of America felt it had proved its case against Farrell.

The defense countered by putting three "satisfied" clients on the stand, all of whom testified they had received their 10 per cent interest as well as the return of their original investment. The three, who had invested $3000, $10,000 and $5000 respectively, expressed reactions including "quite happy" and "very good treatment." Another defense witness testified he invested $3000 and got all his money back plus interest. "They treated me very good."

Oliver Farrell, forty-five, four years older than his brother David, got on the stand and declared that up to the time LATD was placed in receivership no investors had lost any money. He said his own duties in the company were primarily concerned with sales of trust deeds to customers. His brother made the decisions.

The third defendant, controller Stanley Marks, testified he too had no voice in determining LATD policies and except for accounting procedures he knew none of the details of the firm's internal operations.

Then the ex-SEC lawyer Farrell had hired testified he had approved the operations of LATD while he was legal advisor for the firm.

Big gun for the defense was David Farrell himself. Smooth, composed, confident, the picture he sought to paint was that of a businessman who had acted in good faith. He contended that many aspects of his firm's operations were no different than the policies of savings and loan associations and mortgage companies.

Trying to beat down the prosecution's case, he made six major points about the technical operations of LATD.

1. Virtually every mortgage company services trust deeds for

investors and lenders. In the development of subdivisions "it is universal" that money be loaned to developers for improving property and constructing buildings.

2. The use of various corporations to handle specific functions within a development is a common practice not only for tax purposes but also to keep accounting records in order.

3. Appraisals were made on all property on which trust deeds were placed. It was LATD policy to always determine the underlying value of the property before trust deeds were placed on it and to be sure there was sufficient security for every trust deed.

4. It was a standard practice to place trust deeds on raw land because it not only proved profitable but permitted development of property with adequate financing.

5. There were many examples where the company credited investors with early pay-offs—cases in which borrowers paid up the amount due before it was actually due—instead of putting the "windfall" payments into the company's funds.

6. He was "not too concerned" with an estimated $8,500,000 worth of delinquent trust deeds in the accounts of customers because they were composed mainly of trust deeds on tracts under development and eventually would be valuable.

Farrell also said that early in May, 1960—about a month before the firm was taken over by receivers—"large crowds began appearing at our offices" and a large volume of mail came in from investors wanting to withdraw their money.

He said the company honored these requests as fast as possible and paid out about $3,000,000 up to the time the receivers took over.

Regarding his capacity to run a giant enterprise like LATD, Farrell said he had picked up his management background under unique circumstances. "I was a German prisoner of war in 1943–45, and we had classes on financing by men who were familiar with that field in their civilian days. We had a lot of books on financial subjects and we studied vigorously during that period."

On cross-examination, Medvene put Farrell through a withering three-hour session. Farrell admitted that he was given a $6000 airplane, an expensive car and fancy office furniture by land developers his company was financing. He also conceded that on some developments trust deed holders would have no access to

their property except by airplane or parachute! And he acknowl-
edged that he borrowed $100,000 from LATD to buy all the
stock in the Mortgage Insurance Company of America, a Colorado
firm that had no clients other than LATD. Under Medvene's
prodding, Farrell testified he then borrowed $100,000 from the in-
surance company to repay the loan from LATD.

Through it all Farrell retained complete composure.

Summing up, Medvene told the jury: "You must find them
guilty of fraud and conspiracy. They deserve no less."

He asked the jurors to put themselves in the position of the
thousands of investors that had been defrauded. The defendants
materially misrepresented facts or omitted material facts from
investors.

"There are many things the public should have known before
it invested its money. Shouldn't the investors have known how
speculative this program was? That's really what the case is about.
David Farrell was taking it off the top—taking the cream off—as
were Oliver Farrell and Marks, and they said, 'Who cares about
the poor saps who invested their savings.'"

He said documents were jockeyed back and forth so that the
company could take a profit from what rightfully belonged to
investors. He charged that thousands of trust deeds "were created
against raw, vacant land and the pattern grew as they needed
more money to keep going."

Appraisals of land "were just a cover," Medvene said, citing an
example of one piece of desert property "inflated twelve times"
above its appraised value.

In making his final plea for the defense, Dunn declared that
all of LATD's activities were carried out in "good faith while
operating under the American capitalistic system. Just like someone selling refrigerators . . . you buy a refrigerator for one hundred dollars and sell it for two hundred dollars to pay for lights,
heat and employees' salaries."

The defense attorney emphasized that all major operations of
the firm were put into effect only after seeking legal advice, including that of a former counsel for the SEC.

The jury stayed out for three and a half days.

It came back with a verdict of guilty on thirty-one counts for both David and Oliver Farrell. Marks was acquitted on all charges.

The Farrells each faced a maximum penalty of 160 years in prison and $105,000 fines.

Two months after the verdict, David Farrell, now a shaken man, faced Federal Judge John F. Kilkenny to make an impassioned ten-minute plea for probation.

"My religion," he said, "calls for honesty. I now face a paradox. A jury has found me guilty of things I don't believe in doing."

His voice breaking, he made numerous attempts to regain the composure that had marked his appearance throughout the trial.

"I make no claim to perfection. I made many mistakes but I always tried to correct them and take responsibility for them. I can state with sincerity that the mistakes I've made have been those of judgment—not intent. I never intended to defraud anyone.

"I've done my best but I've lost. I fought for the things I considered right. But perhaps you're not supposed to fight against the government."

The speech didn't make much of an impression on the court. "It's obvious to me that you've rationalized and misinterpreted your actions," said Judge Kilkenny. "You have no sense of guilt. You feel you are being persecuted. If I thought so you wouldn't be here. I personally think the jury couldn't have gone any other way. You are of high intelligence and the community should have been able to look up to you, but you have been convicted of high fraud."

David Farrell was sentenced to ten years and a fine of $85,500. Oliver got four years and a $51,000 fine.

The convictions sounded the death knell for all the other ten-percenters. But the tab was astronomical. The scam, invented in Los Angeles, had brought in over $150,000,000. David Farrell had created a gigantic industry. Fittingly, the creator was the first to suffer retribution.

5

DIPLOMA MILLS

The Little Gold Schoolhouses

The holder of a forged degree must not be allowed to tamper with the bodies and minds of Californians.
—San Diego *Tribune*

On February 4, 1836, soldier-of-fortune John Marsh, on the run from the U. S. Army for selling guns to the Missouri Sioux during the Black Hawk War, barreled into an adobe in the Los Angeles plaza to confront the *ayuntamiento,* the Mexican city council.

Marsh made an imposing figure in the cool, tallow-lit room. Six feet two, bulbous-nosed and fair-haired, he towered over the small, alert Mexicans.

Unintimidated, Council President Manuel Requena waited patiently for Marsh to state his business.

"I'm a doctor of medicine," he blurted at last. "I'm told I need your permission to practice."

The council was impressed—and interested. In all of California, there wasn't a single doctor.

"Credentials, *señor!*" President Requena snapped.

Marsh extracted a Harvard diploma from a pocket and thumped it down before the bug-eyed Mexicans. After a few moments of embarrassed consultation, the council apologetically rejected Marsh's credential. It was written in Latin, and none of them could read it. He was asked to have it translated into Spanish and reapply.

Though few in the primitive pueblo could read Spanish or Latin, twelve days after his first appearance before the council Marsh produced a satisfactory translation. President Requena affixed his seal, and Marsh had official permission to practice as a surgeon and physician, earning the distinction of becoming the first licensed doctor in California.

He practiced for six months in Los Angeles, taking his fees in cowhides and beaver skins. Disenchanted, he sold his skins for $500 to a Boston trader and moved north. With his grubstake, he bought a San Joaquin Valley rancho and worked it into a cattle and farming fortune. Respectfully addressed as "*señor-doctor*," he also continued to practice medicine until he was murdered by a vaquero in 1856.

Not until years after his death was it discovered that his foothold in California had been a fraud. The diploma he had shown the Mexicans was a legitimate Harvard bachelor of arts degree, not a medical diploma. His translation was phony. Marsh had picked up a smattering of medicine in his frontier adventuring, but even by the easy medical standards of the day he was unqualified to practice as a doctor.

Precedent thus established in the earliest moments of Los Angeles' history, thousands of the bogusly educated have followed the John Marsh tradition in California. Hundreds of Civil War veterans, yearning for a fresh start after Appomattox, carried phony degrees from diploma mills in Pennsylvania and New York into every corner of the state.

In the 1920s, many Californians took the painless route to education through the mailed diplomas of "Bishop" Holler, potentate of Oriental University in Washington, D. C. Claiming ordination direct from God's angels, Holler sold uncounted diplomas by mail in virtually every civilized country of the world until he was driven from business by postal inspectors.

Ordination mills were a thriving business in Los Angeles during the 1930s. To prove it, a group of ministers from established churches hired an investigator to gather evidence. So flagrant were the mills that for fifteen dollars the investigator succeeded in obtaining a certificate of ordination from an "archbishop" for Joe Penner's famous duck. In two days, a certificate, allowing the bearer to perform weddings, conduct funerals and ride on trains and buses at half fare was duly issued in the name of "The Reverend Drake Googoo." The sleuth then hired a girl to pose as a penniless Swedish servant from Minnesota. Calling herself "Nellie

Poorkluck," she managed to trade a mutt she picked up at a pound for an ordination certificate. The investigator also got a certificate in the name of "The Great Houdini," though the master escape artist had died a well-publicized death years before.

The G.I. Bill of Rights and the postwar surge of population triggered an explosion of diploma mills in southern California. So disturbed were local educators that they petitioned Sacramento for a legislative look-see at the world of bargain baccalaureates and discount doctorates.

A committee headed by State Assemblyman Sheridan N. Hegland came to Los Angeles in December, 1957, for an official investigation.

"According to complaints received by our committee," the chairman announced, "thousands of illicit diplomas are being bought and sold like bottles of gin in Prohibition days. Hundreds of phony degrees are said to carry the official seal of the State of California. Almost every known degree can be purchased. If these charges are true, there may be a bootleg market, international in scope, with every type of diploma for sale."

Said another committee member: "There has apparently sprung up in California the class of person who has been characterized by authorities as the 'diploma mill' operator. He has been described as a 'unique type of con man. Like other racketeers, his business is based on fraud, hypocrisy and huge profits.'"

Diploma mill "psychologists" provided the first sensations. Astonished committeemen heard testimony from a housewife who had visited a "consulting psychologist," an ex-maître d'hôtel and part-time advertising salesman who had hung out his shingle after paying $400 for a diploma mill's "doctor of philosophy in psychology" degree. The woman was advised her emotional problems could be solved by "outside curricula or probably a separation from your husband." She was further advised to "search for adventure somewhere."

Other women testified they had visited counselors who suggested they strip naked, pose for pictures in the nude to "lose their inhibitions" and to engage in sexual intercourse with the counselors. One practitioner had set up assignation headquarters in a desert lair in Palm Springs for those female patients willing to heed his cure-through-joy treatment.

An ex-wrestler told the committee he had obtained a Ph.D. for $200, attending classes in psychology and hypnosis one day a week for nine months in hotel rooms. He set himself up in business with a chiropractor, and they operated as a team for five years, treating hundreds of patients.

Harold Boyle testified he had paid about $1000 for a string of degrees as a doctor of philosophy, doctor of divinity, doctor of naturopathy and physiotherapy and an ordination certificate. His formal education, he said, consisted of graduation from grammar school. Boyle had this exchange with James D. Loebl, Deputy Attorney General of California and the committee's counsel.

Q. You did practice as a consulting psychologist?

A. Metaphysical psychology, yes.

Q. What form did that practice take. Did you treat people?

A. No, you do not treat people. Any more than you counsel them from a religious angle.

Q. What were their complaints when they came to you for counseling?

A. Well as a general rule they want to know themselves better. I do not counsel anyone that's sick.

Q. How can you tell if they are sick or not?

A. Well, I don't know, but if they look sick—

Q. If they come to you and tell you they are sick you don't counsel them. Is that right?

A. Of course not.

Q. What happens if they are not sure whether or not they are sick?

A. Well, I have to trust my own good judgment there. If they look like they need competent work, I don't do anything about it.

The committee found that the religious mills were still flourishing. For $18.50 a housewife had obtained a certificate of ordination from the Universal Church of the Master which allowed her to "solemnize marriages, officiate at funerals, perform and administer divine healing, give inspirational and spiritual counsel, to prophesy, including to warn, exhort and comfort members."

An additional $11.70 bought a charter permitting her to establish a branch of the "mother church."

Committee investigators established that the Universal Church of the Master in ten years had issued fifteen hundred ordination certificates, leading one member to conclude, "More fraud than religion has been practiced by the purveyors of ordinations."

The committee also found that bogus medical degrees were obtained as easily as aspirin.

Archie G. Ross, assistant secretary of the State Board of Medical Examiners, cited the remarkable case of Lester Wilson, who had been arrested for practicing medicine without a license.

"At the time of his arrest, he had in his possession morphine and demerol. You will understand how it was possible for him to have these narcotics in his possession when I outline the circumstances under which he was arrested.

"He was employed as a physician at a clinic in the Los Angeles area. The arrest followed a house call by Mr. Wilson in which he injected shots of streptomycin and demerol. He advised the patient he was on the staff of the Los Angeles County Hospital. For some reason or other the husband of the patient didn't believe that this man was a legitimate physician.

"Subsequent to his arrest the Board of Medical Examiners received information that Mr. Wilson had obtained another position as a physician with another local clinic. He was again arrested and at the time of the arrest he had in his possession a medical license, allegedly issued by the California Medical Board of Examiners. Upon closer examination it was discovered he had in his possession a photocopy of a medical license issued by the board. However, the signature and seals were missing from the document.

"In support of his license, however, he had in his possession another diploma, issued by the Chicago Medical College of Homeopathy of Calcutta, India. This is the document we wish to call to the committee's attention as it is very similar to the other document. . . . Mr. Wilson claimed he found the license in the city dump.

"He says he had inserted his name on the document and rephotographed it so that he could remove the word 'sample' which he claimed was across the original document. To our knowledge there is no such thing as a 'sample' of a Board of Medical Examiners' license.

"Honored with these fictitious documents and a medical diploma he was able to obtain employment in various positions in Los Angeles. Our investigations disclosed the man had no formal medical education. We believe, however, that this is how he was able to obtain the demerol, the narcotics involved. He had completely fooled the physicians he was working with."

Another case, involving a drug addict, was cited by the spokesman of the California Medical Board. Said Mr. Ross: "It is quite amazing how this man has been able to obtain all these degrees covering all these fields in such a short period of time, and covering the different countries that seem to be involved in them."

When he was arrested for possession of narcotics, he had a dozen diploma mill degrees from the U. S., India and Britain. "These documents when you look at them appear quite authentic," Mr. Ross added. Found also on the man was a caduceus, the symbol placed on the automobile of a licensed doctor.

The case cited next involved a railroad waiter with a string of degrees from diploma mills stretching back to 1925. He was tending patients with a form of "zone therapy," a quack treatment of all ailments, from the common cold to cancer, by massaging the sole of the foot.

"He was advised to discontinue and advised of the law," Mr. Ross said. "He readily surrendered the diplomas to the agent of the board. He was further advised that perhaps it would be better if he went back to work for the Union Pacific as a waiter."

The field of nursing, the committee learned, had also been infiltrated by the diploma mill operators.

Mrs. Dorothy Winsor testified that she attended a bogus nursing school one night a week for five months. She paid $200 for the course, received her diploma, and after graduation discovered her training entitled her to only one job in a hospital: mopping floors.

Mrs. June F. Eldon declared she signed a contract with another nursing outfit for $195. The course was supposed to last sixteen weeks with classes of two hours a week. She said she attended eight or nine lessons and then found out that when she graduated she would not be able to get a job in any hospital as a nurse. She quit the course, but her contract was turned over to a collection agency, and though she never completed the "training," she was still paying two dollars a week so that "I'm not put in jail."

Mrs. Barbara Chesler, executive secretary of the Board of Vocational Nurse Examiners in California, appeared as an expert witness and testified to the viciousness and inadequacy of the training offered by the diploma mills. Registered nurses, she pointed out, are required to complete at the very least a three-year course and many of them complete five-year courses. To become a licensed practical nurse a course of about twelve months followed by a period of training in a hospital is required by the state.

Then Chairman Hegland asked Mrs. Chesler:

Q. Is it true that some of the people who take these courses which do not meet your standards do it quite innocently and in some cases go out and treat sick people believing that they are qualified?

A. Yes, they do. They obtain jobs through some of the schools which operate placement services, and they also obtain jobs through the newspapers in private homes.

Q. So actually it is possible that there may now even be some of these people today in some of the homes of Los Angeles taking care of people who believe they have a competent nurse and the nurse herself believing she is competent?

A. That is right.

The academic diploma mill, the committee learned, proved the easiest for operators to run.

Mrs. Hazel Dawson testified she had amassed a total of twenty-one degrees, among them a diploma from the College of Swedish Massage of Chicago and a certificate designating her "Bishop-at-large for the United States of America" from the Inter-National Constitutional Church of Los Angeles. Mrs. Dawson had also opened a "branch office" of Western University in Pomona.

"I had just about got started good," she said, "when the Federal Trade Commission made their complaint." A cease and desist order from the FTC had closed Western University. Mrs. Dawson admitted that she did little or no academic work in order to get the majority of her degrees. Mostly, it was a matter of putting cash on the line.

A teacher from Los Angeles State College said she had paid

$400 for twenty units of work from a diploma mill. She was issued a Ph.D. and part of her current salary was based on that degree. She was now attending the University of Southern California, from which she hoped to get a doctor of philosophy degree. When asked why if she already had a Ph.D., it was necessary to get another, she admitted her first one was "unaccredited" and that "makes a difference, you know, when people ask you."

The most refreshing, candid testimony of the hearing came from Willard Charles Manns, who had previously been convicted of running a diploma mill.

Manns said he founded Greenbriar College because people in this day and age needed a college degree in order to get ahead. He said he had not bothered to get a state charter for the college, and that he had picked the name Greenbriar for his school because he thought it sounded good.

Q. Now, would you tell us a little bit about what you tried to do at Greenbriar College.

A. I tried to make some money.

Q. Now would you tell us exactly what the operation consisted of?

A. Advertising on a national scope, replies were answered with a form letter offering a bachelor's degree in return for passing a test and a fee of $9.50.

Q. Where did you get the questions for the test or examination that you gave?

A. I did the research necessary and prepared the test myself.

Q. What is your own personal education background?

A. Two years at Compton Junior College.

Q. And how are you employed now?

A. I'm employed in construction trades as a steam fitter.

Q. Approximately how many people answered your ads and wrote in to the school during the course of its operation?

A. It was in operation for almost two months and I imagine I received several hundred replies.

Q. And were those from as far away as places like Finland?

A. Yes, Finland, Austria—I got them from all over.

Q. Is it a fair statement to say that your school was just getting started when it was closed?

A. Yes, I only ran the small ad in the *Popular Science* classified section and I was ready to quit work and put all the money into ads I could possibly get a hold of because there seemed to be a crying need. People just wanted to get fleeced and I wanted to take advantage of the market when it was still hot and then, the authorities got me.

Other diploma mill operators were less cooperative. Several took refuge in the Fifth Amendment. But the hearings justified fears that degrees were being sold "like bottles of gin."

In all, the committee gathered evidence that more than one hundred diploma mills were operating in California. Los Angeles, naturally, had the bulk of them—fifty-two.

"The prestige of the genuine degree must be protected by the law," the San Diego *Tribune* declared in an editorial. "Punishment meted out to the crooks should be in proportion to the potential harm they can inflict upon the public."

In 1958, on the basis of the Hegland committee's findings, the state legislature passed a bill that cleaned out most of the fly-by-night diploma mills and tightened loopholes in the state's business, professions and education codes.

The bill's two most important provisions made it a felony "to sell or barter any academic degree of any kind or character whatsoever" and required educational institutions to prove $50,000 in assets. (A school of "personology," seeking to meet this requirement, listed among its educational assets an Indian necklace, four sherry glasses, a set of air pistols, an incense burner, a mother-of-pearl atomizer and a wooden good-luck horseshoe.)

The bill was the death knell for the old-style "printing press" operations, but it had not come in time to net the most successful diploma mill impresario in southern California.

Richard Spencer, Ph.D., was the marvel of the world of education—a Hercules of higher learning, colossus of culture and sachem of scholarship.

The slim, 135-pound Spencer ran an educational empire. Only thirty-nine, he was the don of Oxford Institute, chancellor of Commonwealth, Research and Searchlight Universities, president of the National Board of Psychological Examiners, apostle of New Thought Science, the International Society of Metaphysicians and the Institute of Christian Metaphysics.

Degrees from London, Rome, Calcutta, Buenos Aires, Switzerland and Canada had been heaped upon him. He was minister, doctor, psychologist, philosopher and teacher.

An impressive accomplishment for a lad from Cedar Rapids, Iowa, who had ended his formal schooling in the ninth grade. Spencer had worked as a welder, truck driver, bag factory foreman and sheet metal helper until he discovered the advantages of education by diploma mill.

Once he made that discovery, he dedicated himself to the American ideal of a college education for everyone. Himself a product of virtually every flourishing diploma mill in the world, he set out to spread his sheepskins to all comers.

Operating from a three-room Los Angeles office, Spencer presided over a happy world of learning in which all grades were automatic A's, examinations were sent home with students to be completed at leisure, degrees, diplomas, certificates were handed out overnight and the only text required was a page from a student's checkbook.

In addition to his degrees, he sold titles of chivalry from the "Order de At. Huburt of Lorraine." For fees ranging from thirty dollars to seventy-five dollars, a plebeian could be dubbed a knight, a baron, a viscount or count.

He also ran the Institute of Hypnotherapy, claiming he could cure insomnia, acute neurotic illness, asthma, eczema, bronchitis, homosexual tendencies and other disorders through hypnosis.

His newspaper ads proclaimed: "Hypnosis helps fear, stammering, memory, sleep, weight, self-confidence, emotional and sex problems. Class or private. Free booklet. R. Spencer, D.D."

His Oxford Institute, a "non-profit" corporation, offered a diploma as a "licensed consultant in psychology."

The brochures for this outfit informed both the gullible and incipient con men: "The field of counseling is growing fast and you should not delay in sending in your application for training. *Official Credentials* will be issued to all students who finish this course of instruction with passing grades. Fill out the application and return it *today. Do not delay.* . . . This may be the turning point of your life. Oxford Institute is as near as your postman, for our present method of training is through the extension method and your lessons are sent to you by mail."

Another of Spencer's "non-profit" corporations was The Hermetic Fellowship, established "to give, perpetuate, etc. the scientific philosophy of greater mental and spiritual evolution as prescribed by the most illustrious Master Hermes Trismegistus, who founded the 'Ancient Esoteric Order of Hermes' centuries ago in Egypt."

Promising help for mental, physical, social, financial and spiritual problems through the wisdom of "Hermes Trismegistus," applicants were advised that the "initiate course" of twelve lessons would be mailed, one "monograph" each month, for a $2.00 per month "donation."

One of Spencer's coincorporators in The Hermetic Fellowship was a chiropractor who ran a "School of Craniopathy" in Los Angeles. He claimed he could cure various ailments by his ability to move the bones of the skull—"the greatest discovery of the age."

Spencer also had a follow-up scheme to entice those who had already purchased his degrees to get still another degree from another of his mills, Education Associates.

The mailed pitch, under his signature, said: "Dear Friend: We have made arrangements . . . to confer an honorary degree in your special field upon those of you who have been honored by organizations of which the writer has been an official. These are available at reduced rates. Please make your check available to Education Associates."

From all of this, Spencer lived well. He earned a high five-figure annual income, had a home in an expensive suburb stocked with $5000 in furniture, free and clear. He drove an expensive car. And when it came to the education of his own teen-age daughter he had the impeccable taste to provide her with excellent tutelage at a convent.

His own students were less fortunate. The dropouts, the frustrated, the naïve, the losers looking for a shortcut to educational eminence trooped into his ivy-less campus.

One applicant was Mark Davidson, a young man who turned up at Dr. Spencer's mill on an October morning in 1955.

"I want to become an ordained minister," Mr. Davidson announced.

"You'll need some training," said Spencer.

"That's why I'm here. I want to take your course."

"It's going to take months for you to become properly ordained in the church."

"I can't wait that long," Mr. Davidson insisted. "I have to become a minister immediately."

"Why all the hurry?"

"I have a job opportunity as a lecturer in comparative religion and I would like to be ordained right away, it would help me cinch the job."

"In that case, Mr. Davidson, I'll give you all the lesson books, and you take them home and tomorrow you come back and I'll have your ordained minister's certificate. That will be seventy-five dollars."

"I can only pay fifty dollars."

"Fifty dollars will cover your ordination certificate, the rest is for a degree as a licensed practitioner. You can't become a minister until you become a licensed practitioner."

"I don't want to be a licensed practitioner. I just want to be an ordained minister."

"Don't you realize that if you qualify as a licensed practitioner you can also practice as a faith healer and earn large sums of money?"

Mr. Davidson agreed Dr. Spencer had a point there, and he decided to take both degrees when the doctor settled on a price of fifty dollars for the ordination certificate and only nine dollars for the licensed practitioner's degree.

At home that evening Mr. Davidson painlessly answered the two hundred questions in the lesson books provided by Dr. Spencer. Sample questions: Does prayer change things? Can Bible teaching be applied in everyday life? Can one "run away" from a problem? Can you use the Bible as a textbook? That was the sum of his minister's examination. He now turned to the licensed practitioner's examination. This required answering a number of essay-type questions. He was asked to define "master mind science" and to tell about his previous experience in faith healing.

"My sister once became ill," Mr. Davidson wrote, "and I suggested to her that if she were a good girl she would get cured and she got cured. This experience certainly qualifies me to be a faith healer."

The next day Dr. Spencer agreed. Mr. Davidson was graded A-plus. In exchange for fifty-nine dollars, he received two freshly embossed degrees. He was now a minister of New Thought Science and a duly licensed faith healer, which allowed him to open a church and an office and treat people for everything from emotional problems to cancer. Dr. Spencer congratulated Reverend Davidson on the swift completion of the curriculum, and wished him hearty good luck in his new career.

A few days later, crusading columnist Paul Coates, a specialist in exposing con men, reported the full details of the Davidson ascension to the cloth in his *Mirror-News* column. Davidson was a member of Coates's staff assigned to check out Dr. Spencer's operation.

"He returned to the office as an ordained minister, which was a great shock to us and would have been an even greater shock to his mother," Coates wrote. "The 19-hour delay in his 'graduation,' was because the 'university' needed time to have his diploma engraved."

In a series of subsequent assaults on Spencer, Coates attacked him as "the granddaddy of all con men . . . a first-class racketeer . . . a man with no apparent regard for the welfare of his fellow men . . . more than just a con man . . . a breeder of con men."

The Los Angeles Better Business Bureau joined the mounting chorus against Spencer's operation, zeroing in on one of the doctor's will-o'-the-wisp educational institutions. The bureau's *Data* bulletin, under a headline of "BBB Turns Searchlight On Searchlight College; Much Search, No Light," reported that the "so-called college" was a post-office box in Hollywood.

The bureau also had complaints against Spencer's Commonwealth University. For several hundred dollars, Spencer had sold a degree to a man which made him "dean" of Commonwealth's "graduate school of pharmacy." A lady said she had been offered a Ph.D. from Commonwealth for $200 "without attending school at all."

Undaunted by those who failed to perceive the advantages of instant education, Dr. Spencer continued at the helm of Commonwealth, keeping his presidential door open to all comers— including Robert G. Wells, of Long Beach.

"I'm writing a self-help book on psychology," Mr. Wells explained. "Regular psychology is no good. That teaches such things as thinking of others and learning to love and be loved. People ought to hate more. Nobody ever got anywhere without utilizing his hates."

Dr. Spencer thought that was an interesting theory.

Wells said in order to sell his book he needed an academic degree to convince a publisher that he knew his subject.

"You'll need a doctorate," said Spencer. "The price is $350."

"Too high," Wells countered.

They finally settled on $200 and Wells was awarded the degree of doctor of philosophy in psychology.

But to Dr. Spencer's chagrin, Wells also turned out to be a newspaperman who had decided to find out "if it was really that easy to become a quack."

"My commencement exercises were simple but appropriate," Wells recounted in the Long Beach *Independent*. "Spencer handed me my degree. I handed him $200."

During his brief attendance at Commonwealth, Wells noted that when Spencer wasn't busy selling degrees he was treating patients as a hypnotherapist.

"That's a high-sounding word for quack psychologist. I saw his patients in his waiting room. They were no different from the patients of dozens of other quacks doing business in offices scattered throughout the Southland. There are the women just starting to show their age, sitting composedly but inwardly worrying about why they sometimes burst into tears with no reason. There are the men, quietly studying their fellow patients and wondering if they, too, have problems about sex."

Wells was singing, but not the school hymn of Commonwealth University.

Despite the white glare of publicity, Spencer continued to operate. Legally, he was untouchable. The part of the law applicable to diploma mills was in the state's Business and Professions Code, but the sections—except for those making the sale of a medical degree a felony—were vague and unclear. California's Education Code also exempted from regulation any university, college or seminary of learning chartered prior to September 19, 1939. And most of Spencer's corporations had been chartered prior to that date. The loophole allowed him all the academic freedom he wanted.

In October, 1956, the district attorney's office, not yet armed with the new state legislation that was to come out of the Hegland diploma mill hearings, decided the only way to nail Spencer was to con him into selling a medical diploma. Investigator Robert H. Meng was assigned to the undercover job.

To allay Spencer's suspicion, Meng first applied for a nonmedical degree. After telephoning for an appointment, he went to the Spencer campus.

"I need a degree in architectural engineering," Meng said.

Spencer told him he would need a letter of reference, copies of some preliminary plans he had drawn and $250.

The arrangements were completed in less than three minutes.

When Meng returned with the letter and the plans, Spencer glanced at them briefly and nodded his satisfaction.

"Do you have the fee?"

Meng gave him the $250. In return, Spencer gave him a blank degree, explaining that he hadn't had time to fill it in. He gave Meng the address of a Spring Street printer and told him to take the blank degree there and have it embossed with his name and the degree he was to receive.

It was one of the fastest matriculations in history. The total time that the investigator had spent in his two visits with Spencer was fifteen minutes.

Meng bided his time, waiting four months before telephoning Spencer again. "I'm tired of architectural engineering," he told the doctor. "A friend and I want to go into business, and I think you can help us."

An on-campus appointment was arranged. Meng's "friend" was David May, an investigator for the State Board of Medical Examiners, posing as David Anthony, a Denver shoe salesman, and packing a miniature tape recorder under his jacket.

"What's your problem?" Spencer asked when they met in the office.

"We're planning to open a shoe business," Anthony explained. "A degree for each of us would help."

"What kind of degree would you like?"

"We'll be manufacturing orthopedic shoes," said Meng, "so it should be some kind of medical degree."

"I can't give you a straight medical degree," Spencer shot back. "That's a felony."

"We certainly don't want to involve you in anything unlawful," Anthony said.

Spencer thought it over. "I can give you two honorary degrees in orthopedics, one from a university in Paris and one from a local school. They'll cost one hundred dollars apiece."

They decided to consider Spencer's offer.

The doctor was being cagey. The "honorary" degrees, Meng knew, might not stand up in court. So he applied a bit more pressure.

Reaching Spencer on the phone a few days later, he told him, "I'm sorry, doctor, but we've been doing some shopping around and we've found a school that will give us straight medical degrees for fifteen hundred dollars. We're willing to pay that price because we feel that our business is going to require it. Your degrees aren't adequate."

Spencer's pride was hurt. "Listen to me," he replied, "any medical degree you get in Los Angeles for fifteen hundred dollars won't be worth the paper it's written on! I'll tell you what, I can get you a legitimate medical degree from a university in India and it will only cost you five hundred dollars."

Meng allowed himself to be convinced. He and Anthony resumed negotiations with Spencer.

"I think we can work something out on this deal from India," the doctor said. "Or I might have something else, an Arizona deal. This would be a doctor of philosophy in osteopathy."

"A doctor of osteopathy. That's really going to do it," Anthony said.

Spencer nodded.

"What about the degree from Paris?" Meng asked.

"I've sent for it," Spencer said.

"Since you've already gone to the trouble, we'll take that one too."

"By the way," Spencer asked Meng, "how do you spell your name?"

Meng laughed lightly. "How do you like that? Here he's going to give me a degree and he can't remember how to spell my name. What do you think I am, Chinese?"

"I just wanted to be sure," Spencer replied. Meng obligingly spelled his name.

"That will be seven hundred dollars for all three degrees," said Spencer, proving his arithmetic was better than his spelling.

Anthony counted out a hundred-dollar deposit.

"You don't have any kind of a receipt, do you?" Meng asked.

"I'm afraid not."

Spencer had assured the investigators the degrees would arrive in three weeks, but the time passed without word.

On the phone, Spencer explained to Meng there was a slight delay. "I think I'll get the degrees from Italy instead. I can get them there much faster."

"You mean instead of India?"

"Yes. I won't have to fool around sending wires and everything."

"Whatever you say, doctor, but are you sure you can get them faster from Italy?"

"Yes, I can have them here in three or four days. The ones from India would still take a week or ten days. It won't make any difference."

"Whatever you do is fine with me," Meng said cheerfully.

A week later Spencer phoned to tell Meng the degrees had finally arrived.

Meng showed up at the office and Spencer handed him a cardboard cylinder containing three osteopathic degrees. Meng paid him the six hundred dollars balance.

"You know this is illegal," Spencer said. Meng smiled, the evidence in his hands at last.

"I'm glad you realize that, doctor," the investigator replied as he identified himself and placed Spencer under arrest.

A search of Spencer's office turned up, among other things, a mountain of blank degrees from all over the world, seal embossers from eleven of his mills and five copies of the Hippocratic oath!

At his trial, Spencer refused to take the stand. His defense was based on insufficient evidence and entrapment by law enforcement officers. "The sale of a degree or diploma is not of itself immoral or indecent or wrong," Spencer's lawyer argued. "It is done every day by our leading institutions."

"Applying this attitude to the facts of the instant case," Deputy District Attorney Elizabeth Miller replied, "the defendant is in effect contending it is moral, decent, proper and inoffensive for him to place at large an instrument which could mislead the public into believing that the ostensible holder of the particular degree or diploma had specialized training and upon that basis defraud the public. This position is not worthy of the time which has thus far been spent in stating it."

The deputy district attorney called Spencer "a born con man —almost hypnotic."

The jury agreed. Spencer was convicted of selling the phony medical degrees.

Superior Court Judge Lewis Drucker commented that Spencer had sold his bogus diplomas with "reckless abandon." He sentenced him to four months in county jail, a thousand-dollar fine and three years of probation during which time he was to engage in "no activities dealing with the public, issue no degrees, certificates or fellowships of any kind, and to engage in no instructions offered to the public."

If investigators thought the sentence was mild, they at least were consoled by the breakup of the biggest of the diploma mills. All hands concurred with Probation Officer Karl Holton's evaluation of Spencer and the danger he represented:

"Defendant has perpetrated a gross fraud on the community through his misrepresentation. He has misled countless persons himself and through his operation has spawned and abetted untold numbers of other con men.

"To estimate the injury he has done is impossible. It appears reasonable to assume, however, that many innocent persons have been duped into believing the defendant, as well as those possessing degrees, was well qualified.

"His operation he readily admits was unethical and existed on the fringe of the law for years and was motivated by the profit factor."

Class had been dismissed and the final bell rung for Richard Spencer, Ph.D.

6

THE QUACKS

Snake Oil Scientists

Our goal is to make California an unprofitable—if not an
unhealthy—environment for medical confidence men.
—MILTON P. DUFFY,
Chief, Bureau of Food and Drug Inspections,
California Department of Public Health

In the 1920s, I-on-a-co, a piece of electronic hocus-pocus touted
as a cure for everything from arthritis to yaws, was the hottest
medical marvel of the era. Southern Californians swore to its
effectiveness for man and beast in newspaper testimonials:

"Carleton Everett, Hollywood, claims that his dog had St. Vitus'
dance and was cured by sleeping 'within the influence of I-on-
a-co'!"

"John A. Mooney, 514 El Molino St., Pasadena, claims to have
had nothing but gray hair on his head until he used I-on-a-co,
when about one-third of it 'miraculously returned to the original
color'; and he further reports that his hair 'grows twice as fast as
formerly'!"

"Ramon Martinez, fruit packer, claimed to be paralyzed from
the waist down, legs being always cold. Used I-on-a-co. Circulation restored; legs no longer cold!"

"Otis Williams, 322 South Spring St., Los Angeles. Cured of
cancer of the neck by I-on-a-co."

"Mrs. Annabelle Kelly, 2707 Morsley Road, Altadena, claims to
have tried the I-on-a-co on her husband, who was 'completely
deranged.' After four applications, the husband 'became quite ra-
tional and seemed to have good control of his mental faculties'!"

Mass-produced at a cost of $4.10 each, thousands of the devices were sold for $58.50 cash or $65 on time. Worn like a horse collar around the neck, waist or legs, I-on-a-co consisted of two coils of insulated wire. A small flashlight globe attached to the rim of one coil was lit when the device was plugged into a light socket. The same current that lit the globe supposedly passed through the body and cured illness by "magnetizing the iron in the blood." The control switch, held in the palm, could be adjusted to low, medium or high, permitting the afflicted to regulate the speed of recovery.

I-on-a-co reaped a fortune for its flamboyant inventor and promoter, an eccentric Socialist millionaire who used the profits to indulge his passion for southern California real estate.

Los Angeles has paid him a fitting honor. Its toniest thoroughfare, Wilshire Boulevard, is named for H. Gaylord Wilshire, the charlatan originator of the magic horse collar.

Such high tribute to a "mediconman" is characteristic of a city where the quack is king. Sixty per cent of the local citizenry at one time or another takes its medical problems to illegitimate practitioners, guaranteeing the hustling healers of southern California the lion's share of the nation's annual $1,000,000,000 bill for quackery.

Gordon R. Wood, director of the Los Angeles district office of the U. S. Food and Drug Administration, says his unit receives more complaints about quackery than any of seventeen other district offices. "It's nothing to brag about," he declares sadly.

The gullible are ever ready to plunk down hard cash, no matter how bizarre or hoary the scam.

A sixty-two-year-old construction worker from suburban Canoga Park paid nearly $800 to a woman dressed in gypsy clothing for driving a "devil" out of his stomach. He went to the woman's office in November, 1963, after hearing her spiel on a radio broadcast, a semimystical declaration that she had been sent from Europe by "a higher force" to cure the sick.

The woman told him he was suffering from "witchcraft." He forked over $155 for the diagnosis and the first treatment.

The healer sat him in a chair and applied her medication—a ripe tomato rubbed delicately across his stomach for fifteen minutes.

"Now cut it open and you'll find the devil causing your illness."
The patient's stomach ailment was at least temporarily forgotten by the shock of discovering a shrunken head bedded grimly in the center of the vegetable. His devil thus temporarily exorcised, he was advised to return in two weeks. Payment for the next treatment: two cases of whiskey.

In exchange for eighty-eight dollars' worth of booze, he got another tomato-therapy session, and another shrunken head.

Further treatment, however, was to be more expensive. A permanent cure would cost $1900. The tomato-massaged patient said he had only $600 in his savings account. The healer magnanimously agreed to her vegetable treatment for the reduced figure.

The patient doled the money out for five months. Only when he ran out of funds and the healer refused further treatment, did he complain to the police. An investigation disclosed the tomato and shrunken head therapy had parted dozens of victims, including an aeronautical engineer with a Ph.D., of over $15,000 in a one-year period.

Since 1960, city, county, state and federal investigators in Los Angeles have coped with such medical exotica as:

A Pomona doctor who charged seventy-five dollars for treating heart patients with perspiration baths by means of an electric blanket.

A sixty-seven-year-old Chinese herb merchant who sold a tea drink he claimed would cure stomach gas, constipation, colds, headaches, asthma and hemorrhoids.

A mystic health bracelet sold as a cure for high and low blood pressure, neuralgia, change of life, insomnia and stomach hyperacidity.

A ring that specialized in the "glimmer scheme," an especially vicious racket that collected handsome fees from elderly people for fake eye operations in their own homes.

A Palm Springs practitioner who sold bottles of common dirt for eight dollars each, claiming the soil of the desert spa was so rich that it held all the beneficial effects of a "dozen hot springs mineral baths."

A mail-order slicker who grossed over $50,000 by advertising a device that would make short people taller. It stretched them on a rack something like those used in ancient dungeons.

Smog pills, three dollars a dozen.

Sex pills ("Men! Why Grow Old? Regain Your Youth. Be Confident. Never Be Embarrassed Again! Youth Is Yours If You Act Now. You Will Agree with Others That 'This Is the Best Money You Ever Spent'").

Schemes pitching phony, defective or useless bust developers, dental plates, hair restorers, obesity cures and wrinkle removers.

Medical bunk men calling themselves scientologists, metaphysicians, astrolotherapists, naprapaths and sanipractors.

But most of the important money for the quacks is concentrated in the mass markets for health foods, treatment of arthritis and cancer, and the sale of a staggering collection of weird electric and mechanical cure-alls.

Los Angeles is the land of the health bar, the health food store, the supermarket that sells only "organic" foods, a clutch of restaurants that specialize in health food lunches. It is the land where the latest food fad roots swiftly, the land of yogurt, blackstrap molasses and wheat germ, a vast sucker land for every health lecturer in the world.

Three of the five major organizations taking the lead in spreading nutritional fads are headquartered in Los Angeles, and the area leads the nation as a consumer for the $500,000,000 spent in the U. S. each year for health foods.

Rumors and legends float from the movie-star kitchens of Bel-Air and Beverly Hills of screen idols who have maintained long-lived careers, sexual potency and eternal youth through lifelong devotion to any of numberless offbeat diets and foods.

With movie-star backing and testimonials, the gigantic multimillion-dollar Nutri-Bio promotion was launched in 1960.

"A classic example of food faddism gone wild," says George P. Larrick, a commissioner of the U. S. Food and Drug Administration. "Directly and indirectly, Nutri-Bio was being recommended . . . as the answer to practically all health problems—anemia, arthritis, cancer, diabetes, frigidity, heart trouble, infections, nervousness, etc. On the positive side it promised health, beauty, athletic ability, radiant living and the capacity to stay young and vital. It was even recommended as a cure for juvenile delinquency!"

Before the government put it out of business, more than

seventy-five thousand full and part-time sales agents were selling Nutri-Bio at twenty-four dollars per package for a six-months supply for one person. Lured by the prospect of quick riches from the pyramid or chain-letter plan of distribution, many invested their life savings. For $10,000, an agent could start business as a "General" and get maximum commissions on all sales by his subagents.

Los Angeles authorities in recent years have cracked down on the most vicious of the food quacks—considered as dangerous as other medical charlatans because their claims of magic powers for certain foods keep many with serious illnesses from visiting a doctor.

The crackdown snared pushers of: Vitamin C as a polio cure, cabbage juice to heal ulcers, a honey concoction to ward off cataracts, carrot juice as a cure for leukemia, garlic pills for high blood pressure, royal bee jelly as a sex rejuvenator, kelp for stomach ailments, grape juice for obesity, blueberry juice as a cure for diabetes, and olive oil as a preventative for appendicitis.

The discovery of uranium opened a pseudoscientific cornucopia for the quacks, and southern California arthritics have shelled out for an incredible diversity of such useless products.

A "cosmic radioactive pad" consisting of a plastic bag filled with slightly radioactive rocks and sand was sold for ten dollars and hailed as a cure for arthritis if placed underneath the pillow at night.

Vrilium claimed to have radioactive powers that would draw arthritis from the body when worn around the neck. Retailed for $3000, it consisted only of a brass tube filled with a chemical worth but $\frac{1}{2000}$ of a cent.

The "uranium wonder glove" containing very low-grade uranium dust was sold to thousands of arthritics for twenty-five dollars. A cloud of efficacious dust was supposed to be raised by pounding the glove against the hand before retiring.

In the early 1960s, sad, desperate convoys of arthritics, looking for Lourdes, chartered buses for the "uranium caves" of northern California. The gnarled and crippled were helped into the bowels of the earth and for twenty dollars an hour sat soaking in the "magic" underground radioactivity. Promoters also packaged the "blissful ore" in pillows, mattresses, metallic boxes and cloth bags for shipment around the state to arthritics too twisted to make the journey. Many sufferers claimed they were benefited, even when the caves were exposed as abandoned silver mines.

Though the California Legislature in 1959 outlawed eight alleged treatments for cancer (including the Hoxsey, Koch, Laetrile, Mucorhicin, Bolen and Lincoln Staphage Lysate), new "cures" proliferate.

A Los Angeles cancer clinic, grossing some $250,000 a year, was put out of business by the Food and Drug Administration after six years of investigation. Several hundred persons from nearly every state in the Union and Canada were attracted to the clinic through nationwide newspaper ads, brochures and radio broadcasts. Patients, many of whom did not have the disease, paid $500 to $1400 for a worthless treatment of roots and herbs.

An ex-millworker who mixed a cancer ointment in rusty coffee cans sold his salve for fifty dollars an ounce and $5000 for a course of treatments. The salve unfailingly caused severe chemical burns when applied to the skin.

Another local quack turned up with a mysterious injection he said would cure cancer. A system of treatments cost $1300. He told one victim that thirteen parts of her body were "deficient like worn out gears in a car" and could be replaced by new "cells" only by means of his injections.

Other cancer quacks have made small and large fortunes for treatments involving apricot pits, sauerkraut, apple sauce, table salt and tap water.

As sad as the flight of arthritics to the uranium caves is the traffic of southern Californians to Mexico where several clinics have the reputation of curing terminal cancer. An operator of a flying ambulance service in Los Angeles says he often gets requests to fly cancer victims south, but he turns down business of this sort because he knows that people are throwing away money which could be better used to make the patient more comfortable at home.

The machinery of the modern medicine man in southern California promises cures by music, rays, light beams, tonations and vibrations.

One gadget doctor offered the Sonus Film-O-Sonic, a device that consisted chiefly of the playback portion of a tape recorder without a speaker. Several hundred were sold for $385 each as a cure for cancer. Purchasers were instructed to place electrodes connected by two wires from the machine's front panel over the malignant tumor. The vibrations emanating from an endless tape were disseminated through the wires, causing the tumor to "disintegrate." The machine failed to cure anyone's cancer, but drugged its victims into ennui with a ceaseless playing of "Smoke Gets in Your Eyes."

The southern California distributor of this product—a chiropractor—also claimed he was able to cure cancer by merely passing his hands over the body of a patient. When his hands experienced an extreme chill he knew he had located the malignancy. After a lengthy jury trial on charges of false advertising, he was sentenced to a $500 fine or six months in jail. He chose the jail sentence.

Another cancer gadgeteer used a "magic wand," similar, he said, to "water witch dowsing" used in locating wells. At his trial, he explained that he measured the "electrical impulse of a body" with the wand which was wired to a metal box containing six different minerals. He placed a hand on the patient and with the other hand passed the wand over a large number of vials containing "human tissue." After thus locating the cancer, he treated it with minerals and herbs. Denying he charged for his service, he said, "I help anyone who needs help." But if anyone wanted to leave a voluntary donation, "that's all right."

Midway through the trial, he changed his plea from not guilty to no contest. He was convicted on one count of practicing medicine without a license and another of selling misbranded drugs.

Another popular gadget in southern California is the Spectro-Chrome, invented by the self-styled "Edison of India," Dinshah P. Ghadiali, who founded a nationwide cult on the theory that good health could be won through "attuned color waves."

Ghadiali's victims had to join his cult and pay a ninety-dollar membership in order to get the machine "free." He was convicted on Food and Drug Administration charges and his followers went underground. Investigators are certain some of the faithful are still loyally taking their Spectro-Chrome "tonations" from Ghadiali's marvelous medical machine, a lamplike contraption with a metal box on a stand housing a thousand-watt bulb which emits various colored lights with different colors for treatment of different diseases.

According to the precise instructions, the user must "stand nude in a dark room and choose the proper color for your ailment." The patient should sleep with head pointing north, on white bedding, and never take a "tonation" at sunrise or sunset or during an eclipse.

Then the user is free to match a color with a disease. "Red activates the liver. Orange induces vomiting, stops dysentery, indigestion, ptomaine poisoning, is also a lung builder. Lemon is for abscesses, boils and carbuncles, raises phleghm. Green is a germ killer, prevents decay. Turquoise is a tonic, an alkalizer, makes new cells, tissues, tones the whole system. Blue reduces fever, burns, scalding. Indigo stops bleeding, pain, appendicitis. Violet builds white corpuscles, is good for sleeping and relaxing. Purple removes malaria, lowers blood pressure. Scarlet stimulates sexual desire."

Virility restorers, sex machines and aphrodisiacs are staples in the trade of the medical bunk men. A long line of such promotions has flowed from Los Angeles via the mails.

The Hyperemiator was consigned to the junk pile by postal inspectors in May, 1964, and three men were indicted on twenty counts of mail fraud for selling the sex machine that brought more than $125,000 in orders from all over the country.

"The parts of the Hyperemiator were assembled in Hollywood in an establishment with blacked-out windows, sold to different distributors as 'airplane parts,' and then reassembled in another secret location for resale," said Inspector C. A. Miller. Each of the machines went for $19.95 on the representation that it provided an answer to male impotence.

Various southern Californians are users of various other mechanical panaceas—depolaray (in adult or junior sizes), radioclast, ozone generator, push-button shortwave oscillotron, Z-Ray, tribotron negative ion generator, micro-dynameter and the radiumator (retailed for $10,000 as a cure for heart and kidney ailments, also guaranteed to revive wilted flowers!).

The law struggles valiantly to keep from drowning in this Niagara of contemporary snake oil. The basic weapon against the quacks is the 1939 Pure Drugs Act, which contains general prohibitions against false advertising and misbranding of a drug or device. The act was amended in 1951 to outlaw advertising which claims to cure any of forty-eight serious diseases—diseases for which there is no known cure or for which self-medication is dangerous—cancer, heart and vascular ailments, diabetes, etc.

But violation is still only a misdemeanor carrying a nominal fine, or jail sentence, or both.

The legal and enforcement codes dealing with medical frauds give the quacks "a license to steal," says Francis X. Kemp, of the Los Angeles County Health Department. "The small fines, ranging from $25 to $500, given persons convicted of fakery do not halt these frauds. The fakers pay their fines, consider it only as a license payment and then resume business."

Though hamstrung by the statutes, authorities have still managed to successfully prosecute an average of one quack a month in cases ranging from sales of cure-alls by house-to-house "doorbell doctors" to complex promotions.

One outfit, run by a pair of chiropractors, set up a chain of "diagnostic offices" throughout southern California, offering a complete physical examination for five dollars. The Los Angeles office alone, according to records seized in a raid, showed that during a four-month period 650 victims were lured through its doors.

Investigation revealed that 93 per cent of the patients were given identical diagnoses: enlarged heart and liver, a jellied gall bladder and a high acid or bile condition. The majority actually enjoyed perfect health—but fear was used to persuade unsuspecting victims to take treatments for conditions which they did not have.

The treatments included sine-wave therapy at a cost of six dollars each three times weekly. Various bottles of vitamins and innocuous substances such as bile salts were sold for $6.00 to $7.50 per bottle.

The first series of treatments continued for six weeks. All patients were then informed on a mimeographed note: "You have come along about half-way on the road to recovery. If you do not take another six weeks of treatment you will slide back to your original condition."

The chiseling chiropractors were arrested and tried on multiple

misdemeanor charges of false advertising, petty theft and practicing medicine without a license. Each was fined $500 and
sentenced to six months in jail, a sentence considered laughable
by authorities. The defendants themselves had abundant funds
to send an appeal up to the U. S. Supreme Court, which ultimately upheld their conviction.

To toughen penalties a far-reaching bill has been introduced
in the California Legislature by San Fernando Valley Assemblyman Tom Carrell. It would make quackery a felony carrying a
prison sentence of up to ten years.

"At present quacks are subject to prosecution only for misdemeanors of practicing medicine without a license or petty theft.
Only if he takes more than $200 is the quack subject to a felony
conviction under present California law," says Carrell.

"The medical quack falsely represents that he can diagnose
and cure disease. He is unlicensed and untrained. Every time he
treats someone who must have proper medical care to prolong
or save life, he becomes a potential killer.

"We are living in an age of great scientific advancement. Malig-
nancies which were untreatable a few years ago now are treat-
able. In the hands of a quack a person with a malignant tumor
will surely die; with competent medical care he may live."

Carrell cites a Los Angeles case where an unlicensed quack
treated two persons ostensibly afflicted with cancer. The maximum offense was the misdemeanor violation of practicing medicine without a license. He pleaded no contest to that charge.
"Subsequent investigation showed the same quack had treated
thousands of persons in Los Angeles County," says Carrell, urging
the need for the new legislation. "Quackery is the greatest single
contributor to loss of life and physical injury in California. We
should lead the way in recognizing medical quackery for the
serious crime it is."

John W. Miner, chief of the medical-legal section of the Los
Angeles district attorney's office, goes even further. The fighting
deputy district attorney believes that fines and jail sentences are
not sufficient to stop quacks in cases where a death occurs.

"Except for the public executioner, only the medical quack is
permitted to earn his living by killing people," Miner declares.
"No other kind of murder is so vicious or heartless. Quacks take

hundreds of lives but society kind of tolerates it. How shocking that there is ᴏnly one case in Anglo-Saxon law of a murder conviction where death was caused by fraudulent representation of curing disease."

Stepping up the statewide war against quackery, authorities are using more legal muscle to buttress the weak misdemeanor penalties in the basic statutes.

"We are very effectively applying certain felony sections of the Penal Code, including conspiracy and grand theft" against medical charlatans "whenever the penalty does not seem to be commensurate with the degree of public injury," says Milton P. Duffy, of the California Department of Public Health.

Such strategy was used in 1963 to challenge the high priestess of southern California quackery—an unremitting seventy-two-year-old machine healer whose successful, virtually uninterrupted career bridged the atomic age with the era of Wilshire and his magic horse collar.

Radio was still a novelty in the 1920s, and the medium that was soon to produce Amos 'n' Andy, Kate Smith, Fibber McGee and Molly, Jack Benny, and Franklin Roosevelt's "fireside chats," also produced in December, 1929, Dr. Ruth Drown, perhaps the most incredible purveyor of phony medicine in the long history of American quackery.

Capitalizing on the public's interest in the new medium as well as its ignorance of radio technology, Dr. Drown, a slight, unsmiling, grim-visaged osteopath, by her own reckoning treated more than 35,000 patients.

Investigators estimate her take, conservatively, at over $500,000.

Unlike the usual medical pretender, who cynically bleeds money from patients in exchange for what he knows is worthless treatment, the humorless Dr. Drown was a fanatic believer in her own preposterous theories. Stormy, contentious, self-mesmerized, she clawed like a tigress for thirty-five dogged years at the world of organized medicine and the law.

In 1952, acting as her own counsel, she filed a $5,000,000 damage suit against the American Medical Association and other groups, charging violation of various antitrust laws.

An AMA lawyer, after observing her in court, wrote:

"She is a woman of very severe appearance, obviously with fixed convictions, a firm belief in her imaginary facts and a crusader's determination.

"She was accompanied by a very well dressed, attractive lady of middle age who gave every appearance of being a disciple, and she might well be Mrs. Drown's 'banker.'

"I suspect that Mrs. Drown is going to keep at it indefinitely and no one in the world will convince her that she is completely in error and that the 'facts' which she believes to be true are wholly the product of her imagination.

"The presiding judge attempted to give her a kind lecture, and, in a very nice way, to persuade her to seek legal advice. From the expression on Mrs. Drown's face, while the judge was talking to her, I feel sure she wasn't listening to a word."

Prior to her emergence as a healer in 1929, Mrs. Drown was an obscure employee in the electrical supply department of the Southern California Edison Co. There she stumbled on the idea of radio and its possibilities as an "aid to physicians in the diagnosis of disease." Radio had struck the public fancy and obviously was here to stay. To round out the marriage of crystal set to medicine, she sought further medical background, attending the School of Osteopathy at Kirksville, Missouri, for three years—but without bothering to graduate.

On her return to Los Angeles, she became a member of the American Naturopathic Association and a licensed osteopath, a background sufficient to qualify her as a "doctor."

Over the next few years the hard-working little lady developed a formidable complex of pseudoscientific apparatus, and such companion facilities as a "research laboratory," a manufacturing plant and a "college" to teach her methods.

Organized as Drown Laboratories, Inc., her system covered all the medical bases—invention of the equipment, its production, its sale to other healers, the tuition-based school, establishment of a mother clinic for diagnosis and treatment as well as branch clinics elsewhere in California.

Already hypnotized by what she had wrought, she applied to the American Medical Association in 1934 for "a fair investigation" of her basic machine, the Homo-Vibra Ray.

"Should you find this machine to be scientific, as we know it to be, and it meets with your approval . . . we would deem it a great privilege to give to the good of the cause a certain per cent royalty over a set period of time on each instrument sold, feeling that this money would be utilized for the purpose of assisting humanity, even as we feel our instrument is for that purpose."

The AMA's reply was not encouraging. "Neither in your letter nor in your advertising matter is there any scientific support for the claims made for your Homo-Vibra Ray device. Nor do you give information regarding its physical contents or the electric 'hook-up.' In other words, the device seems to be surrounded with the secrecy common to all nostrums."

Dr. Drown huffily ignored the AMA, and continued her self-styled mission of assisting humanity.

She prospered. By 1936, she had received a patent on the Homo-Vibra Ray, and sold more than 150 of the machines to other Los Angeles healers—chiropractors, osteopaths, naturopaths and some doctors of medicine.

Soon she also had branches in Beverly Hills, San Luis Obispo and Santa Maria. By 1940, the use of her machines had spread to major American cities, England and Western Europe.

She manufactured the machines in various sizes, from a small $250 model sold to patients for home treatment to a large laboratory type for which she charged other quacks almost $5000.

In 1941, she founded the Drown School of Therapy, and sent letters to physicians announcing the "one Known Method at present that will acquaint the doctor with his patient from all angles, and help keep his patients instead of losing them for lack of equipment, and the complete knowledge to use it."

In urging the course for doctors, she said: "The people of the general public are fast becoming educated to the fact that there is some way whereby they may have their physical conditions analyzed, diagnosed, and treated from a purely scientific method. They are demanding that method and it behooves every doctor, whatever the school of healing art he has graduated from, to keep up with the times, and supply the need himself and not have to send his patient to some one else and thereby lose that patient's confidence."

Price of the course was $200. But "if the doctor passes his

examination" the tuition would be applied to the purchase of a Drown machine. "Your business," she assured prospective student doctors, "should never be below $500 per month and can run as high as you desire."

Patients and students flocked to Dr. Drown and her "purely scientific method." The "Drown Atlas," a book of instructions for purchasers of the machine, added some remarkable medical insight concerning the efficacy of shower versus tub baths.

"Any patient who is weak and depleted should never take shower baths and stand in the water over the drain, because the patient's magnetism is washed down with the water through the drain, leaving him depleted."

"Also a weak patient after having a tub bath should leave the tub and have someone else drain the water and clean the tub. . . . Too many people sit in the tub and drain the water before finishing the bath and their own magnetism is drained through the drain pipes to the ground, leaving the patient with much less reserve."

But it was the Homo-Vibra Ray, her mighty medical machine, that was the cornerstone of Dr. Drown's burgeoning medical empire and her foremost contribution to the art of healing.

The black box that she had invented, said Dr. Drown, not only had the unique capacity to diagnose and treat disease, but it all could be done by remote control! Once a sample of the patient's blood was on file in her office, only a forest fire burning somewhere between machine and patient could interrupt the healing power of the Homo-Vibra Ray. In addition, the machine was capable—also by remote control—of *photographing* the tissues and bones of a patient through mysterious "vibrations." It was also able to stop hemorrhaging in patients, and because of this boon Dr. Drown advocated that a portable model of her instrument be made compulsory first-aid equipment in every American automobile.

One visitor reported on the remote-control healing pitch she was given at the Drown premises. She had become aware of the Drown technique through a circular she received that advertised the laboratory's "radio findings for differential blood count, urinalysis, blood pressure, temperature, endocrine gland function, diseases of the body and mind."

"I have an aunt living in the East," the visitor had explained to one of Dr. Drown's assistants. "She's not feeling very well. I want her to take the train out to Los Angeles, but I don't know if she's strong enough."

"If your aunt can't make the trip, we can treat her by radio. All we need is an original diagnosis."

"You mean from another doctor?"

"No, a sample of her blood, taken from the ear. We treat hundreds of people all over the country by radio. We'll send you a blotter and you have your aunt send in a blood sample on the blotter and we'll diagnose and treat her case."

The visitor refused the treatment for her aunt, but most of those who came to the clinic soon became converts.

Over the years, Dr. Drown, who received her personal patients only by referral, perfected her mechanical charade. It was quite a show.

Once inside her sanctum sanctorum, the patient was seated with feet on two silver foot pads. Huddled in white uniform, Dr. Drown sat before the machine, furiously working a system of nine dials with indicators that registered from 0 to 100. With one cotton-covered finger, she rubbed a pad in a corner of the machine until noises or "vibrations" were heard (likened by one patient to the sound of a finger scraping on a balloon). The vibrations bounced the indicators and Dr. Drown gave her "readings" to a somber assistant, also in white uniform, who jotted them down on the patient's chart. The readings were then miraculously transformed into a diagnosis of the patient's ills. Treatment was invariably recommended at prices starting at twenty-five dollars per month. If a patient didn't want to bother making the trip to the clinic, a machine could be purchased for long-distance healing at home.

When Dr. Drown's hocus-pocus machine finally was examined by AMA investigators, they concluded it was a piece of gadgetry with a simple electrical circuit that activated the dials much like a battery tester. An engineer said that by connecting a speaker to the instrument it became a radio set comparable in operation and workmanship to many radios selling for less than fifteen dollars. Oliver Field, director of the AMA's Bureau of Investigation, proved the point by rigging a speaker to a Drown machine and using it as an office radio. The reception, he reported, wasn't bad.

Among the less sophisticated, however, use of the Homo-Vibra Ray was spreading, particularly in Chicago, where a nest of quacks was busily treating patients and selling the machines.

Posing as a patient at the office of a quack with a Homo-Vibra Ray, a Chicago *Tribune* reporter was informed that the machine could tell "if there's a short in any part of your body. It's like static on your radio."

The Drown disciple added: "It's just like tuning in Kansas City, New York, Los Angeles or even Mexico City. There are certain intricate combinations. Turn a couple of knobs one way, and you get Station H-E-A-R-T. Turn them another for programs coming over L-U-N-G-S or K-I-D-N-E-Y-S and so on."

The reporter, prior to visiting the quack, had undergone a thorough physical examination and was found to be in excellent physical health. But she was Drown-diagnosed as suffering from: feverish infection, malaria, undulant fever, afternoon temperatures, weak glands in the neck, bad ears, rheumatism, weak bladder, infected pancreas, infected lung (left lobe; right lobe O.K.), infected liver, possible diabetes, gas on the stomach and constipation.

The reporter's story ridiculed the Drown treatment, but even newspaper exposure of such blatant quackery did not shake the belief of Chicago devotees, many of whom had considerable influence. Among the believers was a society matron whose husband was a member of the citizens board of the University of Chicago. Through her husband, she managed to persuade the august university that Dr. Drown was entitled to an investigation of her claims.

The official announcement from the university was couched in diplomatic language: "On the face of it, the Drown claims appear to be totally unworthy of serious consideration by anyone, least of all a university. However, certain friends who are members of lay boards that have been of great assistance to the university have urged that her methods be investigated so that they may be repudiated if found unworthy or adapted to the benefit of mankind if they should prove to be worthy."

Chancellor Robert M. Hutchins, with a straight face, added that he "considered it a public responsibility" for the university to conduct the inquiry. Five distinguished doctors and scientists were duly assigned to proceed with the investigation.

In Los Angeles, meantime, Dr. Drown had finally run afoul of the law. She was charged by the government with a violation of interstate commerce and misbranding in the sale of one of her machines. But pending the outcome of the Chicago tests, the government agreed to delay prosecution.

Dr. Drown breezed into the Windy City for the crucial confrontation. She took up residence at the fashionable Stevens Hotel. In her entourage was Mrs. Tyrone Power, the mother of the movie star and another devoted follower. Dr. Drown claimed she had once "tuned in" her machine to the screen idol after he was involved in an automobile accident three thousand miles away. On another occasion she beamed her radio-vision device from London, and obtained a picture of a man's stomach as he was undergoing surgery in a New England hospital.

At 4 P.M. on December 30, 1949, Dr. Drown, dripping confidence, walked into the board room of the University of Chicago. Her attorney and an attorney for the university set the ground rules for testing of her claims that her equipment could photograph tissues and bones by remote control, could diagnose disease and control bleeding. The university agreed that blood specimens of ten patients and ten dogs would be furnished to Dr. Drown and she was also to be furnished film for the purpose of demonstrating her technique in "soft tissue" photography.

The tests began the next day in the university's darkroom. A sample of blood and an X ray of a patient with a fracture in the neck of the left femur were supplied to Dr. Drown. The university doctors asked her to make a radio photograph that would show the present stage of healing in the patient's hip.

Using her own compass to line up her instrument so that it pointed in an east-west tangent, Dr. Drown inserted a piece of black paper containing the blood sample into a slot at the rear of her machine.

The morning was spent taking six "photographs." None of them satisfied even Dr. Drown. "It's strange," she said, "that I can get such good results at home and such poor results here."

The group broke for lunch at the Quadrangle Club, then reconvened in the board room. As the doctors watched with barely concealed amazement, Dr. Drown proceeded with her diagnostic readings of the blood samples of three patients.

The final test was made on January 3, 1950, in the animal surgery rooms of the university. The arteries of two dogs were opened and Dr. Drown's two little machines for controlling the bleeding were set up in a corner of the room.

Science had met head-on with quackery, a virtually unprecedented confrontation. The official results of the tests were announced by the university a short time later. They were an unmitigated disaster for Dr. Drown.

Her photographs, the doctors said, "are simple fog patterns produced by exposure of the film to white light before it has been fixed adequately. The so-called radio photographs are mere artifacts and totally without clinical value."

Her machine diagnosis of the three patients by means of the blood samples were way wide of the mark. Patient number one she claimed had cancer of the left breast, was blind in one eye, had defective ovaries and trouble with heart, liver, gall bladder, kidneys, lungs, stomach, spinal nerves, intestines and ears. In actuality, the patient suffered only from tuberculosis. Patient number two, in reality afflicted with hypertension, was assigned a whole series of ailments, including malfunction of the uterus. A particularly remarkable diagnosis, the university doctors pointed out, since the patient was a male. Dr. Drown's diagnosis for the third patient, a perfectly healthy young man with normal blood pressure, was "an ischiorectal abscess, serious trouble with the prostate, probably carcinoma with spread to urethra, pelvic bones, and with loss or at any rate non-function of the left testicle." His blood pressure she reported as 166/78, and his prognosis was "very poor."

So erroneous were her diagnoses that the university doctors didn't bother submitting the blood samples of the seven other patients. Their report said: "The machine is a sort of a Ouija board. It is our belief that her alleged successes rest solely on the non-critical attitude of her followers. Her technique is to find so much trouble in so many organs that usually she can say 'I told you so' when she registers an occasional lucky positive guess. In these particular tests, even this luck deserted her."

In the test of the two dogs, the results were pathetic. "Mrs.

Drown stood in the doorway watching the animals bleed," the report said, describing the hemorrhage control experiment as a "fiasco."

"In the opinion of all observers, including herself, Mrs. Drown failed completely to control or modify hemorrhage," the report noted.

The dogs were destroyed. The wife of the university official who had originally pressed for a hearing for Dr. Drown and had observed the tests on the dogs had bolted from the surgery room in horror as her idol stood by helplessly while the dogs bled to death. "She was thoroughly convinced of the fallacy of all of Mrs. Drown's ideas and never again would be obsessed with them," the university doctors concluded.

On the heels of the Chicago experiments, the AMA branded Dr. Drown "a fake and a fraud." Still undeterred, she puffed back to Los Angeles, ready to face the government's charges.

The case against her had grown out of the purchase of a Homo-Vibra Ray by Wilson Ellis, a businessman from Evanston, Illinois. He had bought one of Dr. Drown's machines in June, 1948, after his wife discovered a lump in her breast.

Ellis had phoned Dr. Drown in Los Angeles and was referred by her to a doctor in Chicago who used her equipment. Mrs. Ellis began visiting the local practitioner, but complained of being tired by the long and frequent trips.

"You don't need to come here," Dr. Drown's acolyte assured her. "Just stay at home and we can treat you by radio wave. That's what's wonderful about the Drown machine; it's just as effective when the patient is miles away as it is when he or she's here."

On a business trip to Los Angeles, Mr. Ellis had stopped by the Drown Laboratories and bought a machine for $423.07. He had returned home with it and his wife had used the instrument to treat the lump in her breast. Dr. Drown had assured Mr. Ellis his wife's illness was not cancer, but was caused by a fungus that had spread through her digestive system into the liver.

The Evanston man had come forth with his story after reading the Chicago newspaper exposure of the Drown quackery.

In court, Dr. Drown, despite the disastrous results of the Chicago tests still fresh in her memory, defended her device and contended that the sale to Ellis was purely an intrastate transaction.

The government put six expert witnesses on the stand, who again proceeded to destroy Dr. Drown's pretensions as a healer.

One authority compared her gimmick "with the voodoo works of medicine men and witch doctors."

Dr. H. C. Pulley, assistant city health officer, declared: "The box is a very pretty thing to look at, but it has no scientific value. It is absolutely worthless as an instrument to cure any ills."

Dr. Moses A. Greenfield, radiologist and head of the radiation physics division at U.C.L.A. Medical Center, testified that the machine was worthless and that it had "an electrical potential no greater than that of a flashlight battery."

Another expert described the machine as simply an "inefficient battery tester" which wiggles its needles better when used with a glass of water instead of a human patient.

Dr. Drown was decidedly getting the worst of it. Then the trial was suddenly sparked by the appearance of a voluntary, unsubpoenaed witness—who came forth on behalf of the healer.

The witness was another of Dr. Drown's highly placed followers, Mrs. Eleanor B. Allen, the prestigious president of the Los Angeles City Board of Education.

Mrs. Allen testified that she was a firm, long-time believer in Dr. Drown's radio therapy. She had two of the Drown machines in her home. She and her husband had known Dr. Drown for eighteen or nineteen years and they both had implicit, provable faith in her methods.

Mrs. Allen said that the Drown device had once cured her of pneumonia when she was in Atlantic City, New Jersey, and the machine was in Los Angeles. On another occasion, the board of education president added, use of the "broadcast treatment" had cured a rash that had appeared on the hands of her son.

Under cross-examination, Assistant U. S. Attorney Tobias G. Klinger posed a hypothetical question to Mrs. Allen.

"Assume you were riding in an automobile in Moscow and Dr. Drown and her device were in Hollywood. You had an accident and received a broken leg, a fractured skull and were hemorrhaging. By telephone, Dr. Drown was informed you had been in an accident—nothing more.

"Using your blood sample on file, Dr. Drown would tune in the machine, which would diagnose your condition. Then she would tune in the treatment device. It is, then, your contention that this would cure your broken leg and fractured skull and stop your hemorrhage?"

"Yes, yes," Mrs. Allen answered. "The way you state it, Mr. Klinger, sounds like black magic, but it isn't. It's science."

The government attorney then asked if she would seek a surgeon instead of the machine if she required surgery.

Mrs. Allen said that use of the machine would preclude any need for surgery.

Klinger asked why, if the machine is so effective, her husband had been ill for five years.

Mrs. Allen replied: "That machine has kept him alive."

The testimony shocked Los Angeles officials. The grand jury, fearful that Mrs. Allen, because of her position, might advocate adoption of the machine for treating the city's school children, prepared to launch a full-scale inquiry. But it never came off. Mrs. Allen stuck to her "machine" guns, and resigned from the board of education.

Dr. L. S. Goerke, Director of the Bureau of Medical Services for the Los Angeles City Health Department, announced the publication of a special bulletin to counteract Mrs. Allen's advocacy of the Drown machine.

"Confusion caused in the public mind by endorsement of such gadgets by the president of the board of education should be clarified and corrected by factual information," he said. "In 1951, in the world's most literate country, we have magic for the cure of disease."

There was no confusion, however, in the minds of the jurors. They convicted Dr. Drown on the misdemeanor charge. She was fined $1000.

Outraged, she then personally drew up her complaint for a $5,000,000 damage suit, naming as the chief defendant the U. S. Pharmacopoeial Convention, an organization chartered by the U. S. Congress, ten other medical groups, including the AMA, plus 154 medical corporations.

In her suit she asked for the dissolution, no less, of the AMA, the California Medical Society, the medical departments of the

U. S. Army and Navy, the U. S. Public Health Service, the U. S. Departments of Agriculture and Commerce and the medical colleges of Pittsburgh and Johns Hopkins universities.

She said the defendants had combined to "engineer" her prosecution. This was done, she said, in order to create a monopoly by the defendants and was in violation of the antitrust laws.

In due course, her complaint, one of America's more remarkable legal actions, was thrown out.

Dr. Drown went back to twirling her dials. Despite the exposure by the University of Chicago and the misdemeanor conviction, she persevered for the next thirteen years, free to pursue her healing and minister to hundreds of patients a year.

Two patients, both attractive young housewives, turned up for treatment at her clinic in 1963.

Mrs. Jackie Metcalf complained of stomach trouble. She was also worried about the health of her three children. Her Drown diagnosis disclosed that she suffered from aluminum poisoning of the stomach and gall bladder, malfunction of the right ovary and left kidney. She was advised to throw away all her kitchen utensils and return for treatment. After submitting blood samples of her children, she was told they had chicken pox and mumps.

Mrs. Concetta Jorgensen complained that she had been diagnosed by another doctor as a cancer victim. On the Drown machine, however, no cancer or tuberculosis showed up. But the machine did find cysts and her salt-sugar ratio out of balance, caused by malfunction of the liver and thymus gland. She was charged fifty dollars for the diagnosis and was offered treatments at either fifty dollars a month on a month-to-month basis or thirty-five dollars a month on a six-month contract.

Mrs. Metcalf and Mrs. Jorgensen were acting as agents for the Los Angeles District Attorney's office and the California Bureau of Food and Drug Inspection.

The two women agents told Deputy District Attorney Miner and Grant S. Leake, supervising inspector of the state bureau, that they had also been shown photographs of astronauts and dogs in orbiting space capsules at the Drown clinic. These were represented as having been obtained by "chance" when the diagnostic machines picked up energy waves from the cosmos.

Dr. Drown had boasted that she had 100 inpatients and 200 outpatients a month, plus about 80 patients a month at her San Luis Obispo office.

Both Mrs. Metcalf and Mrs. Jorgensen had been examined by doctors and pronounced in perfect health before visiting the Drown premises. Mrs. Metcalf's children were not suffering from chicken pox or mumps. The blood samples of her "children" were actually from a turkey, a sheep and a dog.

Armed with the evidence, grand jury warrants were drawn and Dr. Drown's health mill was raided. More than fifty of her machines were confiscated. One investigator said, "Rube Goldberg would be proud of these."

Dr. Drown was charged with three counts of grand theft. Still peppery, she declared confidently, "The advertising will be wonderful for me. When I get back to my office I'll have more patients than ever."

This time, however, it was not to be. The district attorney padlocked the clinic and checkmated Dr. Drown's attempt to have her machines returned.

Her trial was scheduled for early in April, 1965. Miner was confident of victory. Dr. Drown was confident of vindication.

But three weeks before the trial, Dr. Drown died unexpectedly of a heart ailment. Investigators learned she had had her first stroke fourteen months earlier and had secretly been under the care of a legitimate specialist.

In the end, the queen of the quacks had been a physician unable to heal herself.

7

THE CULTS

Prophets, Profits and the Gospel According to George Washington

> Who shall ascend into the hill of the Lord? or who shall
> stand in his holy place? He that hath clean hands, and a
> pure heart; who hath not lifted up his soul unto vanity,
> nor sworn deceitfully.
>
> —Book of Psalms

On the bittersweet morning of September 9, 1964, the San Pedro
harbor of Los Angeles was choked with more than two thousand
chanting, leaping, praying, singing, crying faithful of the Russian
Molokan Christian Holy Spiritual Jumpers, a tormented sect of
conscientious objectors that had made its painful exodus from the
vast Russian steppes to southern California in 1905.

The faithful were on hand to bid good-bye to thirty-two men,
women and children, the vanguard of twenty thousand Molokans exhorted by their prophets to sail to a new Promised Land.

*God protect them. Send angels with them on their long jour-
ney,* a church elder prayed for the eight embarking families.
*Where are you going? Over deep seas and hot sun in search of
God in the name of Christ.*

Paradise had been lost in Los Angeles. "There are too many
worldly activities and too much sin to tempt our children in
southern California," explained Bill Chernekoff, a thirty-three-
year-old member of the sect who was sailing with his wife and
three children. "Our prophets have been telling us that we will
have to move again. A year ago, they began to search for a new
home."

The bearded Molokan prophets, who receive visions from God
and deliver the Holy Spirit's message to members of the sect, had

decided on the location of the new Promised Land, a rural area outside Perth, Australia.

"The bars close at six P.M. in Australia," Chernekoff pointed out. "Everything is closed from Saturday to Monday morning. There is much less divorce. Morals are higher than they are here."

As the families boarded, the two thousand prayed in Russian and jumped "in rejoicement of the manifestations of God." Gifts to the pioneers were prayer books, salt and a large loaf of blessed bread, to be eaten each day of the voyage as a symbolic observance of their faith. The emotional leave-taking reached its height in the traditional kiss by each of the sect members on the cheeks of those departing.

Then the liner *Oriana* sailed for the other side of the world. Hopefully, paradise would be regained—as far from sinful Los Angeles as possible.

The exodus of the devout, sincere Molokans from Los Angeles was unusual. Since 1840, the traffic of small splinter sects, the way-out cults and the fire-breathing apostles of new religions— one eye on heaven and the other on the collection plate—has been a steady in-migration. The City of Angels has restlessly played host to most of the world's freak religions and crackpot faiths, and many another strange altar has sprung full-blown from native soil.

Geography, climate and history help explain the fabled flowering of cults in Los Angeles. The city is the last stop on the gospel trail, the tag end of the continent where the cult con men easily find a place in a blizzard of other exotic faiths among a rootless, questing population already conditioned to bizarre religions.

"It's much easier to believe when you live in sunshine," says Dr. Marcus Bach, comparative religion professor at the University of Iowa. "The influence of many Midwesterners who left behind faiths that no longer excited them is particularly strong in Southern California. They become ripe for the colorful, dramatic shows some of these sects put on. They arrive looking for a new faith."

The only question is which new faith to embrace. The Saturday newspapers offer a bewildering index of the Lord's many mansions. Partisans of everything from astrology to Zen, old-line

Christian churches as well as the most outlandish of the cults, push their path to salvation in the unabashed prose of the huckster. The houses of worship buy their advertising space and hawk their holy wares with the subtlety of a white sale announcement. Salvation comes in many guises and a wide variety of styles.

For those who like their religion folksy there are endless old-fashioned revivals. "Rx for a heart-warming experience in sermon and song," says one ad. "Send for heart-to-heart talk." Another temple, the Wings of Healing, offers a program consisting of a sermon "packed with Holy Spirit Power and anointing," a star from the Grand Ole Opry and an evangelist conducting a revival—"a world-renowned man of God with a ministry of miracles."

More sensation is promised by Christian Science. "Ancient and modern necromancy alias mesmerism and hypnotism, denounced . . . this Sunday!" A competitor, Brother James B. Carr, declares in warning boldface: "A TOTAL BLACKOUT IS COMING. THE EARTH SHAKING! Sea and waves roaring over cities! COME! Be blessed with the Spirit of Prophecy. Have a NEW experience with God! You can receive WISDOM, KNOWLEDGE and FAITH in this meeting."

Imagery is neatly tailored to the local congregation. "Your Picture Career" is the promised Sunday sermon at the Unity Church of Beverly Hills for affluent parishioners from the movie and television industries. "Your personal world is a living, moving picture in technicolor. What kind of pictures have you been taking? You have only to look at the screen of your life!" And the Church of Religious Science of Beverly Hills suggests: "Let's Talk About You, Are You in the Top Ten?"

There is religion aided by slogan. "Temple Baptist Church, The Downtown Church That Cares." The Alvarado Church of Christ declares itself: "*Your* Downtown Christian Church." And the Hollywood First Methodist Church urges: "Attend Church regularly. Your attendance is your vote for the Church's survival."

The never-quite-solved mysteries of the mystics invite investigation of their complexities. "Dr. Seiko Wada, a living disciple of the great Tibetan Master, Djwal Khul, lecturing on 'Esoteric truths, occult anatomy and breathing techniques.' Spiritual Healing and Counseling Wed. Thru Sun. Tibetan Breathing & Calisthenics for Health Every Friday, 8–9 P.M. at The World

Brotherhood of the White Temple." Dr. Dingle's Mystic Christianity advertises: "Our Church is especially for the seeker—he who has searched in vain for the inner Mysteries of the Spirit and desires to discover the Eternal Way. Mentalphysics is what the whole world consciously or unconsciously is seeking." One may also embrace the Temple of Tarot and Holy Qabalah, the "Builders of the Adytum." Sample sermons: "Use of Tarot in Formulating Spiritual Goals," "The Power of Vibratory Sound in Qabalistic Chants" and "The Qabalistic Secrets of Love and Marriage."

The pages of religious ads, observing strict neutrality, also list the Church of Life lectures on "ESP—Your Coming Great Inner-Space Adventure" and "How to Make ESP Work for You."

Salvation in southern California lurks everywhere. The seeker is advised to phone in, tune in, drive in or walk in to the church of his choice.

"Are you searching for a religion which does not insult your intelligence? Call the Unitarian Universalist Church for additional information." Other churches offer "dial-a-prayer," "dial now and just listen," "dial daily devotion," "dial a creative thought for each day," "call toll-free for a message from God." Calls may also be placed for: "Spiritual Reader & Advisor on all problems. One free question answered by phone." "FAMOUS PSYCHIC—You tell me NOTHING. I will tell you ALL on the telephone."

The collection box can be avoided altogether in the comfort of home. "Worship at the only church service on television . . . presented by Forest Lawn Memorial-Parks. Actual services of prominent Southern California churches brought to you by videotape. A different church every Sunday morning."

Some churches have anticipated all the comforts of home and call prideful attention to the exclusivity of their facilities. "California's Only Walk-In, Drive-In Church . . . where 3,000 people worship weekly . . . sitting in their cars . . . or in the great glass cathedral. Located two miles below Disneyland just off the Santa Ana Freeway." In addition to the familiar free parking and nursery care there are additional boons: "inspiring worship in an air cooled sanctuary" and "closed circuit TV for overflow congregation."

Sermons with a zing are a southern California specialty. Provocatively titled, they are linked to psychiatry, bank balances, health, politics as well as religion: "Can a Modern Man Be Happy?" "Conquest of Fear," "Toward Success," "Five Major Steps to Prosperity," "Claiming Your Share of God's Financial Abundance," "Prayer and Penicillin," "Why I Believe in Divine Healing," "Facts and Fictions of Divine Healing," "God's Election—Who Was Elected," "God's Formula for World Peace," "Pray with Authority," "The Final Answer," "Truth or Consequences," "Will the World Last Forever?" "Surprised at Heaven's Door?" "Fractured Faith," "Good People with Luxury Sins," "The Paralyzing Sin of Lukewarmness," "Keeping Out of God's Penalty Box," "Slave of Love" and "The Ten Virgins."

This steaming, bubbling, overflowing caldron of God is a made-to-order paradise for con men fleecing the desperate, the lonely, the defeated and the fearful in the name of religion. Almost everyone in southern California has bought at least one ticket to heaven, and separating the sincere cultist from the con man requires the wisdom of Solomon.

The law has found it next to impossible to act against religious bunco except in the most blatant cases of doorbell-ringing Bible salesmen, and phony nuns and priests who work the suburban circuit, collecting contributions for mythical good causes in rented clerical garb.

For only seven dollars in fees and three signatures scribbled on articles of incorporation, anyone can open a church, seek a following and solicit tax-free contributions, secure in the knowledge that constitutional guarantees covering freedom of religion makes prosecution difficult.

Constitutional guarantees are unfailingly cited by astrologers, agnostics, atheists, cabalists, card readers, clairvoyants, fortune-tellers, mediums, metaphysicists, palmists, psychics, random Jehovahs, phrenologists and yogis.

In October, 1964, a raiding squad of over a hundred Los Angeles police officers netted nine gypsy women on charges of fortunetelling, a bunco offense.

George Adams, self-styled king of the thirty thousand Serbian gypsies in the United States, promptly accused the police of a violation of freedom of religion.

"Gypsies are born with the power to look into the future," he said. "It's part of their religion. We are members of the Palmistry Church."

The day after the raid thirty other gypsy women—obeying the command of their "king"—surrendered. Adams said he had ordered their surrender because "it was a waste of taxpayers' money to have a hundred police officers running around trying to catch our women giving spiritual readings."

"I don't know how my people are going to stop giving spiritual readings," he said. "We've been doing it for two thousand years."

Most of the women were fined twenty-five dollars and released.

Captain John A. McAllister, head of the fraud division of the Los Angeles Police Department, explained the reason for the raid. "We've been arresting gypsies at the rate of one, two or three a month for a long time. But we're finding their fortunetelling to be a rather well-organized operation.

"It isn't that the police department has anything in particular against gypsies. It's just that ninety-nine per cent of all fortune-tellers happen to be gypsies.

"Troubled people, who can ill afford to spend their money, are going to them and receiving spurious advice."

Other communities have set up punitive license fees as a deterrent. County supervisors of Riverside, California, drove out the fortunetellers, palm readers, astrologists and phrenologists by demanding a $2400 yearly license charge.

"For the most part the con man who uses religion as his scam," says one deputy district attorney, "is the untouchable of the criminal world—no matter how ridiculous his so-called religion."

Con man or child of God? From the beginning, most southern Californians have given their favorite cultist the benefit of the doubt.

The first to challenge established religion in Los Angeles was a tough, irascible Scotsman named Bishop William Money. He thundered into town in 1841, preaching the gospel of his self-created "Reformed New Testament Church of the Faith of Jesus Christ," a vegetable-soup theology of Catholicism, Protestantism, Greek philosophy, and astrology, peppered with some quack notions of medicine and geography.

Bitterly anti-Catholic, he won a small following of poor Mexicans. He dressed for the pulpit in a red flannel shirt, miner's boots and a frock coat, and he specialized in sermons that were more profane than sacred. In one sermon, he denounced his wife for infidelity, recounting her fall from grace in lurid detail. The bishop also claimed he was a doctor, having treated more than five thousand patients, most of them successfully. "Only four of the sons-of-bitches died!"

He published the first book in Los Angeles, "Reform of the New Testament Church, by Wm. Money, Deacon and Defender of the Faith of Jesus Christ," blithely claiming he could return from the grave. When a brace of skeptics ragged him into proving it, he led them to a cemetery and allowed himself to be laid in a coffin. Before the shallow grave could be covered, he screamed aloud, "Get me out of this damn thing before I suffocate!"

He drew a map of the world and claimed the earth was fish-shaped. San Francisco, he said, would soon collapse into flaming perdition. A curiosity for most of his career, Money finally put a curse on Los Angeles and fled into retirement in San Gabriel. He built "Money's Castle," a strange six-sided little home, and died there in 1880. Votive candles were found burning at his head and feet, a final tribute from a believer to the eccentric Deacon and Defender of the Faith of Jesus Christ.

The first of southern California's countless séance sellers came to San Diego in 1887. Tall, slender, dark-haired Francis Grierson inveigled a pair of impressionable brothers, local cattle and produce kings, to build him the palatial Villa Montezuma. A fantastic edifice, each of its rooms had a different shade of wood paneling. Appointments included deep Persian rugs, stained-glass windows, expensive paintings, sculpture and candelabra, a Spanish cedar staircase and bronzed ceilings. Grierson's private bedroom, in which he shored up the strength to communicate with the spirit world, had a magnificient bay window overlooking the ocean.

Grierson was a disciple of Madame Helena Petrovna Blavatsky, Russian-born founder of theosophy and the reigning spiritualist of the era. Word of Grierson's séances soon spread, and he became a fad. Governors, society leaders and stage celebrities began turning up in the halls of Montezuma.

Spectators swore they heard voices, drums, tambourines and trumpets—a "simply indescribable effect," said one. Grierson soon came to grief when his patrons had business reverses and could no longer maintain the mortgage on the Villa. Having bled them down to almost their last nickel, he pulled one last piece of chicanery before leaving town. He offered to trade his interest in the Villa for a piece of property in Cheyenne, Wyoming. With borrowed money, the brothers swung for the deal, eventually discovering the Cheyenne property was valueless. Grierson went to Europe, changed his name, and launched a successful career as a concert pianist and writer until his death in 1927.

Grierson's exodus left the city wide-open for a new flame-bearer of spiritualism. The torch of theosophy was relit in San Diego in 1900, by the "Purple Mother," self-proclaimed successor to Madame Blavatsky who had died nine years earlier. With the arrival of Katherine Augusta Tingley, a thrice-married, fifty-three-year-old New Englander, the age of flamboyant cultism in southern California was truly launched.

She came west, she declared, filled with a dream of building a "White City in a Land of Gold beside a Sunset Sea."

Build it she did, with the "love offerings" showered on her by well-fixed disciples. Forty buildings were constructed in Moorish and Egyptian architectural styles on a magnificent five-hundred-acre site. The Purple Mother's White City included a university; a Greek theater; a school of yoga; the Iris Temple of Art, Music and Drama; a "progressive" school for children; and The Homestead, the ninety-room main building. Visitors were piped through the elaborate Egyptian Gate by a bugler.

Some three hundred of the faithful, after turning over all their worldly goods to Mrs. Tingley, came to live in the theosophical utopia. They wore free-flowing Greek costumes, and raised chickens, silkworms, fruits and vegetables.

Mrs. Tingley preached the Hindu doctrine of karma, the belief that the spirit undergoes a succession of earthly lives. And she practiced what she preached. She slept with her dog, Spot, the reincarnation, she claimed, of the most favored of her three husbands.

She ruled her flock like a czarina, floating ubiquitously over the grounds in purple gown and determined mien. But trouble rumbled down the coast from General Harrison Gray Otis, the powerhouse publisher of the Los Angeles *Times*. He called Mrs. Tingley's establishment a "spookery" and charged that "gross immoralities" were being practiced, children were suffering from malnutrition and "the most incredible things happen in that lair." But he couldn't prove it in court, and eventually Mrs. Tingley won a large libel judgment against him.

More trouble came from the wife of a wealthy doctor, one of the Purple Mother's most ardent followers, who had contributed $300,000 to the colony. The doctor's wife sued Mrs. Tingley for alienation of affection and won a $75,000 verdict.

Other followers began to slip away or convert their allegiance to another battle-scarred lady of theosophy, Annie Besant—who had studied at the knee of Madame Blavatsky in India and claimed that she, not Mrs. Tingley, was the true inheritor of the founder's 100,000-member flock.

Annie invaded Hollywood and soon was a prime mover in Krotona, a fifteen-acre hill tract built by a lawyer from Virginia as a spiritualist retreat. She said she was locating her own wing of the movement in southern California because the area was producing a race of supermen, Aryans "not unlike the Greeks in appearance." She branched out and picked up 450 acres in the Ojai Valley to build a rival spiritualist center. Breathlessly she confided to her own followers: "The Christ-spirit is living in seclusion in the Himalayas."

A spirited war for the loyalty of the theosophist faithful broke out between the two ladies. Mrs. Tingley called Mrs. Besant a crank and accused her of "commercializing" theosophy. Mrs. Besant called Mrs. Tingley an "opportunist and usurper."

The brickbats flew back and forth between San Diego and Ojai. But the colorful cultists were both aging, their heyday over, the influence of theosophy waning in the glow of a new female usurper, the unchallenged queen of the sin-busting sisterhood, a veteran of the sawdust trail who rolled into Los Angeles in 1918 with worldly goods of only $100 and a battered automobile.

Sister Aimee was her name and fighting the Devil was her game.

Titian-haired Aimee Semple McPherson, preaching the Second Coming, redemption, conversion and faith healing, became southern California's most famous Satan-chaser, building a multi-million-dollar religious enterprise that still flourishes in Los Angeles.

Aimee wasn't one for theological hair-splitting. She poured color, drama and excitement into her straight-out good-versus-evil sermons. In only five years after her inauspicious arrival, she had preached her way into a $1,500,000 house of worship that seated five thousand.

Dressed in football togs on the stage of Angelus Temple, she declared herself ready "to kick a touchdown for the Lord."

She preached ten times a week, did an enormous amount of good in feeding the poor and selling war bonds. Attractive, feminine, with a toothpaste smile, she drove around Los Angeles in a car as long as the Lord's arm. It bore a sign that asked: "Where Will You Spend Eternity?"

At the Temple, Aimee dressed in white and tossed red roses to the congregation. All she asked in return was that she hear a "rustle" of dollar bills rather than a "clink" of coin when the collection was taken.

On May 18, 1926, Aimee went for a swim at Ocean Park, but no one saw her come out of the water. Her followers were soon in pandemonium and her disappearance caused a wave of unbelieving shock. Thousands went to the beach and prayed for her safe return. In the confusion, one of the more devout was accidentally drowned.

For nearly five weeks the vigil lasted. Then on June 23, Aimee turned up in an unlikely Mexican village with a sensational tale, claiming she had been kidnaped, held captive for $500,000 ransom before escaping from her abductors.

The faithful praised the Lord, and never questioned her story. She came back to Los Angeles in blazing triumph. One newspaper headlined, "Aimee's Home Again!" She was lifted off her train into a flower-bedecked chair, and more than 100,000 lined the parade route and cheered her all the way to the Temple.

The Los Angeles district attorney's office tried to prove her story a hoax. Investigation had turned up evidence that Aimee had spent ten days of her absence with a radio operator from the Temple at a "honeymoon cottage" in Carmel. She was held for trial, but under pressure from local businessmen who feared a public circus, the charges were dropped.

She continued preaching until her death in 1944 from an overdose of sleeping powders. Today the Temple is run by her son,

Dr. Rolf K. McPherson. Leading Los Angeles politicians often address the crowds. A pleasant housewife, the Reverend Jean Darnall, is the only woman preacher on the Temple's ministry staff. She sings the praises of the Lord from where Aimee once stood. But the old-timers still miss Sister Aimee kicking her touchdowns for the Lord.

The harsh days of the Depression thirties nourished three fantastic cults in southern California that mixed religion with politics. All three, Mankind United, the Kingdom of Yahweh and the Mighty I Am, became big business and won enormous followings.

Handsome as a matinee idol, Arthur Bell founded Mankind United in 1934. Los Angeles was soon in an uproar. Proclaiming a hazy theology, he concentrated on his hypnotic economic program, promising a utopia to the elderly who flocked to him and lined his pockets with more than $1,000,000.

Bell called President Franklin Roosevelt a "fathead" and a tool of international bankers. Since the government obviously couldn't take care of citizens in the style they deserved, said Bell, he would, with God's blessings, provide every member of his secret order with a pension of $250 a month, a $25,000 home with a swimming pool, radio, television, unlimited movies and "an automatic vocal-type correspondence machine." There were only two preconditions for Mankind United's heaven on earth. Members first had to surrender all their assets to the movement. Over 14,000 southern Californians complied. And only when the organization swelled to 200,000,000 members could all its promises be fulfilled.

The government cracked down on Bell, convicting him of owing $267,000 in back taxes. The money that had cascaded into his movement, investigators found, had gone into Bell's private investments—hotels, real estate, a resort, dairies and a fish hatchery. The cult was dissolved in complete disenchantment in 1949.

Preacher Joe Jeffers, a little tiger of a man, hit Los Angeles about 1938 with his Kingdom of Yahweh "located on the planet Orion." Spieling a jumble of astrology, Protestant fundamentalism, Nazism and anti-Semitism, he collected some $2,000,000 and thousands of adherents, primarily middle-aged women.

A one-time Baptist minister who had studied acting in a Holly-

wood drama school, Preacher Joe knew how to work a crowd.
Rolling softly on blue suede shoes, he flashed a hand heavenward
and announced, "I ain't preachin' tonight until I get six hundred
dollars!" He got it.

But the pious preacher became famous in Los Angeles for a
reason that had nothing to do with religion. A couple of investigators assigned to check out the man who was collecting money
in rolling green waves found evidence of sensational morals offenses. The investigators said Joe was holding sex orgies in his
apartment.

Joe's trial opened in a jammed courtroom. The overflow of his
faithful in the street sent up chorus after chorus of "Onward
Christian Soldiers" as witnesses testified that at one drunken
party Joe and his beautiful wife had performed an immoral act in
front of others and passed around pornographic photographs.
Mrs. Jeffers confessed, then recanted, that she had had sexual
intercourse with another man in front of her husband and that he
had engaged in a sexual act with three other women while she
observed.

When Joe got on the stand, the judge asked the amount of his
income.

"Anything from nothing up. I live on love offerings."

"Do you own any stocks and bonds?"

"I do. Two or three million—laid up in the kingdom of heaven."

"That's not in my jurisdiction," the judge replied. "Let's come
down to earth."

Joe charged the trial was a frame-up. The jury, after carefully
scrutinizing each line of the testimony, agreed with him. He was
found not guilty.

"Our Messiah is free!" members of the joyful, overflowing congregation shouted the next day as they welcomed home their
conquering hero.

Joe's wife divorced him, but he went on preaching, once announcing that Jesus had a wife and wasn't crucified, but had
gone to live in the Far East and "I know where the body is."

He subsequently got involved in a torrent of other legal action.
A couple of followers sued for return of large sums they had contributed for construction of a temple. His ex-wife sued for non-
payment of alimony. Joe explained to the judge that his religion

did not permit him to make the payments. He went to prison
for stealing his wife's car and later served another jolt for violation
of parole.

But the most eccentric of all the cults to blaze across the Los
Angeles heavens was a weird, wild, whiz-bang operation pieced
together by a Midwestern Mr. and Mrs. team, a broken-down con
man and an ambitious housewife.

On March 25, 1929, a Cook County grand jury in Chicago issued two indictments against a tall, blue-eyed, gray-haired ex-
medium named Guy Ballard. Two elderly women had testified
that Ballard fleeced them of several thousand dollars for shares
in a "Lake of Gold" mining investment in California. It wasn't his
first scam, according to the records. He had also been a fleece man
in the south, selling stock in nonexistent oil wells to gullible widows. Warrants on the Chicago charges were issued, but Ballard
had skipped town. At fifty-one, he was an unhappy, frustrated,
pathetic failure who had spent twenty-five years working as a
paper hanger and dabbling in con games and the world of the
occult.

Ballard turned up in Los Angeles, using the assumed name of
Dick Gilbert. He lived a hand-to-mouth existence, and spent most
of his time wandering from one metaphysical lecture to another.
He made a side trip to northern California to run down a rumor
of a lost gold mine. Ballard had an obsession about gold and had
once tried his hand at prospecting. Even as a child in Newton,
Kansas, his favorite dream was finding buried treasure.

Unable to locate the mine, he moved on to San Francisco and
strayed into a cult meeting that specialized in showmanship
rather than sanctity. He was transfixed as he watched the performance. A high priest and priestess sat in gold chairs as a
scantily clad choir of twelve vestal virgins tossed flowers to the
flock. The backdrop was a giant cross, illuminated by flashing
lights. After the silver-tongued high priest addressed the crowd,
dozens in the audience streamed toward the platform, begging to
touch him. The vestal virgins passed efficiently among the believers at the height of their frenzy to collect contributions.

Ballard never forgot it.

In all, he spent two years tramping through California, soaking up local cultist lore and waiting for the con game warrants in Chicago to be forgotten. When he thought it was safe, he slipped back to rejoin his family.

Edna Wheeler Ballard was a pretty, middle-aged blonde, an ex-concert harpist and one-time clerk in an occult bookstore. She had a consuming drive for success, a drive that thus far had been thwarted. During her husband's absence, she had supported herself and their teen-age son, Donald, by giving spiritualist readings.

Even with Guy's return, the future of the Ballard family was bleak. But as Guy began to pour out the details of his California trip, an idea began to grow. Over the next few years, Guy and Edna patiently hammered out the theology of a new cult. They christened it the "Mighty I Am," and working doggedly at the kitchen table in their cheap brick bungalow, they eventually produced the I Am bible, *Unveiled Mysteries*. It appeared under Guy Ballard's pseudonym, Godfre Ray King.

It was an amazing work, destined to become a best seller and earn millions for its creators. The book, which the Ballards were to claim later had been dictated by the patron saint of their movement, transposed Guy's shabby, hard-times sojourn in California into epic adventure.

According to the revelations in *Unveiled Mysteries,* Ballard had been sent to California "on government business." During his visit to Mt. Shasta, a favorite watering spot for generations of occultists as the abode of various tribes of gods, Lemurians and a race of little men, Ballard had the soul-churning confrontation that led to the founding of the Mighty I Am.

It began one morning at daybreak when he went for a hike, "deciding to follow where fancy led, and in a vague sort of way, asking God to direct my path."

After walking all morning, Ballard stopped near a spring for a drink.

"Cup in hand, I bent down to fill it, when an electrical current passed through my body from head to foot. I looked around, and directly behind me stood a young man who, at first glance, seemed to be someone on a hike like myself."

Ballard guessed, however, that his companion was no ordinary person.

"My brother," the young man said, "if you will hand me your cup, I will give you a much more refreshing drink than spring water."

Ballard passed the cup to the stranger and it was immediately filled with a creamy liquid.

"Drink it!" the young man commanded.

He did and found it delicious. "The electrical vivifying effect on mind and body made me gasp with surprise."

The young man explained that the drink came from the "Universal Supply"—and that through love any material object can be precipitated. "Whatsoever I desire manifests itself when I command in Love. I held out the cup, and that which I desired for you appeared. See! I have but to hold out my hand and, if I wish to use gold—gold is here."

"Instantly," Ballard recounted, "there lay in his palm a disc about the size of a ten-dollar gold piece."

"I see you do not quite recognize me in your outer consciousness," said the young man. "Sit still a few moments—watch me closely—and I will reveal my identity to you."

It took only a moment—and then "I saw his face, body and clothing become the living, breathing, tangible 'Presence' of the Master, Saint Germain."

Ballard's invoking of St. Germain was neither original nor surprising. The legendary, flamboyant Count of St. Germain, an eighteenth-century adventurer, alchemist and booster of reincarnation, had been a made-to-order hero for dozens of other occult movements. In his heyday, Germain had claimed to have a secret for removing flaws from diamonds and for changing base metals into gold. He also claimed discovery of a liquid that could prolong life and said he himself was two thousand years old. Germain had been a confidant of Louis XV, had helped Catherine the Great reach the Russian throne and been a friend of Cagliostro.

Now, according to Ballard, he was back and perfectly intact despite his death about 1780.

"He stood there before me—a Magnificent God-like figure—in a white jeweled robe."

Germain explained his latest reincarnation. "This is the body in which I work a great deal of the time, when occupied with the welfare of mankind, unless the work I am doing at the moment requires closer contact with the outer world of affairs, and in that case, I make my body take on the characteristics and dress of the nation with which I am working at the moment."

Germain added that he was an "Ascended Master," one of less than one hundred in all of history to have attained the power to appear and reappear at will. In previous embodiments, said Germain, he had been on earth as the prophet Samuel, Francis Bacon and "Uncle Sam."

"It is no more effort for us to change the appearance and activity of our bodies than it is for the ordinary human being to change his clothes," Germain said. "The unfortunate condition in human consciousness, that keeps individuals in their self-created limitations, is their attitude of mind which either fears or ridicules what it does not understand, or what is still worse, in its ignorance says: 'This is impossible.' A thing may not be probable under certain conditions, but the God Self, which is the Great 'Light,' can change all human conditions so nothing is impossible."

By willing the "God Self" into everyday life, Germain declared, the "law of re-embodiment" is attainable to anyone.

"The time has arrived, when many of humanity are rapidly awakening, and they must in some way be made to understand, that they have lived again and again in hundreds—sometimes thousands—of lives, each time in a new physical body."

Germain was the Lord and Ballard was Moses being handed the tablets on Shasta instead of Sinai.

The Count was ready to "prove" the truth of reincarnation.

"I will revive these Etheric Records and you shall see living pictures, giving every detail of your life."

Without the least effort, Ballard found himself standing outside his physical body. But he was worried. Would his body be safe on the mountain while he and Germain floated back in time? Reading his thoughts, the Count declared: "Do not be disturbed. Not a thing in the world can harm your body while we are away. Observe!"

Immediately, a "White Flame" flashed, forming a protective circle about fifty feet in diameter around his body.

Ballard and Germain were now free to defy time and motion. "Come with me," said Germain, "and let us review the physical life in which you used a feminine form in France, wherein you were a singer of splendid accomplishment with a voice of rare beauty and power."

With Germain's stout right arm around him, Ballard was free to enjoy the journey. "I saw we were rising rapidly from the ground but I soon became adjusted to his vibratory action. There was no definite feeling of motion through space."

They were soon looking down on a village in the south of France. Here Ballard had been born a woman in the first of his lives. He had made rapid progress as a singer, according to Germain's narration, and performed before the Queen of France. He was showered with fame and riches. But he died young and the fortune he had amassed passed to one of his teachers. Instead of using the money to further the good works that had been Ballard's final request, the teacher turned into a scoundrel. "The last rites were no sooner over, than a complete change took place within him. Greed took possession entirely." Swiftly producing another "etheric record," Germain showed Ballard that this man had himself been reincarnated and Ballard had met him in America as a representative of the Belgian government. "That man," said Germain, "was given a chance to right the wrong he did you in France, but he was not yet strong enough to permit the working out of the Great Cosmic Law of Justice and balance that debt."

Ballard's tour wasn't over. "Now," Germain continued, "let us recall another of your embodiments—one that you had in Egypt."

Moving rapidly over the Mediterranean to Karnak and Luxor, they entered a temple. In this life Ballard's son was the temple's high priest. Entering the inner sanctuary, they saw a beautiful vestal virgin guarding the sacred fire. Ballard recognized her immediately.

"She, whom I now beheld," said Ballard, "was Lotus, my beloved Twin Ray, whom I met and married some years ago and who is the mother of our son."

Germain had timed their arrival at an exciting moment. A critical drama was being played out. A visiting prince from a distant province was rushing forward to seize Edna for his bride. But by raising his right hand and letting go a bolt of lightning the high priest destroyed the nervy prince.

Ballard never explained how his son, the high priest, happened to be available to protect his virgin wife, Edna.

Germain and Ballard now whipped back to Shasta for a rest. The journey, Germain promised, would be resumed the next day.

At the appointed hour, Ballard was waiting for his mentor. But suddenly he heard a twig crack. Looking around, he expected to see Germain. But "imagine my surprise when I saw a panther. I wanted to run so frantic was the feeling of fear within me.

"Then came the thought that one part of God could not harm another part. A feeling of love swept over me and was sent out like a ray of light directly to the panther and with it went my fear.

"The vicious glare in the eyes softened, the animal straightened up, and came slowly to me, rubbing its shoulder against my leg. It looked into my eyes for a moment and then, lay down and rolled over like a playful kitten."

The sudden appearance of the panther had been no accident. Germain, materializing again, explained to Ballard: "My son, I saw the great strength within you or I would not have permitted so great a test. You have conquered *fear*. My congratulations! Had you not conquered the outer-self, I would not have allowed the panther to harm you, but our association would have ceased for a time."

Master and pupil resumed their travels and were soon floating over the Sahara Desert. Their visit was at a point in history when the Sahara was a fertile country enjoying a golden age with a perfect government run by fourteen "Ascended Masters" who controlled all science, industry and art.

Germain recommended to Ballard that America might well emulate the type of government the Saharans had enjoyed. So advanced were these people that they had invented the airplane but had long since discarded it as unnecessary when they discovered how to use their "finer bodies" to travel from place to place. "They were able to transport the physical body at will, for the use of their power to overcome gravity was as natural as breathing is to you."

On their way back to Shasta, Germain filled in the time with a lecture on Ballard's favorite subject—gold.

"Gold is placed upon this planet for a variety of uses. Two of its most trivial and unimportant ones being that of using gold as a means of exchange and for ornamentation. The far greater activity and purpose of it, within and upon the earth, is the release of its own inherent quality and energy to purify, vitalize and balance the atomic structure of the world.

"The scientific world today has no inkling as yet of this activity. However, it serves the same purpose to our earth that radiators do to our homes."

Setting down on the mountain, they broke until Germain could manage the next flight. The meeting was duly arranged by an invitation delivered to Ballard by "a snow-white dove, with a tiny card in its mouth." It read, "Be at our meeting place at seven in the morning" and was signed by Germain. Ballard said he had attempted to preserve the invitation from the Count, but "unfortunately it was made of a substance that disintegrated in a few days."

They traveled this time to the "top of a majestic mountain"— the Royal Teton in Wyoming. Landing smoothly, Germain flicked aside a huge boulder and they entered a cave.

"This has been here since before the sinking of Atlantis, more than twelve thousand years ago," Germain noted.

They made their way down a two-hundred-foot stairway cut from solid rock and entered a "tube elevator" made of a material "stronger than steel." At the bottom, Germain announced, "We have descended two thousand feet into the very heart of the mountain."

Going through a couple of bronze doors, they entered a magnificent room, two hundred feet long, its walls carved from veins of white onyx and virgin gold.

Germain pointed out two Ascended Masters, dressed, Ballard noted, in gold-embroidered robes ornamented with a "sunburst of rubies, diamonds, sapphires and emeralds."

"These two Great Beings were the founders of this retreat," said Germain.

Moving along, they entered other chambers in the cave. "These rooms," Germain declared, "contain only gold and jewels that are to be used for a special purpose which will bless the entire world, when mankind has transcended his unbridled selfishness.

"This is Spanish gold lost at sea and we, seeing it would not be recovered by other means, brought it here through the activity of certain forces which we govern. Later, in a time that is rapidly approaching, it will again be sent forth for use in the outer world."

Germain also showed Ballard gold that had been picked up from the lost continents of Mu and Atlantis, the ancient civilizations of the Gobi and Sahara deserts, Egypt, Chaldea, Babylonia, Greece, Rome and other places.

"If all this gold were to be released into the outer activity of the world, it would compel sudden re-adjustments in every phase of human experience," the Count said. "At present, it would *not* be the part of wisdom. The Infinite Wisdom of those Great Cosmic Masters, who have been the guardians of the race since its first appearance upon earth, is almost beyond the comprehension of the human mind."

In subsequent trips, Germain continued to indulge Ballard's fanatic passion for gold. *Unveiled Mysteries* trails off with visits to gold mines in Yellowstone, the lost Inca civilizations and the buried cities of the Amazon.

Germain, finally releasing Ballard to return to his current embodiment in Chicago, assured him he would be on call as needed. While he returned to dwell in the cave at the Royal Teton, Ballard and his wife should consider themselves his "Accredited Messengers." Their assignment was to go forth and preach his gospel.

Immortality, precipitation, a bit of faith healing, the stumbling back into previous lives of high status, the appetizing fantasy of a world filled with gold and ultimate peace and serenity once the state of Ascended Master was attained became the core of the Mighty I Am teachings.

In the Ballards' social, economic, political and religious utopia, bizarre as it was, all the losers were dramatically changed into potential winners. As Guy and Edna were soon to discover, the promise of the murky I Am paradise was enough to reap a harvest of some 150,000 followers throughout the nation.

Ready now to spread the new faith, Guy, Edna and Donald piled into a beat-up Ford, slipped out of Chicago, and hit the road, stopping to hold meetings and classes in Miami, New York, Boston, Cleveland, and Washington, D. C. At first the audiences were small, the contributions smaller. But those who joined began to recruit others. Loyal I Am cells began to spring up and *Unveiled Mysteries*, with its mesmeric account of Ballard's meetings with Germain, began to sell briskly.

Piece by piece, through trial and error, Guy and Edna added to their theology and the showmanship of their performances.

When they hit California in 1935, they had a smooth-working operation. Before tackling Los Angeles, they held meetings in San Diego, Long Beach and Pasadena, playing to ever bigger, ever more enthusiastic audiences.

When they felt ready to confront Los Angeles, they booked themselves into the six-thousand-seat Shrine Auditorium for ten days.

They were a sensation!

"I have just had a message from St. Germain," Guy announced at the Shrine meeting. "He says he wants us to take up another offering and raise another five hundred dollars. Beloved, you have done fine tonight, but surely you can do better for the sake of St. Germain."

Despite the three nightly collections which became standard at I Am meetings, membership swelled. More than fifteen thousand joined in Los Angeles, the majority middle-aged women. With contributions rolling in, the Ballards bought radio time and won additional converts.

Success made Guy Ballard confident. The movement began to be highly structured. I Am became a way of life. Guy began making strong pronouncements on sex, politics, economics, even on the type and color of clothing that members should wear. At the same time, his theology became highly fluid and he ad-libbed much of it on the spur of the moment whenever it seemed to suit his purpose.

There was enough money now for the Ballards to convert an old tabernacle into an I Am temple. It soon became a Los Angeles landmark, and the meetings were the last word in effective showmanship.

The faithful were beckoned by a giant neon-lit cross. Outside, on a typical meeting night, women dressed in long flowing white gowns offered soft words of welcome, a Mighty I Am songbook, and a little envelope marked "I Am Love Gift." That was an admission fee and the first collection of the evening.

Inside it was all show business, an atmosphere calculated to appeal to the senses and emotions.

The stage was banked with flowers. Colored lights played over the audience. Huge paintings of Ballard, a bearded Germain and Jesus were hung above the platform. According to Ballard, Jesus had returned for twenty-one days for the express purpose of posing for the picture. Prints could be purchased on the way out for $2.50.

The Ballards were always the main attraction, and the crowd was warmed up and worked for the second collection by a glib announcer.

"Blessed Mr. and Mrs. Ballard, the Accredited Messengers of the Great Ascended Master of St. Germain, do not need these offerings. They are merely for you beloved students to 'open up channels for blessings from the great Ascended Masters.'"

Members of the "Minute Men of Saint Germain" and the "Daughters of Light," two I Am auxiliaries, strode down the aisles and picked up the love offerings.

The announcer next called the attention of the audience to the two giant flags onstage, one the red, white and blue of the American flag, the other white, blue and gold—the I Am banner. "St. Germain hates red, he never wears it. Someday when the Ascended Masters rule America there will be gold instead of red stripes in the flag."

Then the announcer raised his hand. A hush fell. The lights continued to play over the audience, and in came Guy, Edna and Donald.

Ascetic and gaunt, Guy wore a dazzling white tuxedo. Gold and diamonds sparkled from his rings and tie clasp. Edna was equally theatrical, sporting a white gown almost covered by gleaming rhinestones with a corsage of orchids pinned to the left shoulder. Donald, appearing somewhat uncomfortable, moved unobtrusively to one side of the stage while Edna seated herself at the harp and began playing.

Guy came stage center to address the audience, his message to be punctuated by the ritual I Am command of "annihilate." A steady buzzing beelike sound signified approval, and applause was obtained by the faithful beating their hands against their chests.

The crowd pressed forward eagerly.

"Picture yourself and feel your body enveloped in a Dazzling White Light," said Ballard. "Recognize and feel intensely the connection between the Outer-Self and your Mighty God within. Focus your attention upon the heart center and visualize it as a golden sun."

Annihilate, annihilate, annihilate.

"Now joyously accept the fullness of the Mighty God Presence —the Pure Christ. Feel the great brilliancy of the Light and intensify it in every cell of your body."

Annihilate, annihilate.

"Then command: I Am a Child of the Light."

The sound of the beelike buzzing filled the hall.

"I Love the Light. . . ."

Annihilate.

"I serve the Light. . . ."

The chest-beating applause began, a loud thud echoing up to Ballard.

"I live in the Light. . . ."

Annihilate, annihilate.

"I am protected, illumined, supplied, sustained by the Light, and I bless the Light."

Annihilate, annihilate, annihilate.

The audience was on its feet, a chant swelling in thousands of throats.

> Turn the darkness into day;
> Kill the sins for Godfre Ray;
> Manifest, manifest, manifest,
> I AM, I AM, I AM!

Then the third collection was taken.

The Ballards took the show on the road again. At a meeting in Washington, D. C., Guy walked out to a mighty ovation. A huge Uncle Sam hat of red, white and blue carnations was passed up to him.

"The drafting of the Declaration of Independence," he told the crowd, "was a direct result of St. Germain's help and influence, and it was his love, protection and guidance which sustained Washington and Lincoln during the darkest hours of their lives."

Ballard announced to cheers from his believing congregation that he had lived one of his previous lives as George Washington! And Edna was the reincarnation, not of Martha Washington, but Joan of Arc, an interesting, if illogical, study in adulterous historic coupling. Donald was revealed as the re-embodiment of Lafayette.

As the reincarnated George Washington, Ballard blandly recreated the perilous crossing of the Delaware through the crashing ice blocks of the raging river. He wrung hearts with the tale of the bitter winter at Valley Forge.

Passing the White House during the Washington meeting, Donald was reported to have told an associate: "That man (President Franklin Roosevelt) has no business in there. My Dad should be the head of this nation right now!"

Ballard had become infected with the idea of becoming President of the United States. "I have instructions to take over the government direct from St. Germain."

He told a meeting in Cleveland that I Am Messengers had saved the Panama Canal from destruction. "The devastation planned for America would have begun more than eighteen months ago if it had not been for the tremendous powers released by St. Germain through the Messengers."

In San Francisco, he declared that intervention by the Messengers had saved the city from disaster. "You may not have known it—but before the Messengers came your city was in great danger."

In private hotel room meetings, the Ballards entertained some of their wealthy businessmen followers by issuing "death decrees" against F.D.R.

They gathered around a golden goblet which held a "black list" of their enemies. They circled the urn, raised their hands, thrusting them back and forth rhythmically, shouting and chanting:

"Franklin Delano Roosevelt and Eleanor Roosevelt—blast, blast, blast their carcasses from the face of the earth forever."

Though the I Am faithful believed Ballard's political rantings and would have gladly voted him into the White House, the big lures were the I Am promises of eternal life and precipitation.

Ballard continually reassured members that once the power of the dazzling light was conquered, they could conjure any object desired. Riches were to be had solely for the asking. Members, however, reported continued difficulties in reaching the required level of precipitation. Ballard convinced them to persevere. He continued to guarantee that they would never die—and if a war should come I Am members would be untouched. They would all "ascend" unharmed in one mass astral flight to the abode of the Ascended Masters. He and St. Germain had made definite provisions for that eventuality.

Still some members began to voice doubts. To keep them believing, Ballard took to announcing in advance of meetings "that Ascensions will be made before your very eyes." When the moment came to deliver, he declared that ascensions had indeed been made, but in private at the secret retreats on Mt. Shasta and the Royal Teton. That was the way St. Germain wanted it.

Non-I Am husbands with wives dedicated to the movement began to raise the loudest complaints of all against the Ballards' views on sex.

"Sex desire is the most infamous thing ever on this earth," Guy declared. He said it was absolutely taboo for members except for procreation and even that wasn't too important. I Am members needn't worry about children since the mass ascension of all the faithful was imminent.

"Those who have the opportunity and the privilege of gaining their freedom from human bondage through their Ascension, should certainly not contemplate sex or family relationships in that respect," Edna added. "You have served a long time in raising children, in exercising undesirable sex force. Is it not time now that you might forget it for a few years? There will be enough of mankind left to take care of the requirements of birth. You cannot seek another for the desire of sex and expect yourself to be free."

The Ballards issued a special plea on the subject to the young people of America. "We ask ALL under this Radiation to stop all practices of what the world calls necking, kissing and hugging those of the opposite sex who are not your own relatives."

Skeptics said that one reason for the Ballards' sexual puritanism was to alibi themselves when ascensions did not take place. They could point an accusing finger and charge, usually with accuracy, that members were participating on the sly and for that reason they could not hope to ascend.

Many husbands remained unconvinced of the advantages of abstinence and divorce in the cult began to be a problem. But the movement kept its momentum. Membership had passed the 150,000 mark and contributions totted up to more than $3,000,-000. The Ballards became polished hucksters. They hawked *Unveiled Mysteries* and two sequels, *The Magic Presence* and *The "I Am" Discourses,* and added to their line of merchandise I Am rings, phonograph records, photographs, lectures, a monthly magazine and binder, even a "new age cold cream."

Wherever they traveled, the Ballards lived in luxury hotel suites. Guy now was drinking only the best Scotch—and too much of it. A fleet of yellow Phaetons had long since replaced the beat-up Ford. Edna traveled with a bodyguard and a chauffeur. Donald had married, and was being supported by I Am funds.

"Dear Donny," his mother wrote in answering a letter from her son in New York requesting more money, "since you got your car in December, which is five months, you have had $11,000. Daddy said the end has now come between Daddy and son."

After four years of riding the crest of all the southern California cults, a major crisis suddenly confronted the Mighty I Am. At a large meeting in December, 1939, Edna appeared onstage alone and explained to the disappointed flock why Guy could not appear. "Blessed Daddy is out with St. Germain."

Not quite. High living and boozing had caught up with Guy. He had collapsed in a hotel room and been secretly moved to a quiet home in the Griffith Park district of Los Angeles.

Ballard was a very sick man. Unattended by a doctor, he lay in bed for nine days, his condition worsening. Edna kept things rolling down at the meeting by insisting he was still out with St. Germain.

With Guy's abdomen swelling to tremendous proportions, Edna finally called a doctor who performed surgery. But it was too late.

Guy George Washington Godfre Ray King Ballard, the man who had faced down a panther on Mt. Shasta and been assured of eternal life by St. Germain, died at 5:20 A.M. on December 29, 1939. The death certificate said he died of heart disease complicated by cirrhosis of the liver.

Edna kept her husband's death a secret for three days. Though Donald broke down and cried, Edna fiercely set her chin and left Guy's body on his deathbed waiting for his ascension.

By New Year's Day of 1940, Ballard was still on the bed. He had not ascended. Edna called in the undertaker and had him cremated.

The newspapers got wind of it, and blazed the story in front-page headlines.

Forced into an explanation, Edna went to the meeting and announced: "Our Blessed Daddy made his Ascension last night at 12 o'clock from the Royal Teton Retreat, and he is now an Ascended Master!"

The audience rose as one and beat their chests for Ballard's good fortune.

"When people of our outer world are discussing what has happened to Mr. Ballard," Edna cautioned the faithful, "please make it clear that he has made the Ascension!

"He can wield Power in that Body which America needs right now.

"And he is doing it with no uncertainty.

"Make your statements with positive force; for I assure you that I am telling you the Truth and will never tell you anything but the Truth. We have nothing to cover up."

Edna had smoothly picked up the reins. She was now in full charge.

"It's all part of the plan," she reminded members as she continued to deify her late husband. Though he was dead, Edna still considered Guy a candidate for President. "Remember—an Ascended Master shall sit in the chair at the White House."

In the *Voice of I Am*, the cult magazine, she called on the faithful to purchase colored photographs of Guy for $2.50 to $25.00. "Contemplation of His Pictures and calls to Him are bringing forth instantaneous answers."

Edna announced that at a propitious moment Guy would return in visible form.

Then in August, 1940, Edna suddenly faced a new crisis. The

government, dismayed at the mighty Mighty I Am merchandising machine, took the view that the cult was producing more profits than prophets. In a sixty-page federal indictment, Edna, Donald and twenty other I Am leaders were charged with eighteen counts of mail fraud and one of conspiracy.

A government spokesman promptly announced: "This is not a religious persecution. The federal officials charged with the investigation and prosecution of the leaders of the I Am movement stand ready to protect all persons in their constitutional guarantees of the right of religious freedom.

"Notwithstanding this constitutional guarantee it is a violation of the law of this land to utilize the mails in the execution of any scheme intended to defraud whether under the guise of religion, education, patriotism or any other movement."

In the view of the United States of America, the Mighty I Am was a massive con game. The cult's leaders did "unlawfully, knowingly and willfully devise and intend to devise a scheme and artifice to defraud and obtain money and property by means of false and fraudulent representations, pretenses and promises from a large group of persons."

Specifically, the indictment charged that Guy Ballard "did in fact die" despite I Am claims that he had "attained a supernatural state of self-immortality"; that it was claimed that teachings promulgated under the I Am movement were absolutely essential to the salvation of mankind; that solely as a result of their teachings and the I Am movement the United States was saved from destruction; that they acquired a hypnotic power over those to be defrauded, causing them to travel great distances in the hope they might see a physical appearance of the "Ascended Masters"; that the world was coming to an end and that it was unnecessary to save money and that members should withdraw their funds from banks and insurance companies and give it to the defendants as love gifts; that many happy homes were disrupted through the advocacy of absolute continence; and that the defendants advocated a condition of harmony and kindliness toward mankind and a utopian state would thus prevail when as a matter of fact the defendants at times quarreled bitterly among themselves.

A government attorney, while admitting the case contained

"unusual features," nevertheless called it "just another fraud trial."

"It's no such thing," defense counsel Charles H. Carr shot back. "The religious issue is bound to be injected. It is strange that in this period of national emergency the government should expend so much time and effort to persecute clean, wholesome people, who wish to worship . . . in a manner a trifle different and perhaps slightly in advance of some orthodox faiths."

Carr promised "plenty of fireworks."

For her part, Edna was undisturbed. "I accept the challenge of the United States government to disprove the 'divine truth' of the Mighty I Am Presence. We ask the public to withhold judgment until they have heard the truth of this law. This Ascended Master activity of the I Am movement is educational and patriotic. We have never asked a human being for a dime to carry on this activity, through the mails or otherwise."

Donald Ballard added: "We have offered only good and love for America beyond all words to describe. It is difficult for me to see how the government could make accusations against us when we have at all times fought Nazism, communism and the fifth column."

Edna and Donald were fingerprinted and released on bail. They entered a not-guilty plea, and prepared to do battle with their accusers in a trial that was to become one of the liveliest in the history of Los Angeles, a trial punctuated by offbeat antics and unorthodox testimony. Nothing quite like it has ever occurred in an American courtroom.

Hundreds of the cult faithful, dressed in white or pastel-shaded robes—the "legions of light"—turned out daily to witness the persecution of their martyrs. They overflowed into the corridors and streets. Those in the courtroom prayed for "annihilation" of I Am enemies and buzzed audibly when points for the defense were scored.

Carr began by asking for a dismissal on grounds that the indictment interfered with the right of free worship and was void because it was returned by a grand jury from which women were excluded.

Turning down the arguments, Federal District Judge Leon R. Yankwich ruled: "It is one of the glories of the constitution of the United States that freedom of worship cannot be challenged by anyone. But this does not stand in the way of charging as the government does in this case, that religion was used as a cloak for the perpetration of fraud in violation of United States law."

The judge also held that "there is nothing in the state or federal constitutions or in any statute which guarantees one accused of a crime a jury composed of men and women, or of only women, or of any definite proportion of either sex."

Thus overruled, Carr questioned prospective jurors carefully, sounding them out on how they might react to "fantastic evidence" and their attitude toward the Bible.

The bench interrupted to remark: "This is a trial for mail fraud and religion does not enter into it. It would make no difference if the religion of jurors or defendants embraced having a woman disappear in the ocean and come up in the desert."

"I don't want any atheists or Communists on the jury," Carr protested.

"For that matter," the judge answered, "if Mohammed should be drawn on the jury there would be nothing to prevent his qualifying."

Finally agreeing on a jury, the prosecution began parading its witnesses to the stand.

T. F. Masters, a thirty-eight-year-old milliner, told of attending more than three hundred I Am meetings. And though he followed the teachings religiously and made love gifts totaling more than $1000 he was "disappointed" that he didn't ascend.

"Are you still disappointed?" Judge Yankwich asked.

"Yes, I am."

"Are you married?"

"Yes, and my wife seemed more inclined to ascend than I did."

The judge asked if he believed the I Am teachings insofar as they concerned the ability to precipitate material wants. Masters said he did and had made calls for worldly goods.

"What did you call for?"

"Shall I tell everything?"

At a nod from the judge, he admitted that he had "put in a call" for a new home, a new automobile and a bank account. His calls, however, were not answered.

Since I Am doctrine demanded a sinless life before precipitation or ascendency was possible, Carr, on cross-examination, probed for a flaw in the character of the witness.

"Before you joined the I Am movement," the lawyer asked, "did you smoke?"

"No, I did not."

"And you didn't drink?"

"No, I did not."

"Well, you must have told just one little lie?" Carr asked in amazement.

"No, I never lied."

"That's too much for me." Carr dropped his hands to his sides in resignation. "I'll stipulate that at last we've found the perfect man."

The widow of a former United States senator, Minnesota's Thomas D. Schall, said she had joined the cult after Guy Ballard promised he could cure her husband's blindness.

"Mr. Ballard told me I must visualize a ray of light from the Mighty I Am Presence down through the top of his head and turning at right angles and going to the eyes," Mrs. Schall recalled. "I tried that without success. Two months later the Senator was killed in an auto accident."

She had first been attracted to the movement in Washington, D. C., and told of following the Ballards on the road to meetings in San Francisco and Los Angeles. She made many love offerings and bought several sets of I Am books.

"Mrs. Ballard said many times, 'Give and it shall be returned to you,' and I believed them."

"Did you think you would receive money?" asked Judge Yankwich.

"Yes, I certainly did."

"Did you ever hear of a church that did return money?" inquired the judge.

"Well, I believed that in this case."

On one occasion, she had uttered the Mighty I Am decree of protection and then went down to the corner. "That was supposed to protect you, but when I got to the corner I fell off the curb, sprained my ankle, broke my glasses and bruised myself."

"You blame that on the I Am presence?" inquired Judge Yankwich.

"I do, because they didn't make good. I asked them to protect me and they didn't do it."

As to precipitation, Mrs. Schall said she was instructed that if she would look into the atmosphere any sunny day she would see particles of light which were the same as the Ascended Masters used to deliver diamond necklaces, money, food, clothing and automobiles.

"Did you ever try?" asked Carr.

"I did, but I couldn't see the sparkles."

"Maybe you didn't have enough faith," the judge observed.

Carr got Mrs. Schall to admit I Am services were conducted much the same "as in the good old Methodist Church."

She also admitted that the I Am instruction to "give and you shall receive" was similar to the admonition contained in the Bible.

"And you believe in the Bible?" asked Carr.

"I do now," she replied, "but I was confused then, my faith was shaken."

The government's indictment also charged the Ballards had sold $2,000,000 worth of books "in a few short years in a complete scheme to defraud by mail" and that the defendants had realized more than $33,000 from the sale of "animated electrical charts" and netted more than $1000 during each of their class days.

Several witnesses gave a behind-the-scenes peek into the cult's financial operations.

Wyatt Richards, former personal secretary to Guy Ballard, said that in July, 1938, during a seventeen-day meeting in Los Angeles, nearly $15,000 was realized from the sale of books and more than $12,000 from love offerings. In other cities the receipts were approximately the same. Personal "dictations from St. Germain" to individual members of the cult brought in another $1000 a day.

Richards also said that Ballard received checks in the mail which totaled from $1500 to $2000 for every three weeks' class. He would cash the checks and give the money to Ballard who would place it in one of his trunks. Mrs. Ballard's secretary had once objected to this procedure because it "balled up her bookkeeping."

Mrs. Janet Kingsley, a bookstore owner and former head of an

I Am branch in San Francisco, said she was told by Mrs. Ballard that "all students should read, read, read" and that each member should have two complete sets of books.

"She repeatedly emphasized that the proper handling of finances was a very important part of the work. Before coming to San Francisco she wrote that I should arrange for six cashiers, each with two assistants, at all meetings where she and her husband were to speak."

A housewife from Chicago, Mrs. Louise Ramsey, testified that she once discussed two insurance policies with Mrs. Ballard.

"One of them had only two years to run until it would be paid off and the other was a straight life policy which had a cash value. Mrs. Ballard told me to keep the policy which would be paid off within a few years, but to cash in the other because there was a cataclysm coming and it wouldn't do me any good anyhow."

She declared that she had repudiated I Am, but at one time was a firm believer. She said the Ballards taught that I Am followers would ascend from their graves in the manner of Christ. "We were supposed to make our ascension as Jesus did. We were to become so spiritualized that we would just ascend to heaven."

Carr objected to the line of questioning. "It's going to be impossible for the government to prove these ascensions didn't take place."

Another disillusioned I Am-er, Mrs. Cynthia Nelson, of Toledo, said Mrs. Ballard had told her "money could be precipitated directly into your hand and that it was just as easy to get a thousand dollars as five cents. And to precipitate an automobile —just visualize the color, kind and make."

The Ohio woman, mother of four daughters, was advised by Mrs. Ballard to buy a set of I Am books for each member of her family because each set held "a particular vibration for its individual owner."

About reaching the I Am heaven, Mrs. Nelson told Mrs. Ballard, "I don't want to ascend. I have a very happy home with my husband and daughters. Mrs. Ballard said that was all right, that I could come back and take care of the children."

After Mrs. Nelson admitted that her husband smoked, Mrs. Ballard declared: "That will have to stop because the use of tobacco in the home will cause dangerous entities that will not leave until Mr. Nelson quits tobacco. If he does not quit you will have to leave him."

"But you didn't leave your husband, did you?" inquired the court.

"No, I did not."

Prosecutor Ralph Lazarus asked what Mrs. Ballard said would happen to her children if she didn't leave her husband.

"She told me that my four children would die, one by one, starting with the youngest."

"They didn't die?" she was asked.

"No, they didn't," was the reply.

Lazarus turned to the origin of the painting of Christ, one of the best-selling I Am items.

Mrs. Nelson quoted Mrs. Ballard: "Jesus appeared to him [the I Am artist] twenty-one times and posed. He came in the early morning and stood at his bedside."

One of Mrs. Nelson's daughters took the stand to relate a conversation with Donald Ballard after an I Am class. "Donald said to me and my sister, 'How much longer are these people going to swallow that stuff?'"

Other witnesses added to the picture of Donald's indiscretions about the faith of his father and mother.

Mrs. Phyllis Lee, mother of Donald's wife, said that at one time he tried to jump up in the midst of an I Am class and denounce the movement as a fake. "But my daughter held him and kept him from doing it."

Walter Fulsum, a former aide of Guy Ballard's, recalled a conversation with Donald in which the son of the founder said: "Whatever my mother wants said—that's what St. Germain says."

Fulsum testified that there was frequent friction among the leaders of the cult. On one occasion he heard Ballard say that the viciousness of one of the movement's members toward Mrs. Ballard had caused a rash to appear on her shoulders.

On cross-examination, Carr asked Fulsum if it was true that among students in the movement he was nicknamed "Cataclysm Walt" because of his belief that the end of the world was near.

"I never heard it before," he answered.

About midway through the trial, word reached Judge Yankwich that I Am followers in the courtroom were disturbed about his black robes; they considered his dark judicial garb a malign influence.

As a gesture to freedom of religion, the judge appeared for one day on the bench dressed in a light-colored business suit.

"Judicial robes do not aid the court in making a sound decision and I feel that if the situation warranted it, I could function as well in a bathing suit as in this court costume of purple and black," Judge Yankwich said.

"But I would not wear a bathing suit to church out of deference to the feelings of the worshipers, and for the same reason I am leaving off my judicial robes today.

"A great many people here honestly believe that light and bright colors have a favorable effect on the soul's welfare, and I am not one to flout another's religious beliefs."

In one of the trial's highlights, the government put a husky chiropractor, Dr. Otto Dunn, on the stand to tell of treatments he had given Guy Ballard. The doctor said that, skeletonically speaking, Ballard had been a bit out of line.

Dr. Dunn had discovered that Ballard was a sick man when he called on him. He had a sallow complexion with a purple cast to his skin which to his trained mind indicated a lack of air.

"His voice was not clear," said the doctor. "He kept coughing. I made adjustments; in fact, I also adjusted Mrs. Ballard and their son Donald."

The doctor said he had also talked to Ballard about various retreats and caves at the Royal Tetons and Mt. Shasta.

"I told Mr. Ballard that the wife and I took a different trip each year and we'd like to have them as our guests sometime when the Ascended Masters were having conferences at one of the retreats."

The witness recalled that Ballard stuttered a bit and said he would have to ask St. Germain's advice as to whether he could take strangers there.

"I tried later to talk to him about it but on each occasion he would walk away," the doctor said.

Carr waded in on cross-examination. "Look at me, is my head on straight?"

"No," Dr. Dunn said critically, "it's not."

"Of course not," said Carr. "There's nothing wrong with that. My head isn't any more out of line than was Ballard's."

"No, Ballard's was worse," the chiropractor declared with professional assurance.

"You say Ballard had bumps on his spine," Carr persisted. "Well, feel the bumps on my spine."

Removing his coat, Carr went to the jury box where the doctor let his fingers wander over the lawyer's backbone. To the lawyer's dismay, the doctor snapped his suspender as he moved away.

"You've got bumps all right," said Dr. Dunn, "and you're also a bit out of line."

"Well, Doctor, as a matter of fact, Ballard was no worse off than I am."

"No, I'm sorry," replied Dr. Dunn, "Ballard was worse off."

Rearing back on his heels, Carr declared: "Doctor, didn't you once tell a class of I Am students that you had adjusted Mr. Ballard's brain?"

"Yes," replied the doctor casually. "Shall I adjust yours?"

Carr accepted the challenge and on Dr. Dunn's instructions sat in a chair placed in front of the jury box.

The doctor gazed soberly at his patient and then deliberately removed his coat and vest. Carr stirred uneasily. The chiropractor moved off a few paces to study the lawyer. Carr fidgeted.

"Now," the doctor explained, flexing his muscles, "I think I better explain what I intend to do."

"I-er-w-w-ish you would," Carr said uneasily.

Judge Yankwich, who had restrained himself thus far to permit the demonstration in the interest of science, could restrain himself no longer. In a measured voice, he said: "Into each life some rain must fall."

Spectators in the rear of the courtroom were standing on their feet, craning their necks for a better view.

"You see," the doctor said and turned eagerly to the audience.

"Never mind the audience," ordered the judge. "Look at the jury."

The doctor shifted his gaze as ordered, and indicating Carr, he diagnosed: "You see, his left eye droops. That means he has pressure on the left side of the cerebellum."

At the mention of "cerebellum," Carr's right eye seemed to droop more than the left.

"And now"—Dr. Dunn's voice became intense as he gathered himself for the attack—"as soon as I release that frontal bone."

Carr bounded out of the chair. "Doctor," he announced with relief, "the examination is over. You're excused."

The audience settled back. Carr mopped his forehead with his handkerchief and returned meekly to the counsel table. He had been unable to shake the testimony of the spunky chiropractor.

Carr was soon tilting with another doctor, a Los Angeles physician who testified on the government's behalf that one Frank B. Kelly had not ascended into the I Am heaven.

When Kelly, a "100 per cent" I Am believer, died on February 21, 1939, Guy Ballard had announced his immediate ascension. But Dr. F. Louis Young told of treating Kelly several years before for hardening of the arteries and said he was called in a few moments after Kelly died.

"Did you make an electronic test after death?" challenged Carr.

The doctor said he hadn't and that he had never seen an electron.

"You don't know how much of the electronic substance departs after death?" Carr persisted.

Dr. Young said he did not and that he knew of no doctor or scientific treatise that could determine such matters.

"But Kelly's body was on the bed and you didn't see it ascend, did you, Doctor?" interposed government attorney Norman Neukom.

"The body wasn't on the bed, it was on the floor," Dr. Young replied. "It had not ascended."

"And you didn't see his soul ascend to heaven, did you?" asked Judge Yankwich.

The physician said that he did not and he never had seen a soul.

As the trial moved into the Christmas season, Prosecutor Neukom told the court that he was puzzled over a Christmas card he had received. The card, contained in an envelope with a stamp bearing a Mt. Shasta cancellation, said: "With sincere regards, and wishing you the kind of a holiday season you'll always remember!" It was signed in ink, "St. Germain."

For the defense, Carr brought in a battery of witnesses from all over the nation, eager to testify on behalf of the cult.

"I was just about ready to believe that human beings once swung by their tails—and then I found myself and joined the I Am movement," said James Newkirk, a twenty-seven-year-old Detroit steelworker.

"In other words," inquired Carr, "you had about reached the state where you believed your ancestors were monkeys?"

"Yes, that was true," replied Newkirk.

A seventy-five-year-old osteopath from Spokane, Washington, Dr. Lyman Hirsch, said that he accepted the movement after reading *Unveiled Mysteries*. He now enjoyed spiritual satisfaction and a feeling of well-being as a result of having questions answered which had arisen all through his life concerning the mystery of the universe.

"I was uncertain before," said the doctor, "as to the procedure after so-called death. Now I have no further fear as to how and what will be the ultimate result."

Lillian Wescott, a woman lawyer admitted to practice before the U. S. Supreme Court, stated she studied I Am teachings for more than a year before she became convinced that the laws and principles enunciated could be applied to everyday life. "I now find that the severe sick headaches I used to have are a thing of the past, that I have more energy and am more calm and poised."

Sea captain Henry Baggett declared that when he found I Am, he "found something he had been searching for all his life" and "something he would not give up for the whole world."

Another witness, Robert Edmonds, known to students of the I Am movement as "Brother Bobby," testified, "I know why I'm here, I know where I'm going and I know how to get there." A former newspaper publisher in Louisiana, he said he had been teaching the I Am creed since 1936 and that men and women from every walk of life were among his students. "Judges, lawyers, ministers, physicians, clerks, nurses, schoolteachers, printers, in fact all types became students of the Mighty I Am Presence."

And since embracing I Am, said Brother Bobby, "I feel ten

years younger. I am a better citizen. I am a better man, physically, mentally and spiritually, and—I am happy."

Dr. C. J. Cornwall, an osteopath from Long Beach, was on crutches when he "set up an I Am healing call."

Then he tossed away the crutches. The "healing call" did the work and cured him completely of arthritis, a heart ailment and encephalitis.

He said he began to notice improvement shortly after reading the I Am books.

"Suppose some patient comes into your office now, suffering from these same ailments, what do you do?" asked one of the jurors.

"I'd introduce him to the principles of I Am, tell him what the I Am study had done for me and I'd feel sure he would be helped," the doctor said.

The most important witness for the defense was Edna Anna Wheeler Lotus Ray King Joan of Arc Ballard. Attired in pure white, her blond hair nearly hidden by the folds of a white turban, she casually dropped a white fox fur on the counsel table and strode to the stand—confident, unwavering, smiling.

"Now, Mrs. Ballard, have you at any time, as alleged in this indictment, or in connection with I Am activity, made any false or untrue statements to any person for any purpose whatsoever?"

"Neither intentionally or knowingly at any time for any reasons whatsoever."

Asked by Carr if one could precipitate an automobile out of thin air as government witnesses had interpreted the teachings, Edna declared emphatically: "No, absolutely not. After all we are responsible people and I try to remain balanced under all conditions."

She went on to explain in detail the concept of love gifts, most of which were turned over to the St. Germain Foundation, except those specifically earmarked for her. "I've never asked a human being for a dime. I want the whole world to know that."

Carr asked her to explain exactly what was meant by the Mighty I Am Presence.

"I mean my own individualized focus of the God-Life of the universe, that divine source of all perfection and all constructive activity."

"Does the divine source of which you speak contemplate destructive activity?"

"It may contemplate them but it does not accept them into itself and does not create them."

"Then the Magic Presence or the Mighty I Am Presence or whatever you want to call it, comes from the source commonly designated by all denominations and all creeds as the ultimate or the divine source, is that correct?"

"The divine source is God and we call perfection God in action. We speak of Light as the activity in action."

"When you speak of the great central sun, is that the same?"

"That is God."

"That is the divine, is it?"

"The divine source of everything in the universe."

"That is not the sun we see every day?"

"It is the great sun behind the sun, the central point from which all proceeds."

On cross-examination, Edna denied earlier testimony that she had once called the Bible "a filthy book" or stated that people in California were metaphysically minded and that I Am would go over big in the state.

She testified she never made any statement "that those persons whom St. Germain might dismiss from the staff as being disloyal would not live six weeks in the outer world."

Lazarus and Neukom brought out from I Am publications that teachings of I Am activity could not come to the world except through the Ballards.

Lazarus read from the I Am magazine: "Jesus and St. Germain have both said that 'St. Germain or any other Ascended Masters are not giving out teachings of the I Am in the western world except through Mr. and Mrs. Ballard and their son Donald and those named by them and under them.'"

"That is true," she answered firmly.

When it was over, Edna sauntered back to her seat, much as Daniel must have walked from the lion's den.

Summing up eloquently for the defense, Carr declared: "This case should be made a cornerstone of liberty. For once and all the government should be clearly put on notice that it cannot interfere with the personal liberties guaranteed people of our democracy by the Bill of Rights.

"Guy Ballard has passed on and it is now impossible to disprove that he had the experiences set forth in the books. And, besides, the main question is not whether he had such experiences, but whether Mrs. Ballard believed them and in good faith presented them to their followers.

"Is it criminal to defraud people of frowns, disharmony, bad habits, fear of the future and lack of faith in a Supreme Being?

"If it is criminal to do these things then the jury should find the defendants guilty of using the mails to defraud.

"And you will convict a new type of criminal, highwaymen who teach people to be good.

"We are not here trying a few defendants. We are really trying thousands upon thousands of persons who believe in the rules of life as enunciated through the Mighty I Am Presence."

For the government, Neukom countered that I Am defendants had not lived up to the tenets of their own faith.

"This project was strictly a gigantic scheme to defraud by mulcting hundreds of thousands of dollars from unwary men and women through the guise of religion. Many persons contributed their life savings, thinking that by so doing they would ascend to heaven. These defendants in their project preyed upon the poor, the maimed and the blind by misrepresentation.

"We don't claim that they don't have good philosophies in many of their books. That isn't what they are on trial for. They are on trial for false representations.

"Let your verdict be a warning to those who use false representations on the subject of religion."

Charges against all but nine of the defendants had been dismissed. If Edna, Donald and the seven others were convicted they faced prison terms of eighty-seven years and fines of $27,-000 each.

After seventy-six hours of deliberation, the jury admitted to Judge Yankwich they were in disagreement on eight separate phases of the case.

"I do not think this jury has deliberated enough," the judge said, "and has not yet got down to fundamentals."

It took four days for the verdict to come in. And when it did, it was inconclusive.

Three of the I Am leaders were acquitted. As to Edna, Donald and the four others, the jury reported itself "hopelessly dead-locked" on their guilt or innocence.

Later one of the jurors disclosed the voting. From the first, they had stood 10 to 2 for finding Edna guilty, and 9 to 3 in favor of convicting Donald.

The Ballards' joy over the verdict was short-lived. Reindictment on the same charges was ordered in Washington, D. C., by the U. S. Attorney General.

The second trial was a replay of the first, except for the verdict. This time the jury brought in a conviction against Edna and Donald.

"You have been found guilty of mail fraud," said Federal Judge J. F. T. O'Connor, "and I want it clearly understood that you were not on trial for holding or expounding any religious belief."

Sternly, Edna replied: "I am not guilty before God or man of these charges. I never was and I never will be. All religious teachers have been persecuted, but have stood by their principles. The world will some day come to realize how true my teachings have been."

The judge gave Edna a one-year suspended jail term and fined her $8000. Donald was sentenced to thirty days, also suspended, and fined $400. Climaxing a long series of legal battles, their convictions eventually were reversed by the Supreme Court. In 1946, Justice William O. Douglas said in the majority opinion that exclusion of women from the grand jury panel that had issued the original indictment was "highly prejudicial to the defendants."

But the two trials in Los Angeles all but destroyed the cult. After her conviction, Edna announced that she and three hundred diehard followers were moving I Am headquarters to Santa Fe, New Mexico. "The work we came to California to do is now finished. We shall continue to pour forth our blessings to Los Angeles and her people regardless of the actions of a few who have seen fit to disagree with the greatest blessing that has come to mankind in two thousand years."

But the old excitement was gone. So was the big money. The post office denied Edna the use of the mails. The Phaetons were repossessed. The Los Angeles Public Library was ordered to remove the I Am books from its shelves. Edna was sued for $62,-000 by a disenchanted follower. A couple of cult members committed suicide, one of whom the previous day had assured her parents that "I Am people never die but are transformed."

Donald's wife divorced him and sold their furniture at auction. He was reduced to going into court to get a sixty-nine-dollar personal property tax assessment shaved to thirty-five dollars. Donald's attorney claimed his client was broke.

When last heard from, Edna was still preaching the gospel according to St. Germain to a handful of followers. Small knots of I Am faithful in Chicago, Boston and Cleveland still keep the faith, waiting for their ascensions, knowing without a doubt in the world that one day they'll be reunited with their Ascended Master and Blessed Daddy—Guy George Washington Godfre Ray King Ballard.

8

MARRIAGE
"Do You Take This Woman . . . ?"

California has still a great need of virtuous, educated,
energetic women. . . . I would advise no woman to pitch
into such a community devoid of the protection of relatives or trusted friends.
—HORACE GREELEY (in 1859)

The white Palace of Bandu beckoned.

Located in an unfashionable Los Angeles neighborhood of aging homes and tacky store fronts, the Palace was a beacon, a
white hope for the despairing. Behind its wood-paneled doors
the "Universal Truth Society Foundation for Development of
Body, Mind and Soul" promised medical, spiritual and, particularly, marital counseling.

Mr. and Mrs. Robert Martin entered the Palace on a November
day in 1962, seeking help for their troubled marriage.

While Mr. Martin sat in the ornate, musty waiting room, Mrs.
Martin, a striking brunette, was ushered into the office of the
resident counselor, Dr. Ahmed Sonji, Founder of the Palace of
Bandu, Ph.D., D.D.N.S., and Director of the Problem Clinic of
the American Association for Family Service ("Problems large
and small treated").

A broodingly handsome man in his early thirties, Dr. Sonji,
wearing a saffron turban and a medical smock, seated Mrs. Martin
near his desk. Holding her hand so that the "vibrations" of her
"aura" could register loud and clear, he gazed meditatively off
into space for a moment, seeking the proper "emanations." Then
he turned to the problem of Mrs. Martin's troubled marriage.

"What do you and your husband do at night?"

"Most of the time we watch television."

"Do you have any friends?"

"No. My husband has taken a dislike to most of the couples we've met."

"What sort of meals do you cook for your husband?"

"I feed him a lot of steak."

"That's not good."

"I bake rolls and biscuits."

"That's not good either."

"We have lots of salads."

"That's good."

"With Thousand Island dressing."

"That's not good."

"I use oil and vinegar sometimes."

"The oil's good. The vinegar's bad."

"How often do you and your husband engage in sexual activities?"

"Once a week."

"Do you or does your husband instigate this activity?"

"I do."

"Do you enjoy sex?"

"Yes."

Dr. Sonji paused briefly to consider Mrs. Martin's answers.

"You and your husband," he concluded, "are more like brother and sister than husband and wife. The reason you married was primarily because you both were lonely people. Actually, you two are more like a brother and sister that sleep together."

Though she had not considered subconscious incest as one of her marriage difficulties, Mrs. Martin gave the doctor the benefit of the doubt. Perhaps he had stumbled onto something significant in her relationship with her husband.

"You will need counseling and special treatment," Dr. Sonji said. "Six treatments for sixty dollars."

"Should my husband be included in these treatments?"

Once more the doctor gazed off into space. "Your husband's psychic emanations from the next room are most unfavorable. He would not respond favorably to treatment. He would be inclined to combat treatment."

Then the doctor looked deep into Mrs. Martin's eyes. "Your

'aura' is not healthy. Your color is not good. You also have a liver ailment."

"I do have a thyroid condition," Mrs. Martin admitted. "I've been under treatment for a number of years and take pills under my physician's prescription."

"The pills won't do you any good. Throw them away."

Dr. Sonji opened his desk and took out a large black book, turning to a page with a drawing of a large eyeball.

Indicating the drawing, he explained: "If you continue to take these pills crystals will form at the top of your eyeballs which will cause blindness! And the bundles of nerves and muscles at the back of your eyeballs will become paralyzed. Then the paralysis will move to the upper part of your brain, then descend into your lungs causing them to become paralyzed too."

Mrs. Martin took a deep, worried breath.

"Moreover," the doctor added, "if you don't stop taking the pills they will cause hair to grow on your chest!"

To solve her medical and marital problems, Dr. Sonji suggested she attend his church every Thursday and Sunday. The church was an integral part of the facilities at the Palace.

"Can I bring my husband?"

"No, your husband would not benefit or be very favorably inclined. Come alone."

Dr. Sonji asked five dollars for the session. Mrs. Martin paid. The doctor didn't bother with a receipt.

And Mrs. Martin didn't bother showing up at the Palace again. Instead she showed up a few weeks later to recount the incredible meeting with Dr. Sonji before an awestruck Assembly Committee of the California Legislature. The committee was meeting in Los Angeles to determine the extent of quack marriage counseling, and Mrs. Martin, actually Louise Sheffield, was an undercover agent for the lawmakers. Her marriage was mythical, a fact that Dr. Sonji's spiritual vibrations had failed to communicate to him.

On subpoena, Dr. Sonji also showed up at the committee's hearing, an attorney at his side.

Committee investigation had unearthed some plebeian facts concerning the exotic doctor. He had an apple-pie American background. His real name was James Smith (changed, he said, "after my rebirth") and he was from Iowa, where he had attended school up to the tenth grade—and then "decided to venture on my own to study the higher realms of life."

Under questioning about his triple-threat activities as minister, healer and marriage counselor, Smith said he had received his "doctor of divinity" degree from the "International Church" of Los Angeles. Founder of the "Health Diet Clinic," he admitted recommending large doses of carrots, spinach and lettuce—the "organic and cosmic" vegetables—to people with everything from leukemia to hay fever. "I do not believe in medicines to heal, for I am a spiritual man."

Asked if he recommended any other treatment for people with such maladies as asthma, heart disease, cancer, cataracts, multiple sclerosis or high blood pressure, he said, "I tell them to eat organic foods and live a Christian life."

He declared that he did not give "marriage counseling" but "spiritual counseling" and was paid only by "voluntary donations."

In addition to private counseling, the doctor said he held group therapy sessions for unhappily married people, with attendance ranging from five to seventy-five. "The therapy consists of people coming to service. By being in my presence they receive therapy." The sessions were silent. "I discover their problems through psychic vibrations."

The committee, under the chairmanship of Assemblyman Lester A. McMillan, had been summoned to investigate mounting complaints against fakes and charlatans passing themselves off as marriage counselors. Under urging from reputable agencies, the committee was seeking legal ammunition to gun down the con men who had overrun the profession.

There were plenty of targets. The Los Angeles phone directory contained more than four columns of marriage counseling ads. And the public, without a scorecard, couldn't tell the phony from the ethical. In volume and vice, the committee soon discovered, Los Angeles led the nation in outrageous abuses among marriage counselors.

Construction engineer Howard Laws said he was advised by a counselor that he had a subconscious need for sexual partners other than his wife. Over a ten-year period, he had paid his counselor more than $1400.

"He moved into the area of sex which had not presented a problem," Laws said. "The first thing you know he had a hold on us."

The counselor did not have an office, but conducted sessions in his apartment or in Laws's automobile. The witness recalled once asking the adviser why there were no degrees visible on his apartment wall. He answered that he had no wish to be "ostentatious."

Despite the ten years of counseling, his marriage ended in divorce.

James D. Loebl, Director of the Los Angeles Department of Professional and Vocational Standards, declared there were hundreds of dangerous, unqualified quack marriage counselors in the Los Angeles area. They were able to operate because of loose laws. In most instances, their offenses were only misdemeanors.

Merely hanging out a sign put a counselor into business. "Many of these people are without moral qualifications and are without professional, educational or experience qualifications," Loebl said, citing a number of specific cases.

An ex-convict, with a seventh-grade education, charged fifty dollars an hour for his advice. "His method of operation consisted of advising women clients to engage in abnormal sexual activities, particularly with him." He had a "very lucrative practice."

Another operator conducted group therapy sessions for people with problem marriages. "The therapy consisted of lectures in spinal manipulation. These manipulations were given by the participants to each other in a state of partial disrobement."

One self-proclaimed counselor advocated abnormal sexual relations involving his wife, himself and his patients. "Complaints were received that he had raped some females. But upon investigation, it was determined that the victims submitted voluntarily."

Several practitioners offered marriage counseling by mail. Others advocated drugs or hypnosis as part of their treatment. One operator had studied hypnosis for only three weeks, but repeatedly hypnotized a young girl in an effort to cure her of an emotional illness supposedly stemming from her unhappy marriage. The result was disastrous. "At the present time," said Loebl, "she is committed to the psychiatric division of the county hospital."

Mark F. Joseff, an attorney specializing in domestic relations cases, appeared voluntarily before the committee.

"In the past seven years I have seen the money-making in marriage counseling," said Joseff. "I used to think we lawyers were expensive, but we're pikers in the ability to make money."

He spelled out in detail the financial rewards of group therapy marriage counseling by con men.

"The way to make money, gentlemen, is not to handle each patient privately, one at a time, at $15 to $20 an hour. A better technique is available. Have groups of six to nine people at $10 to $20 an hour and you have $90 to $180 an hour for one so-called marriage counselor."

Some of the bogus counselors in Los Angeles and Orange counties held ten to twelve group therapy sessions a week. They often were a prelude to orgies.

"Fifteen minutes before each counseling hour starts," said Joseff, "the patients sit around in rather luxuriously equipped rooms, with a nice low coffee table, usually having a marble top, and glasses of champagne are set out, and the parties drink champagne, one or two or three glasses, together with maybe one or two tranquilizers.

"They sit around and discuss their marital problems and it always gets down to sex. They are encouraged not only to discuss their sexual feelings in a rather grandiose way, but they are also encouraged, literally, to have extramarital affairs, but not ordinary sex, gentlemen, perverted sex, perversions. It's safe, you know. You don't get pregnant that way. You don't have to use the typical contraceptives."

Joseff said a thirty-two-year-old girl had wandered into his office under the mistaken impression he could arrange an abortion for her. She was a product of a con man marriage counselor.

"It turned out the counseling was this: that she and her husband were having difficulties being compatible, and she was advised to have an extramarital affair. She did and she became pregnant.

"I discovered one of the techniques of these so-called marriage counselors is that you encourage patients to have sexual affairs, and when they do, they have more problems, and you can get them to come back more frequently. You create problems. You don't get resolutions of problems, you encourage a creation of problems."

Joseff added that not only were "people who call themselves ministers of the gospel" dispensing marital advice, but they were publicizing the use of LSD (lysergic acid diethylamide), an experimental hallucinatory drug.

He said a client of his with marital problems "had stood in line" at one church to receive LSD.

Dr. Bertram F. Capp, of the Church of Advanced Metaphysics, readily admitted his church had sponsored two lectures about LSD and that he offered counseling on marital problems.

McMillan: Doctor, would you tell this committee what your qualifications are? What your educational background is?

Capp: Primarily I am self-taught. My only qualification is as the minister of the church; so far as legal qualifications, this is the extent of my qualifications. . . .

McMillan: Did you study for the ministry?

Capp: I am the founder of the church of Modern Philosophy.

McMillan: Did you issue yourself the degree?

Capp: The church issued it to me.

McMillan: It's your church, though.

Capp: Yes, I am the founder of the church.

McMillan: So, then, you received your right to call yourself "Doctor" from this church that you founded.

Capp: That is correct.

The minister denied advocating the use of LSD to members of his congregation. "I have never administered it nor have I been responsible either directly or indirectly for its administration." Two "public interest" programs concerning the drug had been held at the church, one lecture entitled "Knowledge of God Through LSD-25." The lecturer had told Dr. Capp's flock that "many times individuals taking LSD had developed a greater spiritual awareness, that to some degree it had made a profound difference in one's belief or disbelief in God."

Dr. Thomas T. Boyd, minister of the Christ Christian Church, told of taking LSD himself for experimental purposes.

"Well, I had an amazing experience," Dr. Boyd related. "I

was able to see for the first time the reality that I had been preaching and teaching about for so many years. I came back completely amazed by this thing as being one of the most remarkable things that I had ever seen in my life. With my eyes covered and my ears covered I was able to look at reality in a way that is beyond all possible description. It was an amazing experience. I was so amazed by it, that I felt that I should share it with my congregation."

McMillan: Have you ever recommended it?

Boyd: Yes, sir. I have said to people that I thought it was a very remarkable drug. I still say it is a very remarkable drug. . . .

McMillan: Do you devote a great deal of your time to marriage counseling?

Boyd: Oh, no. I don't have time to. When people come to my office with marriage problems I talk to them. All ministers do that. But if their problem is very deep I send them to a counseling service.

McMillan: Do you charge for—

Boyd: Oh, no. I make no charges. I do the normal thing that any minister of an orthodox church does, what your pastor does, I am sure. Catholic priests, rabbis, ministers of all denominations. They are bound to counsel on marriage. I have counseled on marriage since I was seventeen years of age. People naturally come to you when they have problems.

McMillan: Are you still having this great experience [LSD] with people, advising them of your—

Boyd: No, it hasn't come up at all.

McMillan: Those people who come to you, most of them have problems. Don't you recommend this?

Boyd: No, I do not. I don't recommend this.

McMillan: You used to, didn't you?

Boyd: No. I had people ask me specifically if I thought they would be benefited by it, and I have said yes, just as I would recommend the Mayo [Clinic], would recommend some important surgeon. . . .

McMillan turned to a charge that Dr. Boyd had also recommended an aphrodisiac to parishioners having difficulties in their sex lives.

McMillan: Now, Doctor, do you know anything about this other drug called Pego Pela or something?

Boyd: Yes. That was an amazing thing, too.

McMillan: What's that stuff?

Boyd: I never heard the word aphrodisiac until after someone spoke about this. It is a drug that is very fine for older men.

McMillan: Have you ever used it?

Boyd: I tried it and didn't care for it, and threw it aside.

McMillan: What did it do to you?

Boyd: . . . It had no effect, and I don't need anything like that, I assure you.

McMillan: Are you advocating it for any of your flock?

Boyd: Oh, no. Absolutely no. I consider it worthless.

McMillan: I never tried it.

Boyd: I would get into trouble if I offered to get you some.

Judge Roger Alton Pfaff, of the Los Angeles Superior Court, urged the committee to establish high standards for marriage counselors.

"I saw one down in Ensenada about a month ago, with a big neon sign that says 'Marriage Counselor.' I looked inside this little shacky place, and here was this old boy sitting in there. I suppose he also got divorces for married people as well. I am sure his standards were not very high."

In addition to expert testimony from Los Angeles social workers, family relations specialists and bona fide counselors from university and private clinics—all of whom favored creation of licensing standards for those who give marital advice—the committee also heard from Philip O'Neal, a representative of the United States Personology Practitioners, a group that offered its own form of marriage counseling.

"Personology is a specific approach to the individual. It is called personology because we are setting the individual alone. Not in relationship to other people, not in relationship to his environment, or to any sort of other relationship."

The important thing, O'Neal pointed out, is "torso percentage."

"We measure the length of the individual's torso as compared to the length of his legs. Now this comes out as people who are long torsoed and short torsoed."

When McMillan asked what torso analysis had to do with

marriage problems, O'Neal gave a case history of a mailman who was having difficulty with his wife.

"In the course of the analysis, it was determined that this individual was not meant to stand. At the end of the day, he was worn out, irritated, and annoyed. He'd go home to his wife and have all these fracases, the kids would annoy him, the dog annoyed him. He was just tired and irritated. He didn't know what was the matter."

He was advised by his personology counselor to change his job—to drive a mail truck instead of walking a route "because this is the way you are naturally constituted. . . . He did this, and his irritation, his difficulties were soon taken care of by one simple factor that he had not respected with his own build."

Advice from off-brand counselors, according to additional testimony, included the suggestion to unhappy husbands that they consider homosexual relationships or sexual gratification with prostitutes.

Then Perry Sinclair explained to the committee his "patented" system of marriage counseling through magnetic tape recordings.

"I do not use psychic radiations or vibrations or telepathy to ascertain the nature of a problem of the people who contact me. I don't require donations. I have fees and they are very explicit, and there is no hemming and hawing about it."

His explicit fee was ninety-five dollars for a "metaphysical" two-track tape.

After checking a client on the "electropsychometer, I very quickly and without any guesswork, and without any psychic thing of any sort, I arrive at the probable basic problem, or the problems as they were implanted in childhood."

"I consider most of the problems that come to me are people who are now hypnotized by what they have been through as children, through having been abused, kicked around, called no-good, being disfavored, being disbanded. I have one now coming up whose father strangled him with a towel when he cried, so now he won't talk. . . .

"The tape is all positive affirmation, affirmation that you are reversing, canceling, releasing, de-hypnotizing the problems of childhood."

McMillan: Then the idea is to continue playing that, and repeat the playing of it?

Sinclair: The tape runs an hour. At the end it has instructions. For instance . . . "John, you turn off this tape recorder and move into restful sleep." The next day they turn the reels over and run track number two. Sometimes it is different, sometimes it's similar. . . .

At the conclusion of the hearings, the committee declared that there undoubtedly were more unqualified than qualified marriage counselors operating in California.

The hearings resulted in the nation's first law regulating marriage counseling. Its key provisions required a state license to practice and banned the advertising of marriage and family counseling services.

Some of the quacks were driven out, but they soon turned up in the phone book and newspaper classified ads as "personal advisors" and "psychic readers." Most of the charlatans, including some who testified before the committee, are still in business.

"The point is that they are not selling themselves as marriage counselors any more," says Dr. James J. Rue, Director of the Sir Thomas More Marriage and Family Clinic in Los Angeles.

He says that "southern California and New York City have been the two top areas—and I am afraid we are number one—in abuse. But California has stepped in to do something. New York is in bad shape with no legislation at all."

The law is still weak in that it exempts ministers, doctors, lawyers, and nonprofit organizations from its provisions, thus allowing many diploma-mill charlatans to slip through.

One of the most informed spokesmen for toughening the law is Dr. James A. Peterson, of the University of Southern California, a highly regarded sociologist and marriage counselor. He advocates upgrading of educational standards for counselors—a master's degree in one of the behavioral sciences and at least two years of supervised internship at a recognized clinic.

"With half of California's marriages ending in divorce," says Dr. Peterson, "the marriage counselor is needed as never before. But the con men must be driven out. There's too much at stake for too many troubled people who need qualified help.

"Beware the counselor," he declares, "who tries to sign you up for a set number of consultations, who refuses to give details of his training, who makes outrageous claims in his advertising and who overemphasizes sex."

It is not only the unhappily married who are preyed upon in southern California. The unhappily unmarried are also fair game for the social clubs, introduction services, lonely hearts meeting places, dance studios and the polished bunk men who fleece their women victims shortly before or after a trip to the altar.

"Selected Introductions," "Jewish Introductions," "Catholic Introductions," "Beautiful Spanish Girls," "German Introductions," "Meet a Girl Tonight—All Races," "Meet the Right People" run the siren-song ads of the high-fee, no-satisfaction-guaranteed social clubs. Trading on loneliness and despair, matrimonial agencies also offer such new wrinkles as "scientific mating" and "computer matching."

Warns the Better Business Bureau: "Persons who patronize matrimonial agencies or correspondence clubs may expose themselves to manifold dangers. Some of these have been shakedown rackets, used by adventurers and swindlers of all kinds."

Amassing a list of 340 women that he'd met through lonely hearts clubs, a thirty-seven-year-old ex-Navy warrant officer sent them letters informing each that she was a beneficiary of a $20,-000 estate and asking for twenty dollars in probate fees.

Contending his client was the dupe of a mysterious San Diego attorney who offered him $10,000 to write the letters, the defense lawyer claimed his client actually was the victim of a "stupid, crass, obvious bunco game." The judge recommended a psychiatric examination, saying the defendant was "either very clever or unbalanced."

Lifetime contracts for payments in excess of $500 for lessons have been outlawed in California, but the dance studio dodge is being worked with a new twist—the selling of 1 per cent interests in studio franchises for $10,000 or more. "At that rate," says the BBB, "the franchise would be worth $1,000,000. This may make dollars for the promoter, but no sense to cold-blooded investors. This is another example indicating that we can't legislate honesty or erase lovelorn companionship by lures."

Southern California has been a long-established Eden for the timeworn, basic marriage bunk.

The undermanned bunco squad of the Los Angeles Police Department handles hundreds of complaints a year. In fifteen years on the detail, Sergeant John Di Betta has investigated five hundred cases—but says the figure could be ten times higher, estimating that nine out of ten women who have been victimized are too ashamed to tell the police.

The marriage bunk men are the most notorious repeaters of all flimflam artists. They are cut from the classic mold of con man—well-read, well-groomed, versatile conversationalists, excellent dancers, personable and resourceful.

"Unless they have a very beautiful woman, they seldom go to bed with their victims," says Investigator Kenneth Scarce, who worked the detail for years. "The pitch is, 'Sweetheart, I think so much of you that I'm not going to touch you until we're married.' All this does is make the woman think the bunk man is a wonderful person."

The professional Don Juans are usually not physically handsome, but their success springs from the deft caroling of the wedding march. The variations on the scam are endless.

After talking a series of women out of sums ranging from $500 to $15,000 "to pay the interest on business loans," one marry-'em-and-scram expert staged fake drowning accidents to cover his trail.

An ex-Salvation Army clerk known to the bunco squad as the "dancing romeo" was a veteran of seven trips to the altar. He fleeced cash and jewels from his wives by promising to repay them as soon as he received "my father's $18,000 estate." He admitted staking out victims in dance halls. The passionate letters from some of his wives, even after he was exposed as a con man and given one to ten in San Quentin, would have wrung the heart of a loan shark.

A one-time Los Angeles policeman also tried his hand at the scam, obtaining money by promising marriage and getting women to invest in a honeymoon yacht he called "The Dreamboat."

Another operator enticed $20,000 from a woman he married under an alias by telling her it was an advance against $270,000 from his "Philadelphia investment syndicate." At the time he was caught he was on probation for a similar offense, having bilked two women of $3300 to compete in a nonexistent $250,000 pool game. He told the sentencing judge, "If women are stupid enough to believe my stories, they deserve to lose their money."

It took only six months for a fleece man to gobble up nearly $65,000 from two women he met in bars and wooed separately with promises of marriage and bullish descriptions of his mythical business interests. The pitch was that he needed immediate cash to save his hotels, motels and other property holdings in Bermuda. One victim had parted with more than $60,000, the other with $4700. He was undone when one of the women phoned him at his flossy Hollywood hotel and the other woman answered. They got to comparing notes. After his arrest, he admitted using the money to gamble and "live it up" in Las Vegas.

The champion human marriage machine in local history was Emil Drake, who rang up at least thirty trips to the altar ("Maybe more, I'm not certain") in a lifetime dedication to the marriage scam.

Passing himself off as a brigadier general, a psychiatrist, plastic surgeon or just plain doctor, Drake was sixty-eight years old when he was nabbed for taking his thirtieth (?) bride.

Short, gray and of dignified mien, the brigadier was transferred to a jail cell with the echoes of Mexican wedding bells still ringing in his ears. Out of a cell for less than a month on a previous bigamy conviction, the brigadier had violated parole by remarrying. He was arrested while hiding in the bushes at the rear of the motel owned by his new wife.

A few years earlier, bunco squad men had walked in on him while he was living with another wife. When the detectives told the woman her husband was a famous fleecer, she quickly emptied his pockets and found $3. He was, however, $29,997 short. She had turned over $30,000 to him as a wedding present.

It was a point of professional pride to the brigadier that all of his thirty some-odd marriages were one-way affairs—he had never been divorced.

On the occasion of his last arrest, ever natty and sniffing a still-fresh boutonniere, Drake indulged himself in a bit of vanity.

"I'm the last of the old-time con men," he said with quiet pride. "I knew Francis Van Wie. But he was a piker alongside of me."

Observers of the southern California bunko scene would have gladly contributed a month's pay for the privilege of eavesdropping on the shoptalk between Brigadier Drake and Van Wie—the fabled "Ding-Dong Daddy of the D-Car Line." But concerning the latter, no one was ever quite certain if he was or wasn't a con man, although some of his best friends and unabashed admirers were officers of the bunco squads of San Francisco and Los Angeles.

On a blustery December afternoon in 1944, Francis Van Wie tooled his trolley along San Francisco's Market Street, a contented man filled with the joy of living.

At the helm of his streetcar, the short, chunky, balding, fifty-eight-year-old motorman was unfailingly polite and efficient. He smiled and sang out a hearty greeting as each of his passengers boarded. For the ladies who chanced to ride the rails with him, Francis snapped a smart military salute, a habit acquired during his days as a doughboy in World War I. Though he prided himself on keeping his car to a tight schedule, he always had a moment to spare while his female fares settled themselves comfortably.

His warm blue eyes scanning the traffic and the Christmas decorations festooning the city's major artery, Francis picked up a little speed thanks to a tailwind from the Bay. The car rattled slightly in the strong breeze, but Francis kept her steady as she goes, a part of his mind devoted, as it was each day, to deciding where he would spend the evening after his shift was over.

Francis was fortunate. He had a great many choices. If somewhere along the route his trolley happened to break down, it was an easy jog from anywhere he happened to find himself to a home, a hearth and a wife.

This convenient arrangement was possible for Francis because he had providentially provided himself with a string of wives, scattered carefully throughout the city like a squirrel with nuts buried all over the back yard.

As Francis now smoothly tethered his trolley to pick up a new load of passengers, a burly man in a tweed jacket hopped aboard and shoved a paper into his hand. It wasn't a transfer.

The man vanished as swiftly as he had appeared. And when

Francis took a moment to examine the paper, he discovered, to his chagrin, that it was a notice of divorce.

Francis Van Wie, ex-circus lion tamer and wounded combat veteran, was for the first time in his life really frightened. He was so upset that he brought his car into the shed several minutes late.

In shock, he headed for a home, a hearth and a wife, turning up at the quarters of Mrs. Leona Simmons Van Wie, his latest bride. He took to bed, deep in melancholia, refusing to talk. His worried wife of two weeks, knowing Francis only as a gay, jovial *boulevardier,* forthwith called a doctor. Francis was told he had indeed suffered a shock and the doctor suggested he abandon his job and turn his changemaker in to the streetcar company.

Francis began a slow recovery. In two days, he was ambulatory. He obediently handed in his resignation, and then, without so much as leaving a note for Leona, he fled to Los Angeles.

His ignominious departure came only a step ahead of the law. Bunco detectives had been diligently amassing a growing file on Francis. They had complaints stacked up from three of his wives, and now issued warrants for triple bigamy against the missing ex-motorman.

The southern California air seemed to agree with Francis. His recovery was rapid. He soon felt well enough to take a job as a painter in a stamping plant. After five weeks, the shock of the divorce action had almost worn off. He was beginning to feel secure. Then his world collapsed again. The chief of the security police at the plant remembered Francis from a picture in a newspaper. He tipped detectives, who were waiting for him when he next reported for work.

The carbarn Casanova, who had, according to police, been thrice a bridegroom and never an ex-bridegroom, began to tell his story. The police, it soon appeared, had underestimated him. By his own admission, Francis had, not three, but at least eleven wives! Five of them had been stashed along his trolley route in San Francisco.

Awaiting the arrival of officers to return him to San Francisco, Francis declared, "I've been a respecter of womanhood all my life—ever since I was a little boy."

Francis had been a little boy in Madison, Wisconsin, and had spent his youth in Milwaukee. In his teens, he had run off with a circus, gradually clawing his way up to lion tamer.

He had married for the first time when he was nineteen.

"That was Margaret Windsor, but I can't remember if it was 1904 or '05," said Francis, honestly straining his memory. "Anyway, I was young then and it was romance. But it didn't last long. I'd say about a year and a half. Then in 1912 there was Sally. That was Sally Morgan. We made it till 1915 and later Sally and Margaret got together and between them they had me in court on bigamy. Margaret said she was going to divorce me, and I was under the impression she had. It was all straightened out in court, but not until after I had spent three months in jail in Chicago. Then I convinced the court Sally's child was not mine and I was released."

At this juncture, his romantic career was interrupted while he fought in France. Francis never got a chance to propose to a *mademoiselle;* he was injured in battle and sent back to a convalescent hospital in Milwaukee. Into his life now came red-haired Jane Sullivan, a former artists' model, working at the hospital as a waitress.

Romance blossomed. After his convalescence was complete, Francis married Jane. The strongest thing going for them was that they both were ex-circus performers, Jane at one time having worked as a mind reader.

Naturally, they teamed up. Jane thought lion taming was too dangerous, so she taught her husband card tricks and mind reading. They joined a circus and became a sideshow attraction.

The marriage lasted seventeen years. But, according to Francis, in the end he had misread Jane's mind. All of a sudden she disappeared. "She found someone else and ran away. If she divorced me, I never heard about it."

After Jane's departure, Francis tried to console himself. "I had worked hard all my life and all I wanted was a happy home and contentment. I guess that's why I married all the time."

Wife number four was Annabelle Wall. "We were married in some small town in Nevada, near Reno, in 1941." It was this wife's divorce action that had been served on Francis that wind-whipped day on the trolley car, precipitating his decline and fall.

Life with Annabelle had proved a sad detour for Francis, and finding himself in Sacramento in April, 1942, he married Hungarian-born Eva Fedrova, his fifth bride. She proved to be an undigestible goulash.

"Often when I was married to Eva I went to work with a scratched face. I had enough of her and told her that I was going for good." That was in 1943.

He took two other brides that year, marrying Dorothy Astin in Reno. Then he tied the knot with Kathryn Dawson in Las Vegas, the highlight of that ceremony being Francis' polite prompting when the justice of the peace momentarily lost his place as he read the vows.

But it was 1944 that proved to be the banner year for Francis. He strode proudly to the altar four times. The wedding bells rang, rang, rang, and rang as he said "I do," "I do," "I do," and "I do," with Melody Moore and Maxine Garwood early in the year followed by an Easter ceremony with Virginia Codel and a pre-Christmas nuptial with Leona.

"Leona was the sweetest of them all," Francis declared, breaking into sobs. "I got acquainted with her a year ago at a whist party. In Leona I found the happy home and contentment I was always searching for. Then I found it was too late. I was served that divorce summons while at work on my streetcar." He admitted that it was fear of arrest that had prompted him to leave the hearth he had shared so briefly with Leona.

"I just felt that I was going to be caught up with one of these days, and I had a hunch that it was going to be soon. But I'm no bum. I've always worked and it was my intention to send Leona some money after I started to work here but it was just too late."

Totaling the score, it made Francis an eleven-wife man. With some justification, police said it also made him a bigamist.

"I believe in divorce," Francis declared, "but I just never got around to getting one."

Up in San Francisco, meantime, things were humming. A Chinese woman claimed she also was married to Francis (he denied it).

Captain Bernard McDonald spurned a suggestion that he send a policewoman to fetch Francis from Los Angeles. "They probably would be married when they arrived."

County Clerk Herman Van Der Zee checked the records to

determine how Francis had managed so many marriage licenses. But he was at a loss for an explanation. "It's not our fault. Some people get divorced that fast."

E. T. Cahill, manager of San Francisco's streetcar system, said that Francis could have his job back any time the police let him go. "All I hope is that he can persuade his wives to go to work for us."

In his Los Angeles jail cell, Francis turned stoic. "I'm guilty of bigamy and ready to face the music. I don't think I'll get out of it. I don't expect the court to show me any mercy, but I've dished it out and I can take it."

He began to sob once more about Leona. "I hope she won't hate me too much for what I've done. She's too good a woman to get mixed up in all this."

Leona proved she didn't hate Francis at all. She came down to Los Angeles to join him on the train ride back to San Francisco. Also aboard, for added consolation, was Mrs. Virginia Van Wie, the wife Francis had married immediately prior to Leona.

Francis arrived in San Francisco to find himself something of a hero. A crowd of nearly a hundred women and a number of men greeted him with scattered applause and whistling as he stepped from the train to a police car. Francis paused a moment to introduce the two wives that had made the trip with him—"the last two."

The swain of the streetcar system also found that he was not to face his ordeal in court without powerful friends. A "Ding-Dong Daddy Defense Fund" had been formed, sponsored by millionaire real-estate man Louis Lurie and several prominent Nob Hill citizens. "I am by no means condoning bigamy," said Lurie. "I guess we got into this thing at first purely from a sense of humor."

The Ding-Dong Fund hired noted attorney Jake Ehrlich, later to be immortalized as television's Sam Benedict. "I find in this case a man who had the courage to marry too many women," said Ehrlich. "His crime was that he loved widely, and perhaps too well."

Ehrlich added that he was defending Francis because he "believed that any man brave enough to marry eleven women should have some help."

At the arraignment, Francis promised Judge Leo Cunningham that prior to trial he would curb his penchant for fast courtship and whirlwind honeymoons.

He lost his poise and shed a few more tears when Virginia and Leona both affirmed that he had always been kind and gentle to them. Leona, asked if she objected to Francis' release on bail, looked at Virginia, and answered: "It's all right with us, judge. If you can trust him, we can, too."

Even the judge felt called upon to say kind words about Francis. "He may have been generous in his accumulation of wives, but he never intended to harm anyone." Ehrlich said his client "was just an unfortunate old man who was looking for something he could never find."

Francis was released on $1000 bail.

Mrs. Dorothy Astin Van Wie, who had filed one of the bigamy charges, did not make it to the courtroom in time for the arraignment. "My streetcar was too slow," she told a reporter. "When Francis was on those cars they were on time."

Prior to the opening of his trial, it became apparent that Francis, in recounting his marital career, had neglected to mention two small details. It hardly seemed possible, but those details consisted of two more wives. Digging into its files, the California Bureau of Vital Statistics announced the records showed he had married Grace Lewis on December 12, 1917, in Oakland, and Diane Colfax in Berkeley on November 14, 1920. That brought the total to an unlucky thirteen.

Four wives turned up at the trial to testify against Francis. Recalling his marital merry-go-round from the witness box, he said in his own defense: "I must have been insane. I'm also troubled by a loss of memory."

The twelve jurors (one less than the defendant's collection of wives) brought in an unsurprising verdict. Francis was found guilty and sentenced to three consecutive ten-year terms and a token fine of three dollars. Dead broke, he borrowed the money for the fine from Judge Herbert Kaufman.

Francis decided on a grand entrance through the forbidding walls of San Quentin. Dressing himself in his white painter's uniform and his motorman's cap, he told the escorting officer, "Now I can go to the Big House in style."

In the Big House, Francis was a model prisoner. Fellow cons treated him with the awed respect due a man of his prowess. Word came to him in his cell that Mrs. Annabelle Wall Van Wie had finally gotten her divorce. It was a unique experience for Francis. But he still had twelve other wives to warm his memory through the long prison nights.

On the outside, meantime, sympathy was building up for Francis. Reviewing his case, Judge Kaufman declared: "The trial attracted nationwide publicity. My feeling at the time was that a great moral issue, much more important than the defendant, was involved. It is my considered judgment that it would be in the interest of justice to set a maximum of two years for this defendant, less any credits for good behavior."

Francis was paroled—on condition he would not remarry for five years without court approval.

He tried toeing the marital mark, but the world would not let him forget. He came back before Judge Kaufman seeking a way to avoid being called "Ding-Dong Daddy." Since his release from San Quentin, he had been working on a ranch, loading produce on trucks. The high-school boys working alongside him were making life miserable for him by their constant reminder of his nickname.

"I just can't stand it any more. I want some kind of job in San Francisco where nobody will recognize me, where I can bury myself." The judge said he would try to help.

But Francis himself didn't do much to change his "Ding-Dong Daddy" image, especially when he soon popped back before Judge Kaufman with a new bride-to-be, Sylvia Markham, a forty-two-year-old waitress.

Unwilling to fight the inevitable, the judge officially lifted the ban on Francis and performed the nuptials. Francis tried to repay the three dollars he had borrowed to pay his fine. "Consider it a wedding present," the judge said.

Francis was as happy as he'd been at any of his weddings. "No, this isn't *A Streetcar Named Desire*," he chuckled over the explosion of photographers' flashbulbs.

"How many weddings does this make?" a newsman asked.

"Well, to be honest with you," said Francis, "I don't rightly know. I think this is the fourteenth—or maybe the twentieth. Let's just say it's my last one. We're going to live happily ever after."

But, alas, things did not go well at Francis' fourteenth honeymoon cottage. Only three weeks after the wedding, his latest bride turned up teary-eyed before Judge Kaufman.

She complained that Francis was too amorous.

She also said he was a penny pincher and spending too much time at Bay bars. When she remonstrated, Francis became abusive.

Judge Kaufman called his old pal in and got Francis to promise he would mend his ways. After all, the judge told him, he was no stranger to marriage and by this time he should know some of the requirements—and restraints—of wedded bliss.

Reconciled, Mrs. Van Wie the fourteenth said, "It was just a lover's quarrel. It's all a thing of the past."

But the honeymoon cottage was soon rent asunder once more. Back before the judge a few months later, Mrs. Van Wie the fourteenth said that "Francis just can't seem to make a go of marriage. It's all over, it's ended. I've moved out of our love nest." The judge wearily suggested she contact the Legal Aid Society for information on divorce.

Francis was beginning to think San Francisco was his hard-luck town. He moved to Los Angeles and soon met and married Susanne Knotts, a spunky seventy-three-year-old milliner. She was Mrs. Van Wie the fifteenth, but she tossed him out when she learned from the newspapers that Mrs. Van Wie the fourteenth was suing for divorce.

Francis' spirits were buoyed, however, by an unexpected windfall that proved to him he was still in demand in northern California. An Oakland burlesque theater offered him a two-week engagement at $500 per week to narrate for audiences the story of his bigamous love life. He accepted and titled his address: "My True Love Life."

Francis got into an airplane and flew back to San Francisco. Several strippers from the theater were at the airport to meet him. "If Francis ever becomes a free man," said one of the runway queens, "I'll marry him myself."

Francis had no sooner set foot on stage when, to no one's surprise, another wife materialized. Mrs. Marie Kelly Van Wie, sixty-seven, of Long Beach, number sixteen on Francis' hit parade, was charging him with cruelty and desertion before the district attorney in Los Angeles. She had married him in Yuma, Arizona, in 1951, and separated from him four months later.

"I was a frail little woman, and he was a charming man," Mrs. Van Wie the sixteenth said. "So, I married him. He said he had been married once before in Oakland, but his wife divorced him. He told me he would take me off the old age pension but instead of supporting me he made me pay half the rent, five dollars for moving and buy the food. He never did anything for me."

Pressed for comment at the burlesque emporium, Francis declared sheepishly, "All I can say is that after my fifth wife—with whom I lived for seventeen years by the way—I just seem to have gone haywire. I can't explain anything right now."

A pair of investigators from Los Angeles came to serve him with two bigamy warrants on behalf of wives fifteen and sixteen, catching Francis right after a performance.

He was returned to Los Angeles, and at train side he announced, "I'm glad to be back. I always did like it better down here than in the Bay area. I call this my home now. I just went north to fulfill a theatrical engagement."

Asked if he really had married sixteen times, Francis answered, "That's what they say. But on advice of my attorney, I'm not answering any questions."

In his second bigamy trial, Francis didn't fare too well as a lover. Wives fourteen, fifteen and sixteen all testified against him.

Mrs. Sylvia Markham Van Wie recalled their strife-strewn marriage. Though she had sought a divorce, she said, "I'm still married to him."

Mrs. Susanne Knotts Van Wie said she had "kicked him out" within a few days of their wedding and filed for divorce a week later.

Mrs. Marie Kelly Van Wie rated Francis a poor successor to a former husband, the late Henry Devon.

"My Henry," she said, "was the best husband in the world." As she said it she gazed huffily at Francis, huddled unhappily at the counsel table.

Francis pled insanity again. The judge ordered a psychiatric examination.

Dr. Marcus Crahan, county jail physician, found that Francis was an "incurable romantic" who had long sought a woman who would "be a pal" and would be "as interested as he is in home life."

But the doctor said he was sane. Francis therefore withdrew his insanity defense and pled guilty to one count of bigamy.

Seeking leniency, Francis spelled out his unorthodox views on marriage. "What I wanted was a real pal and companion, which I found in Mrs. Knotts," he told the bench. "I loved her. We would be happy today and together if I had not been arrested. I still don't think I've done so much wrong in marrying and giving the ladies a name instead of just living with them. I never did believe in living with a woman without giving her a name. That's why I married them. I did not marry them for their money."

With a touching note of personal sacrifice, Francis ended his plea by saying he would obey all of the probation department's rules "even if it means I can never marry again."

The judge gave him six months in the county jail and a seven-year probationary ban on marrying again without court permission.

As Francis went off to the Wayside Honor Farm at Castaic, Mrs. Van Wie the sixteenth had her membership in the Francis Van Wie Wives Club annulled.

Francis was allowed one day of liberty from the honor farm to spend a memorable day in the courtrooms of the Los Angeles Hall of Justice. He set a local record by obtaining two annulments in a few hours. Judge Henry M. Willis severed his marriage to Mrs. Van Wie the fifteenth and then Francis walked across the hall to the courtroom of Judge A. A. Scott where he came to the end of the line with Mrs. Van Wie the fourteenth.

He was released after serving five months of his sentence and warned by his probation officer that if he should get interested in another woman he must be sure to tell her about the terms of his probation so "she won't expect too much." The probation officer also took him out of show business—forbidding him from appearing before an audience to tell of his admittedly remarkable career.

Francis settled into a quiet hotel and lived on his service pension. He spent a good deal of his time commuting to court trying to straighten out his matrimonial affairs, piling up annulments and divorces from most of his wives.

Judge Samuel R. Blake granted him a divorce from the wife he remembered as number three, though Francis didn't seem entirely sure. "I just can't remember all of them," he apologized. "They say I've been married sixteen times. I can remember only twelve. But then, I've gone over my history so many times that maybe I'm confused."

"Let me admonish you," said Judge Blake, "that this is only an interlocutory decree and cannot be made final for a year. Meanwhile, don't go out and get married. You would just be in trouble again."

It was good advice, but Francis didn't take it. In March, 1959, he tied the knot for the seventeenth time, with seventy-three-year-old Joan Brody, in Sacramento; and only a month later he tied the knot for the eighteenth time, with Fay Lesser, a blushing bride of eighty-one. It was bigamy again, and the bunco squad, acting on a complaint from Mrs. Van Wie the seventeenth, found Francis sharing household expenses at the Long Beach home of Mrs. Van Wie the eighteenth.

Francis got four months for violating probation and wife number seventeen got an annulment. "He led me to believe he had only been married once before," she testified.

But Mrs. Van Wie the eighteenth said she was going to wait for Francis. "If the Lord can forgive him and give him another chance so can I."

In his last interview, Francis, now seventy-two but still a firm believer in Cupid, looked back on his career of eighteen marriages. "I guess I'm a desperate criminal," he sighed. "One thing I want everybody to know, I never married a woman for money. I can honestly say that. And no woman ever had to work for me. Some of them didn't have any money at all, and I took care of them. You'll find that's true, all the way along the line."

He didn't quite know why he had married so often. "I do things in an impulsive way," he offered. "I was always lonely."

Why had he left all his wives? "Sometimes women are hard to live with. Yes, that's a fact."

He still bristled at the "Ding-Dong Daddy" tag. "What kind of name is that for a man?"

Had he a favorite among them all? "The one I really loved," he said, "I do remember her name. But I'm not saying." Gallantly, the old Romeo added, "There's been too much publicity. I might as well protect her."

Francis went off to serve his sentence, the name of his true love unspoken. No one would ever know for sure if it was Margaret, Sally, Jane, Annabelle, Eva, Dorothy, Kathryn, Melody, Maxine, Virginia, Leona, Grace, Diane, Sylvia, Susanne, Marie, Joan or Fay Van Wie.

9

AUTOMOBILES
The Chrome-Plated Cons

California, here they come:
Doctor, lawyer, merchant, bum. . . .
Here they come, and here they are,
Living, dying in a car,
Ever moving, dawn to dark,
Looking for a place to park.
—RICHARD ARMOUR,
Excerpted from *I Loved You, California* and reprinted with the permission of the author and *Look* magazine

By 1883, stubby, derby-hatted Black Bart, the merchant prince of highwaymen, had eluded capture by northern California lawmen for eight years. Wearing a long linen duster and a flour sack with cutout eyelets, the trim-bearded nemesis of Wells Fargo had commandeered twenty-seven strongboxes. Bart was finally taken after his twenty-eighth robbery by a detective who traced the laundry mark on a handkerchief he had dropped at the scene.

The terror of the trails turned out to be mild-mannered, Bible-reading Charles E. Boles of San Francisco, masquerading between holdups as a successful mine operator. As "Black Bart, the Po-ate," he authored the oft-quoted quatrain that many a latter-day Californian has fondly dedicated, after being gouged and fleeced, to his friendly neighborhood auto dealer:

I've labored long and hard for bread,
For honor and for riches,
But too long on my corns you've tread,
You fine-haired sons of bitches!

With Bart's capture, the colorful era of stagecoach banditry in California came to an end. But the Black Bart tradition has lingered on among the modern breed of highwaymen who rent, park, repair and sell automobiles.

Contemporary California is the well-publicized horror of the automobile age. It has more drivers, more automobiles, more freeways and more auto con men than any state in the nation.

More than three million cars are registered in the Los Angeles Metropolitan area—one for every 2.2 persons—a higher ratio than that of any other major city on earth. Reliance on the automobile is total. Mass transportation, save for a spotty bus system, is nonexistent. Suburbanites whose cars break down and somehow manage to navigate home via the bus system write victorious letters to the newspapers, logging the wondrous journey in the same loving detail as a ship's master sailing through uncharted waters.

Lack of efficient mass transit has made the taxi franchise in Los Angeles a rolling gold mine. But the tourists and natives forced to rely on the city's taxi system discovered in 1964 that they had been taken for a five-year $1,800,000 ride.

The Yellow Cab Co., enjoying a monopoly franchise in the downtown area, was charged with using rigged meters by another taxi firm seeking a competitive foothold in the local market.

Three former officials of Yellow Cab promptly admitted that incorrect gear ratios had resulted in the prolonged overcharging. They said it was the fault of factory-installed transmission gears. Attorneys for the rival company claimed the faulty meters resulted from "intent and design on the part of officials and employees of Yellow Cab."

The controversy flared into headlines. Mayor Samuel W. Yorty blamed the city's inspection department. The meters, he said, hadn't been checked since 1947. The city's chief taxi inspector denied the charge, claiming "spot checks" of Yellow Cab meters had been made, but that records of the inspections had vanished.

"This is the worst case of laxity in enforcement of a city ordinance that I have ever seen," the mayor shot back.

The scandal soon widened. "Yellow Cab should move over. It has lots of company," said Mayor Yorty after receiving police reports that four other suburban taxi companies operating under city franchises had also rigged their meters.

In addition, Chief of Police William H. Parker discovered that auto rental customers were being overcharged in much the same fashion as taxi riders. His investigation disclosed that odometers on rented automobiles were running 7 to 9 per cent fast. The chief's figures were based on a survey of 162 rental agencies operating from 209 locations in the city. "Renters are paying on a mileage basis for more miles than they are actually traveling," he said.

It was also suspected that private ambulance services, speeding helpless passengers to emergency hospital treatment, were running on fast meters.

Investigating the case against Yellow Cab, a grand jury held two weeks of "in depth" hearings, calling more than forty witnesses. Prosecution for the overcharging hinged on whether the current owners of the company, who took control in 1962, had knowledge of the rigged meters.

The grand jury cleared the new owners of criminal intent to defraud the public. It agreed with the mayor and blamed city employees for shirking their duties. "Had the department been run with the efficiency expected of it, or had there ever been a knowledgeable and efficient inspection group," the report declared, "this unfortunate situation could not have occurred."

New state and county laws were subsequently passed to require annual inspection of meters on taxis and "for hire" vehicles. Cab riders were now assured they would be allowed an extra 120 feet on each mile compared with prior standards.

In 1965, the ubiquitous Los Angeles parking lots—which consume one-third of the choice downtown building area—were attacked for fraudulent practices by no less an observer than Municipal Court Judge Nancy Cannon.

"In a city that moves on wheels, this type of pickpocketing becomes big business," said Judge Cannon, ticking off the variety of con games practiced by the parking lot impresarios.

Tickets are "backtimed" (clocked out before the patron is on the lot). Lots whose signs indicate they accept validations from a particular business establishment refuse to do so when presented with the validation. The customer is kept waiting before his ticket is clocked in and an attempt to clock in one's own ticket is met with a rude rebuff. Advance payments for parking are not refunded with validation as promised—unless the customer makes an issue of it. The six-minute grace period required by law is not given. Lots are overparked and underserviced so that patrons are held captive during the lengthy and leisurely unblocking process. The price on payment is increased over that displayed on parking.

County-owned parking facilities were also gouging customers, according to Los Angeles attorney Phil Silver. He filed a formal, unsuccessful claim of one dollar with the clerk of the County Board of Supervisors for "excessive and unlawful" parking rates. Silver said he was charged $1.50 on two separate occasions when he parked at a county lot and "damaged" for fifty cents in each instance. He said the parking fees were a "misuse of publicly owned land" and a violation of the due process and equal protection clauses of the Constitution.

Fraud is so rampant in California's auto repair industry that the state legislature is drafting statutes to curb the abuses of unneeded repairs, overcharging, unnecessary replacement of parts as well as repeated incompetency of mechanics.

In 1964, police in Porterville, California, found one fed-up customer leaning against the wall of a car dealer's service department. He held a shotgun in his arms while employees busily finished repairing his car. He had already fired one shot through a window and swore to put the next one through the manager unless repairs on his transmission were made to his satisfaction. The customer was booked on assault with intent to kill. "At least," he shrugged on his way to jail, "I made them fix it right."

"Auto repair is an open invitation to the criminal masquerading as a businessman because it involves fairly large sums of money," says Mrs. Helen Nelson, of the State Consumer Council in Sacramento and spearhead of the new legislation. "Such a person finds it quite easy to practice fraud without being detected. *Caveat emptor*—let the buyer beware—doesn't work here. Consumer education cannot solve the problem because it calls for expertise."

The legislation will establish policing units with state-hired mechanics to act on complaints and muster evidence for prosecution against offending repair shops. The state units are expected to do a land-office business.

Even the fabled foul ozone in Los Angeles inspired an extremely successful scam. County Supervisor Frank G. Bonelli exposed the "suede-shoe boys" peddling phony automobile smog control devices for two dollars less than state-approved models.

County supervisors unanimously adopted Bonelli's motion to alert state, city and county law enforcement agencies to apprehend the door-to-door salesmen of the dangerous, inferior and illegal devices.

Some of the devices had no bypass or safety valve. A flame, caused by a backfire sent to the oil pan, could trigger an explosion.

"Hundreds of San Gabriel Valley motorists may also have let themselves in for costly engine repairs by purchasing these cheap devices," Bonelli said.

In southern California, car dealers are a special, tangy breed. Inveterate sponsors of dreadful late-night movies on television, many delight in spieling their own commercials, even more dreadful.

In competing for the consumer's dollar in the nation's number one automobile market, the sell is hard, raucous and attention-getting. The air is splattered with cries of "liquidation sales," "end of the month sales," "beginning of the month sales," "consolidation loans," "get up off the couch and come on down," "our inventory must go," "name your own deal" and "we beat any other price." One dealer delivers his commercial with a German shepherd at his side and buyers are invited down to talk a deal over with the dog. Another salesman appears nightly in Superman costume. Others are content to stay with the time-honored sales subtleties of kicking tires, walloping hoods, slamming doors and pounding fenders.

Despite their self-created Barnum image and circus sales techniques, southern California car dealers are enormously sensitive to criticism. They hunger for respectability. Says one: "I don't like to have people snicker when I say I'm an automobile dealer."

In 1965, New York advertising executive David Oglivy told the National Automobile Dealers Association convention in Las Vegas that car dealers ranked at the bottom of an "honesty poll" of

American businessmen (undertakers and plumbers rated higher in public confidence!). Oglivy shorted the dealers particularly on bargain-basement advertising and poor service.

Reacting painfully, a spokesman for the dealers in southern California said, "Only 3, 4 or maybe 5 per cent do business that way." A bulletin issued by the dealers' association added: ". . . It is essential that we face up to the hard, bitter facts. Not all dealers are without sins as Mr. Oglivy charges. This then should be of prime concern to those who are willing to join in a crusade for total ethics in this wonderful business."

The subject of "total ethics in this wonderful business" also concerned Better Business Bureau official Carl D. Dalke, who urged local dealers not to publish or broadcast advertising that is dishonest, immoral or misleading.

He pinpointed three basic types of dealer delinquents: the con man . . . "the outright fraud who crops up in any industry"; the fringe operator . . . "the dealer who plays as close to the line as he can, using a fast pencil and fast talk, regularly and systematically going from one 'gimmick' to the next"; the honest dealer . . . "who occasionally makes an error or seeks to meet the 'gimmick operator's' methods by fighting fire with fire.

"It is not enough to proclaim that the vast and overwhelming majority of dealers are honest," Dalke concluded. "It is necessary to correct incidences of abuses and [regain] public confidence."

Scared down to their hubcaps that the state will pass tougher laws to regulate them, southern California dealers are backing a legislative bill that would allow them to police themselves.

But judging by past performance, the public is not entitled to a sanguine view of the dealers' self-limiting restraint.

In 1962, the Los Angeles Better Business Bureau counted 4728 man-in-the-street complaints or inquiries concerning sales of new and used cars and auto repairs. How many customers failed to complain or inquire about their treatment by the auto men is anyone's guess. The following year, the BBB prepared a special automotive report covering the first nine months of 1963. It found the number of complaints and skittish customers on the increase. A total of 5106 automobile purchasers and prospects had contacted the BBB—3424 for information about the reliability of individual dealers, 1173 to report unsatisfactory dealings with auto salesmen and 509 to inquire about the validity of various claims and practices by dealers.

While most of the 3424 inquirers were assured dealers they planned to do business with were ethical, many were warned against lots that had refused to change such practices as "bushing," "packing," "bait and switch" advertising, flamboyant oral claims made in connection with cars sold "as is" and failure to honor warranties and other service guarantees. It was the same story in 1965: complaints to the BBB against auto dealers led all other categories.

"Bushing" a customer begins with a salesman offering a much higher than usual trade-in allowance on a new or late-model car, knowing the deal will later be turned down by the manager. But the first offer is so attractive it detains the mark and prevents him from looking elsewhere. He is gradually "persuaded" to turn in his trade at a lower price.

One form of "packing" is for the dealer to raise the selling price of a car in order to offer a higher trade-in allowance or a fictitious discount if no trade is involved. Another is for the dealer to inflate the finance charges and obtain a rebate from the finance company.

The bait and switch scam was worked by one Los Angeles dealer by advertising a new car for "cash"—at a lower than wholesale price. His ad appeared on television on a Friday night before Labor Day—a time when the banks would be closed for three days. A customer who came to the lot to buy the car found it had been smeared with grease and dirt to discourage the sale. He still wanted it and offered his check. The dealer refused on the basis that the ad said "cash." The customer offered to leave both the check and the car in the dealer's hands until the check had cleared—but he still couldn't buy it. The dealer insisted his interpretation of "cash" was greenbacks, that a check was not acceptable. Strange to report, however, the dealer would accept a check for any other car on his lot.

Another variation on the bait and switch was worked by a sports car dealer who advertised an enticing price on a popular car. Potential customers discovered the advertised car was for sale—but without front seats. Adding $350 for the seats brought the price above that of competitive dealers. The dealer had run his lure ad to get people down to the lot, then tried to sell them another full-priced model. This same outfit also advertised itself as the largest agency in Los Angeles handling that particular make of car, basing its claim not on volume but on the area of its lot.

One dealer outfoxed himself in the sale of an "as is" used car for $125. A trial court jury awarded the buyer $35,000 for personal injuries suffered in an accident caused by faulty brakes. The appeals court sustained the award, holding that the dealer was obligated to make a reasonable inspection of the brake system before selling the car.

After a blizzard of offers to "consolidate outstanding bills" with the financing of a car, the practice was curtailed by forcing the auto dealers who used the gimmick to obtain licenses as personal property brokers.

Several Los Angeles dealers were prosecuted and lost their franchises for using referral plans, a scheme overwhelmingly weighted against anyone naïve enough to try for a "free automobile." The idea is to induce thirty-two friends to buy a new car. For each friend who buys, a credit of $100 is allowed toward the free car. In one case, a jury ruled the scheme was actually a lottery after a prosecutor pointed out that a successful referral plan could make a dealer a multimillionaire. Assuming that thirty-two purchasers each referred thirty-two other purchasers, who also referred thirty-two additional purchasers, 32,768 individuals would be involved. If each paid $3200 for a car, sales would total in excess of $100,000,000.

Says the BBB: "Referral selling is not wrong, per se, but readily lends itself to deceptive selling and it is almost impossible for an honest dealer to prevent abuses by his salesmen."

Dealers have discovered they need protection from their salesmen in other areas. The point was forcefully brought home in 1965 when police, acting on information supplied by dealers, all but emptied a room at a downtown meeting of Cadillac salesmen. Armed with complaints on six hundred misdemeanor counts, they arrested fifty-seven salesmen.

According to evidence amassed by investigators for the Department of Motor Vehicles, the salesmen had bypassed the 4 per cent sales tax on ownership transfers involving trade-ins. The

salesmen accepted the cars as trade-ins, resold them independently for a profit, then turned the amount of the trade-in over to
the dealer as part of a "cash transaction." Registration slip transfers appeared as direct sales from original owners to buyers with
no intermediaries listed. State law does not require sales tax on a
private sale of a car if no more than one a year is sold, but does
tax resale of an automobile by an intermediary buyer.

One dealer in Hollywood, a former movie producer and director, had a scam going that sent forlorn car buyers all the way
to West Germany, England and France before they realized they
had been swindled. Buyers paid from $2500 to $5700 for cars, but
when they arrived at the European factories they were told that
no money had been advanced from America. The scheme had
brought the dealer in Hollywood over $50,000.

With flags flying and banners waving, the Horatio Alger of
car dealers hit the southern California auto bazaar in the 1950s
with awesome impact. He built a gigantic empire, but, according
to the district attorney, he did it by ignoring most of Horatio's
rules. H. J. (Hank) Caruso became the second largest Dodge-
Plymouth dealer on earth, second only to a multiple dealer in
New York who sold primarily to a taxi company.

With $2000 he had saved in the service, Caruso, a tall, likable,
wavy-haired, bushy-eyebrowed ex-G.I. with wide-set eyes and
smile, bought a half-ownership in a used car agency, then moved
up to a Hudson dealership. From there he went to Dodge-
Plymouth. In only three years, he had broken almost all sales
records for the manufacturer.

The mayor and city manager were on hand for the traditional
hoopla when Caruso opened a new showroom and service center
in Compton. Also on hand was the Dodge director of marketing
who had come out from Detroit for the event. "If energy, drive
and sound experience are the fundamentals of success in our
business," he said, "Hank Caruso has a great future with Dodge
because he has these assets in bountiful quantity."

Soon much of southern California was rolling on wheels sold by
the whiz-bang wunderkind. Nearly ten thousand families bought
from Caruso each year, more than eight hundred sales a month
in the world's most competitive automobile market. His sales

figures were at least thirty times what the average dealer sold.

"On good days," said a newspaper personality sketch of the dealer-titan, "business is so heavy that his biggest headache is the paper work involved."

"Caruso's success," the story continued, "stems from a natural business talent and a belief in the power of advertising. Since his first day as a dealer, he has invested at least one-third of his business costs in advertising.

"'He's the Greatest' is a slogan people recognize throughout the Southland. His face is a familiar sight to thousands of TV viewers, his advertising and sales policy stress one thing: savings!

"At thirty-three, Caruso says America still provides opportunity for success, and his own story should be an inspiration to all young men because he has proven it!"

A few years later, Caruso was in jail, barred by court order from selling another automobile for ten years.

"The Greatest" had somehow stumbled badly along the way.

But while he rode high, life was beautiful. He married a pretty Chicago girl at flower-bedecked Blessed Sacrament Church, the ceremony performed by his brother, Father Lawrence Caruso.

He lived in a $100,000 swimming pool estate in the Hollywood Hills, and had all the impeccable, costly status symbols of a millionaire. Money was so plentiful in the Caruso household that a piggy bank, strewn randomly in one room of the house, held $400.

His empire peaked to four agencies—in Compton, North Hollywood, Long Beach and Pasadena. One wag said, "If all the cars that Caruso has sold somehow disappeared, the smog, freeway snarls and the parking problem would vanish from southern California."

All of this had come on the wings of a $2000 grubstake and a story that "should be an inspiration to all young men."

In 1953, with business running at full throttle, the first puffs of black began to form in Caruso's cloudless sky. A letter of complaint drifted into the district attorney's office. "Mr. Caruso has not only built a bad reputation for himself but also for Chrysler products which he sells," it said. "If you were to make an investigation you would find many unhappy customers. No one I have spoken to has a good word for Mr. Caruso, they all seem to have come out on the short end of the deal."

Though it was perfectly understandable that some buyers were bound to be displeased, other complaints, many unique even for the razzle-dazzle car business, began piling up.

On the evening of October 23, 1953, two officers from the Compton Police Department were dispatched to the Caruso emporium to answer a call from one of his salesmen that a customer was causing a disturbance. The salesman asked the officers to get rid of a man sitting in a 1951 Plymouth station wagon in front of the lot. As the officers moved toward the car, they observed a neat, hand-lettered sign held in place by gummed tape on the windshield. It stated briefly and directly:

THIS IS ONE OF THE LEMONS SOLD BY H. J. CARUSO

The officers listened to the man's story. The car he was sitting in was purchased from Caruso. Part of the agreement was that it would be put in first-class condition. But the work never seemed to get accomplished though he brought the car back on five separate occasions for the promised repairs. On his last visit, a Caruso salesman had given him the option of leaving the lot or "beating the hell out of him."

The officers informed the Caruso representative that since the man's car was not in motion he had a legal right to remain where he was, sign or no sign.

The Reverend Albert B. Pierce had a more harrowing experience with Caruso. He traded in his 1946 Ford for $450 on a 1951 Plymouth, which was to cost him $1250. As part of the arrangements, the minister gave Caruso $200 to pay off a loan on his old car but discovered later that the payment had not been made to the holder of the note. The minister was forced to pay the balance again to the Kern County School District Credit Union.

Moreover, Rev. Albert Pierce's complaints to Caruso that the Plymouth wasn't functioning properly were ignored. When he asked for his old car back he was told Caruso had "sold it for fifty dollars for junk." However, the minister was later notified by a lawyer that the Ford, still registered to him, had been involved in an accident in New Mexico and that he would have to pay for the damage.

While still trying to get the Plymouth in good working order, the minister received a call from Caruso.

"Where are you preaching? I want to come and hear you," Caruso said.

The following Sunday, after his sermon, the minister discovered that the Plymouth was missing from the church parking lot. Police found it at one of Caruso's establishments.

An elderly couple filed a grand theft charge against Caruso, claiming he had misrepresented the amount he was willing to pay for their Chevrolet as a trade-in on the new 1954 Dodge they had purchased. Caruso, they said, had personally offered $1900 on the trade-in, but when they received their contract they discovered a credit of only $1566.37, a disparity of $333.63.

About seven months after the "lemon" incident, Compton officers were again summoned to the Caruso lot. Another dissatisfied customer was acting up. A short blond man of about twenty-seven had been in an argument with Caruso about the car he had purchased a few days earlier. As the argument grew more heated, the angry man called Caruso a few unflattering names and finally took out a knife "to clean his nails." No violence occurred, but Caruso filed a complaint against the overwrought customer.

In July, 1954, a customer who admitted to a Caruso salesman in Pasadena that he was barely literate signed a blank contract for the purchase of a car. The deal was $150 for his trade-in on a newer car costing $1050. When his wife later read the terms of the contract to him he was dismayed to learn it called for payments on a car priced at $1300. He called the Caruso salesman and was told he had to come up with an additional $250. He managed to raise the money—by borrowing on his furniture.

A crippled tailor was another who signed a blank contract and discovered it varied considerably with the oral promises made to him on the lot. When he came back and complained that his trade-in price had been downed and the price of the new car upped, he was thrown off the lot by a pair of Caruso's salesmen.

The Bureau of Investigation began looking into Caruso's operation. They turned up sixty dissatisfied customers who were willing to tell their stories in court. The district attorney prepared to file charges of conspiracy and multiple counts of grand theft. But word of the move reached Caruso. Shortly, some fancy legal talent turned up at the D.A.'s office. Caruso's lawyers said their client was willing to make restitution to any of the complaining witnesses who felt they had been defrauded or unjustly treated.

The district attorney agreed. Caruso was brought in a few days later and sternly warned that the settlements would have to be fair and just to all concerned and unless he changed his selling methods the case would be reopened.

Caruso contacted the complaining witnesses, paid their claims, and sent in signed statements from the victims that satisfactory settlements had been made.

The case was marked closed. But a laconic note was added to Caruso's file by an investigator: "He will probably be back again shortly."

And so he was. In addition to more complaints of ballooned and altered contracts from customers, a woman who had been employed as a salesman by Caruso turned up at the D.A.'s office with an amazing account of how the engine entrepreneur had sold many of his cars.

A unique "school for salesmen" had been established and presided over by Caruso, and the detailed curriculum had made a science of selling. "The Greatest" left nothing to chance.

Mrs. John C. Callahan, of Harbor City, California, said the lessons covered every contingency from the moment a customer walked in.

The first step was to get the customer to turn over the key to his old car. The key then was transferred to an appraiser while the floor salesman showed the customer new models. (Some customers later complained that even when they managed to regain possession of their own cars, the tires or battery, or both, had been changed.)

Once the customer indicated interest in a car he was hustled as quickly as possible into a salesroom. The salesman immediately began jotting figures down on a contract.

"Under no circumstances was a customer allowed to have a pencil or paper," said Mrs. Callahan. "If he attempted to follow the negotiations with his own pencil, the salesman was instructed to purposely break the point of his pencil and ask to borrow the purchaser's. That way the prospective buyer never knew exactly where he stood.

"When we were through with the contract, nine out of ten people had signed before they actually read it. It is surprising how many will sign without reading it through."

Other instruction emphasized the importance of confusing buyers by throwing figures at them in lightning succession. Salesmen were told to push the highest-priced extras and a copy of the contract was not to be given to the customer. The contract was to be mailed so the "shock comes later."

Those little old salesrooms were man-traps in more ways than one.

"Mr. Caruso's office was upstairs and it was wired to all the [sales] rooms and if he wasn't there one of his salesmen was there. They heard everything you did," said Mrs. Callahan. "If you had a customer in there and they thought you were not doing just right they would knock on the door and say you were wanted on the phone and another salesman would take over, then if that salesman wasn't selling another salesman would come in and then finally Mr. Caruso himself came in."

A former secretary at Caruso's Compton lot was also questioned, and she told how she was instructed to erase the pencil figures on the signed purchase orders and type in new altered figures.

The evidence went to a grand jury and Caruso and a fleet of his salesmen were indicted on one count of conspiracy and eighteen counts of theft and forgery. When the news hit the papers, all hell broke loose. In three hours, Deputy District Attorney Herman Arterberry tallied thirty new telephone complaints from others who had dealt with Caruso. In all, some six hundred complaints piled up.

Out of this welter of customer dissatisfaction, a second case was presented to the grand jury. That resulted in twenty-five new counts against Caruso, a total of forty-four felony charges.

In a half-page newspaper ad, Caruso, somewhat emotionally, declared his innocence: "I have been deeply touched by the warm expressions of support and confidence we have received in the past few days. . . . From my family, and from each of the 700 families in my company . . . our heartfelt thanks. God bless you all. I want you to know that I hold no bitterness toward those few who have been sought out to breed grievances against us. . . . But now this attack has grown out of all proportion. . . . In fact, might not this same attack happen to any company which attempts to save folks money through volume selling? . . . With your help, we shall continue to serve the people of Southern California—*honestly* and *fairly*."

But Caruso was out of gas. On the eve of going to trial, he pled guilty to four counts. He was sentenced to a year in county jail and fined $10,000. Seven of his salesmen were also fined and given lesser sentences.

As Caruso began his jail term, his house was robbed of $18,000 worth of furs and jewelry. Also taken was that piggy bank with the $400. The police never determined if it was a professional job or revenge from a dissatisfied Caruso customer.

Several salutary things came out of the Caruso case. The state enacted a law requiring the price of an automobile to be displayed on the windows of new cars and salesmen were required to be licensed.

"The case also brought to the attention of the buying public," says Bureau Investigator Donald L. Lundquist, "what they are up against when they go out to buy an automobile. It proved that the chances of outwitting a salesman whose livelihood depends on selling automobiles are pretty slim."

Caruso at least had operated in the guise of a respectable businessman, but several years later an unlikely gang of grifters whipsawed through a fast, fancy fleece game that was, from the moment of its inception, pure confidence—an ambitious $3,000,000 blitz con.

A couple of the boys were standing around the exercise yard of the California Men's Colony at Los Padres, neutralizing their prison pallors in the warm sunshine of a summer afternoon in 1962.

Smooth-tongued Murry Thomas Evans, a slim, handsome convicted auto swindler, turned to his famous cellmate—now forty-eight, a little shabby around the edges, but still an underworld aristocrat whose past achievements ranked him in the top echelon of prison society.

"Harry," said Evans, his eyes dancing with malice, "we're both getting out soon. How'd you like to spend the next couple of years in South America, living like a fat-rumped millionaire?"

"Who wouldn't?" Harry answered, only half-listening. As a seasoned con and former big-time operator, he had a righteous contempt for the small-time grifters who brought him their shop-worn little scams.

"I got the angle," Evans declared.

Harry's round, chubby face wore a weary look. "So did all the losers in this joint—this time I'd as soon check out for good."

"A three-million-dollar angle!" the Louisiana-born Evans added in the honeyed drawl that women had always found irresistible. "And it won't take but thirty, no more than forty days, to make the score."

Harry's skepticism gave way momentarily to natural curiosity. "How?" he challenged.

"In the used car business."

"That cuts it," Harry said indignantly, straightening himself up to his full five feet four. "Used cars! I ain't a crook. I'm an honest bookmaker!"

At least half of that last statement was true. The speaker was Harry Gross, the ex-kingpin New York bookie who was convicted in 1951 of running a police-protected $20,000,000-a-year betting empire. The stench from his nationally headlined trial had fouled the city's civic air and helped send Mayor William O'Dwyer into political oblivion.

Harry had served four years on the bookmaking rap. After his release, he drifted to Los Angeles. But things hadn't gone well. He was broke and doing his stretch in the Los Padres pokey on a voluntary manslaughter charge for the fatal shooting of his wife's grandfather.

In Evans' eyes, however, Harry Gross still had glamour and class—and something more important. He had a reputation for paying off his debts and could be trusted to handle the kind of money his scheme involved. Evans had also guessed—correctly— that Gross, despite giving lip service to going straight, would be looking for action as soon as he got out.

Back in their cell, Evans kept after Gross. It wasn't that a slice of $3,000,000 didn't appeal to Harry—he just didn't believe it was possible to rake in that much loot so quickly without storming Ft. Knox in a Sherman tank.

"Besides," said Gross, trying to shake off his persistent cellmate, "I don't know nothin' about the car business."

"Leave that part to me," Evans replied. "I was raised on black-eyed peas and the automobile Blue Book."

Harry was still skeptical. "Even if I did go along, I don't see that kind of money in a bunch of old junkers."

"I'm talking about late-model used automobiles, top of the line . . . Cadillacs, Lincolns, Thunderbirds."

Evans modestly informed Harry that he was the originator and sole practitioner of the scheme. He might have added with complete accuracy that the dodge added up to the most inventive wrinkle to hit the automobile business since Henry Ford put the assembly line together. Evans claimed that a few years before he'd made $350,000 working the scam, but his wife had forced him to give all the money back. Now he was ready to try it again and this time enjoy the profits with a perfumed stable of dark-eyed *señoritas* in luxurious exile.

As Evans laid out the plan in minute detail, Harry's eyes grew bigger and bigger, wider and wider. His respect for Evans also began to grow. At least he thought big. And Harry liked the sound of his mathematics.

"I figure we work twelve hours a day, seven days a week for a month to six weeks," Evans said matter-of-factly. "We can grab at least twenty to thirty cars a day at a profit of three to four thousand dollars on each car. That means a daily take of sixty to one hundred twenty thousand dollars. Then when things get hot, we skip."

In their remaining time in prison, Evans and Gross whiled the hours away going over the plan. They refined and honed it, tore it apart and put it back together again, making sure each piece of the mosaic fit snugly into place. They rehearsed it ceaselessly— Harry playing the mark, Evans staying in character as the bunk man. Though Harry endlessly probed for weak spots in their carefully thought-out strategy, he couldn't find any. He was finally convinced and agreed to the partnership on the outside.

It was a fateful agreement. Starting from scratch, Evans and Gross were about to build a complex, intricate blitz of an operation that was as carefully calculated for a quick killing as a German Panzer attack. It would have its moments of comic opera, its improvised touches straight out of the Lavender Hill Mob, and a colorful cast of six shifty, mutually mistrustful Damon Runyonesque characters all trying to con one another as well as the public at large. But for all of that, it was the smoothest, most flawless con game this side of Yellow Kid Weil. And it succeeded, despite some unanticipated handicaps, in bilking a small army of prosperous southern Californians out of the gleaming, high-priced status symbols that filled their garages. Some of the autos they hustled still had that beautiful new-car smell; some were so new, in fact, that the ash trays weren't yet dirty.

The grand strategy began in earnest as soon as the boys were released. Evans was freed October 1, 1962. Gross got out two weeks later.

To keep up appearances for their parole officer, they both got legitimate jobs as salesmen with a car-leasing firm and Gross moved into Evans' expensive two-bedroom apartment on Hollywood's flashy Sunset Strip.

As with many other would-be tycoons with a multimillion-dollar idea, Evans and Gross needed capital to get them rolling. They also needed a distributor to handle their merchandise. Evans decided to approach an old friend in the used car business, a shrewd, barrel-chested, rough-featured forty-two-year-old car dealer named Val Culwell who ran two lots, United Motors in El Monte, California, and Motorland in Phoenix, Arizona.

There was still a bit of bad blood over a debt that Evans owed Culwell, but the presence of Harry Gross impressed the car dealer.

"I know all about you," said Culwell admiringly to Gross as the trio met in an El Monte bar.

Harry smiled modestly.

Evans sketched the plan to Culwell. "Would you be interested in taking the cars?"

Culwell considered for a moment. "Well, how many do you think you can get?"

"At the start, twenty to twenty-five, up to thirty or forty a day."

"I guess so," Culwell said. "What's the deal?"

"How about two hundred dollars below Blue Book? If the car wholesales for three thousand, you've got it for twenty-eight."

"That's fair enough," Culwell agreed.

"Will you take everything we give you?"

"Yeah."

"Will you have cash every day?"

"I'll have the cash every day, or as near to it as I can," said Culwell. "What do you fellows intend to do when this is all over?"

Evans mentioned South America. "We'll cool it down there for a couple of years until the beef blows over."

"That's all right with me," said Culwell thoughtfully. "But I want to cover myself. I'll tell you what I will do. I'll get you fellows to sign some receipts for the cars I take off your hands. A week after you're gone, I'll run down to the district attorney and scream and holler that I was robbed."

"We don't care what you do after we leave," Evans said agreeably.

"Okay," said Culwell, "you get it off the ground and call me. I'll take the cars."

That took care of distribution. But they still needed capital. They were considering the possibilities the next day over lunch at the Thunderbird Motel across the street from their apartment when destiny suddenly beckoned. Evans heard his name called in a familiar voice from a back booth. He turned, a look of delighted surprise on his face. "Friend of mine," he told Gross, "a rich friend. Let's go and meet him."

The friend was Thompson Ellsworth Elwell, a tall, thin twenty-eight-year-old sharpie with a receding forehead and a degree in business administration from the University of Southern California. In his undergraduate days, Elwell had worked with Evans for a time on a car lot.

After the introductions, Evans told Elwell that he and Harry were now in the car-leasing business.

"I'm a building contractor and could use a car for one of my salesmen," said Elwell. "Give me your number and I'll call you."

"Can't we call you?" Gross asked.

"No, my phone isn't in yet," Elwell explained.

Harry, recalling his days as a bookie, was very sensitive to the utility of a telephone. "How come," he wondered idly, "you ain't got a phone?"

"To tell the truth," Elwell said with a crooked grin, "I owe a couple thousand on the bill and I haven't gotten around to writing a check."

After Elwell left, Evans told Gross, "This kid's a millionaire."

"If he's a millionaire, why don't he pay his phone bill?"

"He's a very eccentric kid, but he's all right."

Elwell's eccentricity was confirmed in Harry's mind the next day when he and Evans visited his home, a plush $150,000 mansion in ultraexclusive Trousdale Estates in Beverly Hills.

Gross, as he looked around the spacious home, was flabbergasted. It was almost barren. In the living room, there was nothing but a couch and one log in the fireplace.

Evans whispered to Gross: "I told you this kid is eccentric—don't mind this."

Waiting with Elwell was Robert (Duke) Hall, thirty-two and dark-haired, a fashion plate addicted to $300 tailor-made sharkskin suits. He and Elwell were friends and business associates.

"What'll it be to drink?" Elwell asked hospitably. The boys ordered and Elwell went to the pantry. He came back in a moment with a sheepish grin on his face. "Sorry, somebody drank everything up. How about coffee?"

The boys nodded.

Elwell went out again and came back almost immediately. "Looks like we're out of coffee, too."

"Gee, Murry," Gross asked in a quick aside, "you sure this guy has money?"

"Pay no attention," Evans said reassuringly. "He's always been this way."

They closed the deal to lease Bob Hall a car. Evans then decided to broach Elwell and Hall with the scheme. He ran it down for both of them.

"I don't think it'll work," said Elwell.

Hall was doubtful, too. "There can't be that many cars free and clear that you claim you can get."

"I'll tell you what I will do," Evans said. "I'll bet you fifty dollars that it checks out."

"I won't bet," Hall answered, "but Tom and I will check it out."

A couple of days later, they met again. Hall was now bursting with enthusiasm. "We got like ten dollars' worth of dimes for the public telephones. Tom used one phone and I called on the other.

We checked and qualified these people and you are right. We can get all the cars we want."

"How much front money do you need?" Elwell asked.

"About forty thousand dollars," Gross said.

"You've got it," Elwell assured them with a careless wave of his hand. "Go ahead and look around and get the lot and then come back and I'll give you the money. By the way, how are we going to divide the profits?"

Evans and Gross said they each wanted one third. The other third could be split between Elwell and Hall.

Elwell objected to splitting a share when Gross and Evans were each getting a full share.

"You gotta understand," said Harry, "we're going to take the heat. We're going to take the whole beef. All you're doing is putting up the money."

Elwell decided to go along. But, to protect his interests, he insisted on having Hall around when the business got going. Evans and Gross agreed that Hall could be useful as a telephone pitchman and they threw in an extra $100 bonus for each customer he brought in.

With financing in sight, Evans and Gross cruised around looking for a location. They found exactly what they needed on Culver City's Washington Boulevard, across the street from MGM Studios. Soon the performances of the hardy little band of con men would provide more drama than anything the directors were putting on celluloid inside the neighboring movie factory.

The lot was abandoned, but the landlord refused to rent it to them since the prior occupant's lease still had some time to run. But the deal was closed when Evans offered $1000 a month in rent, $400 over the asking price. The only condition, to which the landlord agreed, was that the existing signs on the lot be thrown into the deal.

"I don't understand, Murry," said Harry. "What do you want with the signs?"

"Geez, look at those signs. It's a shame to waste them. We can save a few thousand dollars."

Harry looked, still uncomprehending. There were signs all right—big attention-getters, but they all read: CRENSHAW CADILLACS.

"I got it!" said Evans, explaining his sudden brainstorm with the logic of a cost-cutting expert. "We'll drop the CREN and paint in TOM. You will be Tom Shaw and I will be John Shannon."

"It sounds like a vaudeville act," said Harry.

"It's perfect," said Evans.

Harry Gross was thus christened Tom Shaw. Evans' pseudonym came from a television hero he admired.

They now reported their progress to Elwell and Hall. A meeting was arranged for the next day. Elwell promised he'd have the first $2000 in front money.

The four tycoons met at a chrome and plastic coffee joint on the Strip. There was an immediate disagreement about which bank they should use. Elwell and Hall favored a handsome, recently built institution on Sunset Boulevard, but Evans preferred a bank closer to the business.

Gross stepped in as mediator. He told Evans, "He just wants the account in his bank so he can check on us."

"Okay, what's the difference?" said Evans. "Go ahead and open up at that bank."

Elwell gave Hall a roll of bills. "You better go with them, Bob, and make sure they deposit the money."

But Harry insisted they first count the capital. Hall handed the roll over and Harry counted. When he was finished, Harry angrily pounded his stubby fist on the table. "There must be a mistake! You were supposed to give us two thousand dollars. There's only fourteen hundred here. I can't open a Cadillac agency with fourteen hundred. That is a fine agency. What are people going to think?"

Elwell said that was all he could raise at the moment. But he'd come up with the balance of the $40,000 he had promised in a day or two.

Momentarily mollified, Gross, with Evans and Hall flying along at his heels, went to the bank and opened the account under the name of Tom Shaw Cadillacs.

With the advance from Elwell, Gross and Evans paid the first month's rent, got a couple of telephones, went to a legal printer for contracts, stationery and business cards. They bought a check-writing machine and had the lights turned on at the lot. They also ordered the signs repainted.

Evans called Culwell, reaching him in Phoenix. "We are ready to go," he reported.

"Fine," the car dealer said, "let me know the minute you have the cars and I will be there to pick them up and I will have the money."

It was early November, less than a month since Evans and Gross had been paroled. Practically everything was set now except the balance of the front money.

But Elwell was still having trouble fulfilling his obligations as financial angel of the plot. At their next meeting, he whipped out a roll and announced, "Five grand. It's all I could raise."

Gross, who from the first hadn't been enthusiastic about Elwell, was plainly disappointed. "You should have told us in the beginning you didn't have the cash."

"We can get it off the ground, don't worry," Elwell said.

"Well, Murry, what do you think?" Harry said doubtfully.

While Evans thought, Elwell explained he had barely managed to scrape the $5000 together by getting a loan on a piece of property. The fact that he didn't own the piece of property he had mortgaged had him worried. "I can go to jail. I'm breaking the law doing this. But it's all I could get."

"Geez," said Murry, "the first deals should be legit. We need a little time to get momentum. Another twenty, thirty grand would give us a shot at an extra million at the other end."

Elwell said it was impossible for him to raise another quarter.

"It will be a little close working with just five thousand dollars," said Murry, "but we will do the best we can."

Elwell turned to Hall and handed him the roll. "Bob, I still don't trust these fellows. Get in the car and go down to the bank and make the deposit with them."

The trio trooped to the bank and solemnly deposited the $5000.

For the scope of the operation Evans and Gross had planned, the total of $6400 in capital from Elwell was a shoestring. Running that into $3,000,000 in the allotted time was going to take all the ingenuity they had.

Undaunted, they went to work on the final trimmings. The lot had to look impressive. To dress it up, Evans leased six new cars, Caddies, T-Birds and a Continental. Two boys were hired to keep the leased cars spit-polish clean. Missing no detail, Evans got them white uniforms with the legend "Tom Shaw Cadillacs" emblazoned in front. Three girls were also hired, an office manager, a bookkeeper and a secretary. Those five salaries alone were an expense of over $600 a week.

All the preliminaries were now out of the way and the forty eventful days that were to shake the high-priced used car market in Los Angeles began officially on November 9.

The three girls were put to scanning the used car ads in the classified section of the high circulation Los Angeles *Times*. They underlined every ad in red pencil that offered an expensive car no more than two years old. Then they transferred the owner's name, phone number, make and year of the car to 3 by 5 cards and gave them to Hall.

But Hall soon felt he was being overworked. "I am bringing in a friend and I'll run down the pitch to him," he told Gross and Evans.

On Hall's word, they accepted a new confederate, tall, wavy-haired, thirty-year-old Larry Mathes. He came in as a phone pitchman, and, like Hall, he was to receive a commission of $100 for each customer he snagged. He also had a private arrangement with Hall for one half of his one-third split with Elwell of the total profits.

Both Hall and Mathes insisted, to alibi themselves, that Gross sign their commissions over to them as payroll checks. For a time Harry went along, but then changed his mind. "I am getting writer's cramp signing all these checks," he said grandly. "Besides, it's lousing up the bookkeeping."

Despite the bickering, infighting and crosscurrents of motives among the boys, the operation now settled down for the common purpose of fleecing all the suckers that could be dragged onto the seemingly solvent Tom Shaw lot.

One of the first victims was Owen R. Carter, a wealthy official of a toy factory in Los Angeles. Carter's experience was typical of the way every other victim was taken.

On November 11, he received a telephone call from Hall at his office. The conversation went like this:

"Mr. Carter, I see you have a '61 Cadillac Sedan de Ville for sale. Can you tell me the color?"

"Red."

"That's perfect. What color is the interior?"

"Yellow."

"That's perfect, too. Air conditioning?"

"Yes."

"Good. What price are you asking?"

"Six thousand dollars."

"That's not too far out of line."

Actually, it was about $1000 more than the car was worth, but Hall and Mathes had iron-bound instructions from Evans that they were never to negotiate price. Under no circumstances was there to be any quibbling over the amount the pigeon asked for his car. "Let them think they are putting it over on us," Evans had said with the instinctive grasp of psychology of the professional con man.

"Mr. Carter," Hall continued, "why don't you bring the car down? Maybe we can make a deal. I think I have a customer interested in your car."

An appointment was arranged. Since several other pigeons had by now been contacted in precisely the same way, each appointment was carefully staggered so that none of the marks would run into each other and have a chance to compare stories.

When Carter arrived with his Cadillac, he was met by Hall. "That is a beautiful car, sir," he purred. "I have a customer who is looking for exactly this model and color. I think I can sell it."

"Fine," said Carter, already hooked at the prospect of a quick deal at his asking price.

"If you can leave the car here for a few hours," said Hall, "I will call my customer and have him look it over."

"I can't do that," the executive replied. "I need a car for my business."

"We will be happy to give you a loaner—"

"Why can't I stay and meet the buyer?"

"It's not allowed," Hall explained. "The Motor Vehicle Department does not permit us to do this. We have a license, and sales tax is involved. We think we have it sold. It is the color we are looking for, and we want to satisfy the customer."

Mr. Carter was still hesitant. But Hall was ready for him. "I will sign a twenty-four-hour consignment slip for your car."

"Well, in that case, I guess it'll be all right."

Mr. Carter drove off in the loaner. His Cad was parked in a corner of the Tom Shaw lot where it remained—unviewed, uninspected and untouched by any prospective customer. In a few hours, Hall made the follow-up call.

"Mr. Carter, I sold your car at your price!"

"Happy to hear it."

"If you'll bring down your papers I think we can close the deal right away—this evening. Bring your pink slip and we will work it all out."

When Carter returned, Hall shuttled him into the office. Gross and Evans, now masquerading as Tom Shaw and John Shannon, were waiting—pearly shark's teeth agleam.

"Congratulations!" said Tom Shaw, pumping the hand of his obviously satisfied customer. "It was a little rough, but we got your price. This is Mr. Shannon, our sales manager."

Shannon, smiling pleasantly as he invited the mark to have a seat, rang the buzzer on his intercom. "Please bring in Mr. Carter's file," he told his secretary. In a moment, the girl appeared with a 9 by 11 folder.

"Now here's the deal," Shannon began smoothly. "The fellow who bought your car is an engineer working at Douglas Aircraft Corporation. He's just been transferred out here from Wichita, Kansas, and his home is in escrow. It will be tied up for thirty days."

Mr. Carter began to shift restlessly in his chair.

"He has given us a deposit on your car," Shannon continued, "and he wants to make this a one-payment deal at the end of the thirty days." Shannon removed a check, already signed, from the folder and passed it across the desk to Carter.

"This is Tom Shaw's personal check for one thousand dollars, good at this moment. You can cash it at the bank and we will give you a draft for the five-thousand-dollar balance payable in thirty days."

"Well, why can't you give me all the money now?" Carter wondered logically.

"Remember, sir, you are dealing with us—Tom Shaw Cadillacs, not with the man who bought your car," Shannon explained. "There is no money in this deal for us. You got top dollar for your car and the only reason I am interested in the deal is I hope to sell the engineer some insurance and convert him to a twenty-four-payment deal so we can make a little profit from the financing."

"I don't know. I've never sold a car this way before. . . ."

"If you like, call our bank or your attorney." If the sucker made the calls, the bank informed him accurately that there was a "four-figure" balance in the Tom Shaw account. His attorney would advise him that a postdated draft was a customary way of doing business.

"I'd still prefer to have the money now," Carter insisted.

"Well, if you want to forget about the whole thing—"

"No," said Carter quickly, now on the defensive. "But what guarantee do I have? Suppose my car is in an accident before the draft comes due?"

Shannon, the ever resourceful closer, had designed a clincher for precisely this moment in the negotiations.

"We have allowed for that," he said, pulling an official-looking document from the folder. "Here is a loss payment insurance policy which I will throw into the deal free. It protects the car until the draft becomes payable. So you have nothing to worry about."

Shannon handed the "insurance policy" to Carter, mythical coverage drawn on a company that had no existence outside the con man's fertile brain.

But to Carter it was the convincer. He signed his car over to Tom Shaw Cadillacs. He also signed a power of attorney, thus giving up forever any legal claim on his automobile.

The next morning Carter presented Tom Shaw's $1000 deposit check at his bank. It was good as gold.

But what Carter and all his fellow victims didn't know was that the postdated draft, the big check for the balance, would not be good. The heart of the scam was to scram before the promissory notes became due.

Shannon-Shaw *et al.* had bought Carter's year-old Cadillac for a mere $1000, all the money he would ever get for it. The rest of the value in the car would be divided among the crowd of con men under the agreed formula: at $200 under wholesale Blue Book, Culwell would get the Cad for $4300. Retailing it out he could expect a reasonable price of $5000, giving him a $700 profit.

The Evans-Gross-Elwell triumvirate (after subtracting the $1000 in front money, Hall's $100 commission plus the operation's overhead) would easily clear over $3000. If they could take in only twenty-five cars a day at this approximate figure for forty days, the $3,000,000 nut was assured.

Now that the cars were beginning to roll in, everything hinged on how fast they could be turned over. Evans called Culwell and told him to pick up the first half-dozen cars the swindle had thus far produced. Culwell arrived shortly with a half-dozen drivers who promptly wheeled the bargain chariots off.

Culwell gave Gross $6000 as an advance against the sale of the first six cars. "I'll bring the balance soon as I liquidate," he said.

"Six grand only covers the money for the front checks," Harry pointed out unhappily.

"Look, I have got to sell these cars. It's going to take a few days," Culwell countered. "But I'll keep you up to the balance you need at the bank to make good the deposit checks. I'll throw in a little extra for overhead."

Harry wasn't exactly overjoyed with this arrangement, but he was a businessman in the unenviable position of having only one outlet for his product.

In the next few days, the busy bunco artists on Washington Boulevard increased their inventory to sixteen cars. Culwell became a regular visitor to the lot, turning up with his drivers and hauling off the cars as soon as the deals were closed. But he kept insisting to Evans and Gross that he couldn't sell them as fast as they were taking them in.

Evans and Gross, however, kept the pressure on Culwell, who finally ponied up about $40,000 for the first twenty-two cars. But that barely allowed them to keep the business going. They had to deduct $22,000 in front money, commissions, salaries, etc., and still keep a modest balance at the bank.

The arithmetic wasn't adding up for anyone except Culwell. Under the original formula, he still owed the rest of the mob about $55,000, possibly more since he was selling some of the most expensive, prestigious cars in America.

In addition to the payments lag from Culwell, another problem developed unexpectedly when Harry, who had been growing more and more restless with the way things were going, gravely called a staff meeting of the motor Mafia.

"Boys," he declared, "I am leaving!"

"For God's sake, why?" Evans asked with genuine shock.

Harry explained that he had been seeing a young lady and that he was in love. He had told her what he was involved in and she was urging him to get out.

But Harry had even more compelling reasons for leaving and those reasons he kept to himself. He didn't understand the car business and felt uncomfortable in it. The operation had been disappointing from the beginning and he was disenchanted with his confederates. Elwell had unnecessarily handicapped their chances for success by coming through with so little front money. Hall and Mathes were annoying. Evans was a major disappointment. Harry realized, even if he hadn't fallen in love, that the trip to South America with Evans was out. His old pen pal by now had several apartments stocked with lady friends and he was spending money faster than it was coming in. Harry was especially fed up with Culwell, who still hadn't paid the $55,000. He was also astute enough to realize that Evans didn't really need him and that Evans and Culwell could easily double-cross him and make a deal behind his back.

Though the boys tried to change his mind, Harry had made his decision. He told them they could split his one-third of the future profits, all he wanted was out.

Gross and Evans went to the bank to close the Tom Shaw account. The bank had already requested, politely but firmly, that Mr. Shaw take his account elsewhere. There had been too many inquiries about postdated drafts and the bank was getting nervous.

Despite the fact that they had taken in twenty-two cars, representing at retail more than $100,000 in merchandise, there was only a cash balance of $12,000 to be divided. All the cream was still tied up at Culwell's end.

Gross, Evans, Elwell and Hall had another meeting at the Thunderbird to split the cash. Harry, scrupulously maintaining his reputation for honesty, gave Elwell his original $6400 plus $1000 in interest. Elwell claimed it was costing him that much to pay off the loan on the piece of property he didn't own. To Hall, who was under the gun to pay his ex-wife's alimony or go to jail, Harry gave $750. There was about $4000 left.

"Okay, take that for your end," Evans said, "and we get you out. Don't worry about nothing."

Gross moved out of Evans' apartment. As a last gesture to his old cellmate, he warned him that he didn't think Culwell was going to come across with the balance of the money he owed them.

Harry dropped from sight, but Evans, having decided to take his chances with Culwell, continued at the helm of the car cornucopia. The scam itself was humming along beautifully.

A couple who ran a nursery school in Downey were talked into leaving their Lincoln. A Beverly Hills doctor contributed a Jaguar. A young movie idol left his racy Porsche. And the wealthy, attractive wife of a Bel-Air attorney provided lady-killer Evans with a pleasant interlude. She fell head over heels in love with him and he spent three weekends with her, taking precious time away from the lot.

The smitten lady even offered to bankroll Evans in a business of his choice, but he refused and further tarnished the legend of Southern gallantry by swiping her Chrysler Imperial and adding it to the operation's car kitty.

Though the scam never approached the volume originally anticipated by Evans, it could have made millionaires of Evans and Gross if it had not foundered on the rocks of human weakness. Evans' amatory indulgences made him unavailable on three high-volume weekends. And Harry's prediction about Culwell's failure to pay off was proving all too accurate. Following Harry's departure, Evans, Hall and Mathes gulled thirteen more gullibles out of their expensive cars. These also went to Culwell—but the payments lag from his end continued. Evans had good reason to suspect a double-cross.

He therefore decided to squeeze as much from the scheme as possible, but now it was all ad lib. Instead of feeding the cars to Culwell, he began merchandising them helter-skelter around town. Over the next several weeks, he bagged another sixty-two of the toniest cars in southern California. But under his revised plan he peddled them way under wholesale to suburban car dealers or tossed them into the Los Angeles auto auction at desperation prices.

Finally, the time to pay the piper rolled around. It was December 11 and the first postdated drafts were falling due. Evans had opened an account at another bank and the drafts were bouncing like a chorus line at Las Vegas. Mr. Carter was only one of a stream of outraged customers who invaded the lot, demanding their money.

Gross's departure gave Evans a handy excuse to fend off his creditors. He suavely explained that Mr. Shaw had left the business short of funds. But the business was in the process of being refinanced and all of the drafts would be made good. Incredibly, Evans not only managed to sell this bag of hot air to the pigeons, but he also convinced them to accept new promissory notes which, he guaranteed, would be honored on December 19.

Eight more days were thus eked out, allowing Evans, Hall and Mathes, with Elwell still hovering in the background as a silent partner, to keep milking the operation. They took in another twenty-eight cars—which Evans also peddled at auction and to dealers in the Los Angeles area.

Finally, inevitably, December 19 loomed up. That was Evans' D day—D for departure. Telling no one, he vanished.

The forty-day blitz was all over except for the shouting. And there was plenty of that. Pandemonium broke out on the lot. Hall and Mathes were confronted with a frantic gaggle of customers, waving their unhonored bank drafts. They lamely explained that all the drafts would be made good, the sales manager would be down at any moment to straighten everything out. Meantime, the leasing company came and took back its cars. A few lucky customers found their autos still on the lot and drove them off.

The swindled suckers now did all their shouting to the authorities. An investigation was begun under the direction of Deputy District Attorney Richard W. Hecht. His task was helped along considerably when Harry Gross surrendered voluntarily and agreed to turn state's evidence.

Thin as their concocted alibis were, Culwell, Hall and Mathes chose to remain in Los Angeles and bluff it out. But Elwell, like Evans, decided to skip. He was rumored at first to be in Peru, then in Puerto Rico negotiating for a gambling ship. He was finally nailed in New York City. He waived extradition and was returned to California.

Evans was picked up in a bar in Shreveport, Louisiana, by the FBI, acting on an all-points bulletin issued by Hecht. He also was returned to Los Angeles after waiving extradition.

It took Hecht almost eighteen months to untangle the complex swindle and bring his case before the grand jury. He presented thirty-two witnesses and 172 exhibits in a masterful step-by-step reconstruction. His star witness was Harry Gross—who sang like a bird.

The grand jury returned a forty-one-count indictment against the five con men. All were charged with grand theft and Culwell alone had twelve counts of receiving stolen property filed against him.

In the face of the overwhelming evidence, all five pled *nolo contendere* in Superior Court. Evans drew one to ten. Elwell was sentenced to concurrent ninety-day and one-to-ten terms. Culwell was given five years' probation and fined $3000. Hall and Mathes each got five years' probation and individual fines of $1500.

The no-contest pleas removed the necessity for any of the boys to testify and give an accounting of the final proceeds from the scheme. Despite all the complications and the paltry $6400 in front money, the final audit was quite respectable. In all, 125 Californians lost their expensive cars in the swindle. Figuring each of their cars was worth an average of $5000 and deducting a total of $125,000 they received collectively in front checks, their over-all loss was still a stunning $500,000. Most of the marks protested in vain to their unsympathetic insurance companies. The majority of the claims for recovery were denied on grounds that the victims had voluntarily signed their cars away to the grifters.

The grifters themselves never came close to the anticipated score in their Jags-to-riches bunk. But Gross's testimony and Hecht's investigation showed that Culwell had received thirty-five cars from Evans, approximately $175,000 worth of merchandise at retail.

The ninety cars that Evans didn't deliver to Culwell would have brought him a profit of at least $3000 each, over $270,000 under the original ground rules. But his take was cut way down by dumping the cars at fire-sale prices, the unpaid debt from

Culwell and his spending on the ladies. According to Hecht's estimate, Evans had barely $30,000 when he left Los Angeles, hardly enough to enjoy a prolonged exile in South America. And when he was arrested, Evans didn't have a kopek.

Elwell denied profiting beyond the return of his original venture capital plus the $1000 in interest. Hall and Mathes had almost nothing to show for their trouble.

Only the honest bookmaker, Harry Gross, admitted a profit— the $4000 he made as he left the operation. This was a far cry from the $3,000,000 pot he and Evans had dreamed of. Harry wasn't prosecuted for his share in the scheme because he had told all to the State. But he ended up in San Quentin for another year as a parole violator.

10

Business

Bunco, Incorporated

One-third of the people in the United States promote,
while the other two-thirds provide.
— Will Rogers

"I've got three hundred forty-seven million dollars available in
Eastern money," Frank T. Murrell cooed convincingly into the
phone. The silver-thatched, forty-seven-year-old money man was
talking to the vice-president of a large drugstore chain from the
headquarters of the Cornucopia Finance Company, located in a
plush office building near Hollywood Boulevard.

Murrell explained that the financial power he represented
would provide the executive's firm virtually unlimited credit—up
to several hundred thousand dollars for purchase of merchandise
from wholesalers.

And when Murrell added that he would charge only 2 per cent
interest on his loan money and required a mere $2000 deposit to
run a credit check on the firm, the vice-president found the offer
too attractive to turn down.

Murrell, who had been in Los Angeles only two weeks, had
phoned a long list of other executives and offered the same heady
terms. He had also hired four of the best legitimate credit salesmen in the city to hustle up additional "unlimited credit" business.

Away from the office, Murrell, his twenty-three-year-old wife
and young son, were sampling the accommodations at the best
Los Angeles hotels, including the Ambassador and the Biltmore.
Only when one of his salesmen became suspicious and reported

Murrell to the Los Angeles Police Department's Bunco Squad did the good life fall apart.

Murrell's *m.o.* and description matched a bulletin received a few weeks earlier from Lakewood, Ohio. One William Dixon had taken twenty-five businessmen for $2000 each in an identical scheme—luring victims with low interest loans and then scramming with the credit check fees.

The suspicious salesman set up a meeting with Murrell and the bunco squad men at a bar. Dixon and Murrell were one and the same. He was an ex-convict with a record stretching back to 1937.

His scheme was so beautifully laid out that it had not only proved irresistible to Murrell's victims, but won the admiration of the bunco officers. "If he could have put it over and extended the credit, he'd have been dealing in millions every month," one officer said. "Actually, if he had had the backing he could have made it—and collected a fortune."

Murrell, carrying a cashmere topcoat, was booked at the jailhouse. And when the high-rolling financier with "$347,000,000 available in Eastern money" was asked to empty his pockets, he produced a personal bankroll of fourteen cents—a dime and four pennies.

As a business community, southern California lolled in the sun until the 1880s. An 1850 census, taken by marshals on horseback, showed that the fourteen southern counties had only 6 per cent of the state's population and little wealth. The rip-roaring real-estate boom of the eighties, followed by the big bust, still left 75 per cent of California's population concentrated in the north. Things picked up by 1910, and sparked by successive waves of new settlers through the twenties, the World War Two defense boom and the continuing postwar influx, the population pendulum swung decisively. Today almost 65 per cent of Californians live in the south.

"California, here I come . . . and come . . . and come," says a research report prepared by the Security First National Bank. "Now it takes computers, rather than marshals on horseback, to keep up."

Population means business. Ceaseless migration has made southern California a financial powerhouse, fast approaching megalopolis, a continuous business and residential colossus extending from Santa Barbara to the Mexican border.

A financial center second only to New York, southern California's combined banking resources and savings and loan assets total $35,000,000,000, outranking all states but New York and California itself.

Los Angeles leads the nation in, among other things, retail sales, defense-space-electronics employment, building construction, dairy output, motion picture and television production and advertising linage for a single newspaper.

But good times and furious competition have created an atmosphere for the proliferation of crime among businessmen, according to Dr. Joseph D. Lohman, Dean and Professor of Criminology at the University of California.

Southern California also leads the nation in bank robberies; more than one was committed for every business day in 1964. "But bank robbers actually make off with less money than do bank employes who embezzle funds," says Dr. Lohman. "There's no way of estimating the cost of crime in business, but it is enormously profitable and may be the biggest industry today."

To help counteract business and other frauds, Los Angeles courts, with increasing frequency, are providing for restitution to victims. The details are administered by the Los Angeles County Probation Department.

"I'm a firm believer in restitution," says one probation officer. "It's the best tool we have. If they didn't have to be concerned with paying back what they've taken, these guys would be back at it again. Taking the profit out of illegal activity is essential."

More than eight thousand men and women in Los Angeles are making restitution payments to nineteen thousand victims. Individual payments have ranged from one cent (to close out an account) to $15,000. From 1962 to 1964, about $1,600,000 was collected and returned to those who had been fleeced.

The probation department contacts each known victim who is invited to submit a statement of loss. But many decline to submit claims for reasons of their own. Says the department: "Some are embarrassed. Others consider themselves lucky to get off with just a financial loss. Some decline because they still have faith in the person who swindled them."

Restitution is likely to be an albatross hovering over a fifty-one-year-old Los Angeles accountant for some time to come. He was handed a repayment bill for $520,334.99—the largest on record in Los Angeles County.

He's paying it off at the rate of $100 a month. On that schedule, it will take him some 430 years to get out from under. ("I don't think I'm going to make it," he says with grim humor.)

His debacle came as the result of a Ponzi-like scheme that began with borrowing from friends to "invest" in short-term industrial loans. When they went sour, he borrowed from others to pay the "dividends" he had promised his first group of investors. He continued to lose and continued to borrow. In a last-ditch effort to recoup, he made a series of desperate plunges on the horses.

When it was all over, he had gone through more than $700,000 of investors' loot. Claims were made for $416,184.06 of the total and the government slapped him with an added fee of $104,-150.93 for back taxes.

"I guess there's a rosy side to everything," says the man who can barely expect to make a dent in his half-million-dollar-plus debt. "It's better than prison."

The time-honored Ponzi scam of robbing Peter to pay Paul also appealed to a successful $25,000-a-year salesman named Irving Belmont. Finding even that generous income too little, Belmont devised a mythical import business—raising some $250,000 in three years by promising investors 15 to 20 per cent return on their money within 90 to 120 days. He sweetened the scam by telling investors he had "signed deals" for the television sets, transistor radios, golf balls, artificial flowers and milking stools he was bringing in from the Orient.

Things went well for a time. He found enough investors to meet the interest payments as the obligations came due. Many happily reinvested their dividends since Belmont's business seemed to be going well. He continued his payouts until the inevitable day that he ran out of victims who would supply him with new principle.

Not all investors lost everything. Four of them reported the following payouts and returns: $21,000–$8000, $49,125–$17,000, $40,000–$20,000 and $10,000–$750.

One victim was so angry he hired a local gangster to drop by and warn Belmont to repay. Belmont's wife also got prophetic, anonymous newspaper clippings in the mail, stories of embezzlers and thieves who had been sent to prison.

Fleecing his victims was comparatively easy. Belmont's suckers weren't strangers. They included some of his best friends—his dentist, an uncle, his next-door neighbor, one of his children's schoolteachers and a pal who had paid his rent when he had arrived, penniless, in California.

Says Investigator Aksel Petersen: "He took advantage of his friendship with each of the victims to the extent that they did not do business with him at arm's length as one would do with a stranger. They believed implicitly in his representations."

At his trial, Belmont offered an incredible defense. He said his victims had attempted to "extort" repayment by threatening criminal prosecution and that they are guilty of "usury" by agreeing to his offer of 15 to 20 per cent interest.

Belmont admitted he had used the money to buy an expensive home, a full-length mink for his wife, and a Cadillac, and to host cocktail parties attended by more than a hundred guests. "They all thought I was making money hand over fist," he told the judge. "I just had to live on a high standard."

Belmont now is living in state prison, convicted on three counts of grand theft. His wife and three children are living in Florida —on welfare checks.

Promoter Roger C. Muir had another system for finding victims to put their funds in six real-estate and investment companies he controlled. He founded the Muir Academy of Success in Los Angeles, taking large newspaper ads which offered courses in personality improvement, how to succeed in business, how to become a memory expert, how to increase happiness and how to double income.

Those who came to hear the "free lectures" were talked into paying fifteen dollars for the next five dissertations. Muir had each of his students fill out personal history forms and a questionnaire titled "How to Retire in Ten Years." The answers gave him a rundown on each student's financial condition. Those with savings were encouraged to consult with him regarding their investments.

And so it was that Muir extracted $5000 from a dentist for a couple of lots in Oregon. He promised he would double the money in a year. But the only word the dentist received from Muir after making the investment was a little note, "Dear Doc, have a positive thought. Roger." Other victims got personal notes from Muir on "appreci-o-gram" stationery (which he offered to sell in packets of two hundred for two dollars, claiming the money "would help little children meet life's problems").

On a promise to triple her money in twenty to twenty-seven months, Muir convinced a schoolteacher to withdraw $5000 from a savings account and invest in a senior citizens project. He also convinced her to invest another $4000 in a deal which would pay 10 per cent. Another schoolteacher and her husband lost $30,000 on similar promises.

On the basis of evidence gathered by Securities and Exchange investigators, a court issued a permanent injunction against Muir, three of his associates, and his corporations.

In a bankruptcy hearing, the SEC said Muir's books and records were incomplete, some of the general ledgers had not been posted for about a year, that monies received for a particular company were often indiscriminately deposited to the account of another company and that frequently disbursements of one company went for payment of expenses of another.

Asked to give the details of one deal which involved $75,000 advanced by two investors for a piece of land in Antelope Valley, the self-proclaimed memory expert said, "I don't recall."

Finally hailed into court on charges of defrauding more than $1,500,000, Muir was convicted and sentenced. "You are a complete fraud," the judge said, handing him an unforgettable eight-year jail term.

"Well-established corporation with a history of success in a three-billion-dollar-a-year industry, requires an investment of only $2,880 in the sale of franchises," was the come-on ad by one of a covey of con men who currently are using the franchise angle to round up suckers.

The inexpensive ad, placed in the business opportunity columns of newspapers all over the country, brought more than $300,000 to a Hollywood promoter of vending machines. Tagged "Santa Claus" by bunco detectives for his white hair, paunch and ruddy cheeks, the deals he gave his victims were not exactly Christmas presents. He was finally jailed on testimony of one victim who discovered that his string of cigarette machines weren't doing anywhere near the volume Santa Claus had predicted. Eighty per cent of his route was located in a cemetery.

In 1965, California Attorney General Thomas C. Lynch cracked down on eight outfits publishing fraudulent classified business directories. Promoters were bilking businessmen who thought they were buying ads in the Pacific Telephone & Telegraph Company's Yellow Pages. Instead, the phony directories were distributed only to the firms that had bought space.

"Over the years, we estimate this sort of scheme has defrauded our businessmen of millions of dollars," said the attorney general.

One of the outfits had solicited advertising from 150,000 southern California businesses using invoice-type forms similar to those of PT&T. Lynch said the forms were used to make customers think their ads, for which they were charged phone company rates of twenty-five dollars to forty-five dollars, would appear in the Yellow Pages. The outfit earned $70,000 on each of its annual publications.

Twenty-seven firms submitted statements that they had paid for ads in the bogus directories. They included the Beverly Hilton Hotel, Jerry Lewis Productions, the French National Railroads, a hospital, a savings and loan firm and the Bible Institute of Los Angeles, Inc.

Los Angeles authorities have received complaints from every state in the Union about phony mail-order firms operating locally. Seven of them, grossing $11,000,000 annually, were run out of business in 1964. They were enjoined from misrepresenting the nature of their business and the quality of their merchandise. The firms specialized in novelties, small appliances and hardware. Leading brand names were offered for sale in their advertising but orders were filled from cheap, substitute lines.

One firm, to lend a businesslike aura of credibility to its operation, used IBM cards as order blanks. Though it did not have equipment to process the cards, the company regularly ordered one thousand a month from IBM. In anticipation of heavy Christmas business, it stepped up its order to one million cards a week!

Postal con comes in many guises, none more brazen than a Los Angeles firm whose three top officials were indicted on one count of conspiracy and fourteen counts of mail fraud for selling worthless and secondhand truck parts as new to the government of Iraq.

Promoters have discovered that a Hollywood postmark has lost little of its luster. It's a big plus, implying movie-star endorsement of such useless products as bust developers, sex rejuvenation pills and baldness cures.

For more than thirty years Hollywood has been the home of one song shark after another, the con conducted exclusively by mailed replies to pulp magazine advertising. "We have started to fame and wealth many hundreds of people like YOU who have wisely PUBLISHED with us." It's a hopeless swindle for the thousands of amateur song writers who send $50 to $110 on promises their songs will be published and their fees returned when "royalties begin."

The Los Angeles Better Business Bureau has a bulging file on one song shark who grossed an estimated $1,000,000 before he was finally put out of business. The BBB through the years has tirelessly pointed out that legitimate publishers and recording companies do not charge composers for their services.

Of the 200,000 songs copyrighted annually in Washington, D. C., less than two hundred achieve success. Never has a song published by a shark been one of them.

Prosecution against the shark is difficult. He easily fulfills his obligations under his trick contract for a few dollars by printing a small supply of "professional copies" and mailing them to a number of record companies where they immediately wind up in the wastebasket. One highly successful Hollywood bandleader-singer confesses that when times were rough he worked for one of the sharks, recording twenty or thirty of the amateur songs at a session for a fee of one dollar apiece. That fulfilled the shark's promise of getting the song recorded by a professional vocalist. "The most horrible sounds this side of heaven," the bandleader commented, wincing in memory of the songs by would-be Cole Porters.

A companion racket is solicitation in nationwide publications for movie and television scripts: "Every day studios are accepting more and more stories from hitherto unknown authors. Submit your stories, hundreds of new writers are suddenly springing into prominence." All of this is news to many of the hard-pressed, established members of the Writers Guild of America, West, Inc., who wait nervously for their agents' calls for the verdict from producers about their own polished submissions. (Most members of the Guild earn less than $10,000 a year.)

When the scripts from the amateurs pour in, a "board of professional advisors" invariably finds them worthy of "further development" for fees scaled into hundreds of dollars.

Of the more than 42,000 unsolicited stories and scripts submitted in one recent year to the Hollywood film factories, only four were purchased.

Movie stars themselves are the natural prey of con men. Who steals their names steals anything but trash. Stars often find themselves involved in bunco schemes of which they have no knowledge.

Singer Dinah Shore in 1963 testified before a Los Angeles grand jury that she had never met a glib Hollywood promoter who had swindled a number of persons by claiming to have big-name stars—including her—under personal contract.

The promoter had sold 157⅔ per cent of a corporation after assuring investors he himself was a writer of many hit songs and also had under personal contract Doris Day, Hedy Lamarr, Joan Crawford and Frankie Laine. He raised between $25,000 and $50,000 by dropping those potent names.

Bob Hope and Bing Crosby, costars of many a "Road" picture, were also taken down the "Road to Con." An outfit selling a "secret" skin care lotion that supposedly helped prevent women from showing their age was accompanied by the representation that Hope was a financial backer and faithful user of the product. The comedian had never heard of the product or the promoters.

The former manager of Bing's Things, Inc., a Bing Crosby enterprise, was convicted of bilking a model of $13,000 for the production of a plastic dishpan. Though he had already been fired from his job, he told his pretty victim he was still working for Crosby and the singer's firm was backing the household gadget. In the words of Bing's brother, Everett, their ex-manager was "inclined to have difficulty with the truth" and "the result was the ruination of Bing's Things, Inc., at a cost of a good piece of money." The loss was placed at more than $100,000.

The phony talent and charm schools still abound on the Hollywood fringes, selling shortcuts to stardom. The racket is especially vicious when mothers are cajoled into paying fees for "professional training" of offspring for television commercials and movie parts that never materialize. Legitimate auditions are open to all through referral by a recognized agent who requires no fee except the standard 10 per cent once a job is obtained.

Despite their palace guards of agents, managers, business advisers and lawyers, movie stars have been frequently victimized in straight-out bunco schemes. One bunk man tore through the Beverly Hills–Bel-Air circuit with a scam tailor-made for Hollywood acceptance. He clipped dozens of big names for $5000 apiece by telling them he had developed a foolproof hangover pill.

Fourteen entertainment figures—producers, writers and stars— were taken by a Hollywood agent for about $7000 in 1957 when he convinced them all that he had an option on Frederic Wakeman's novel, *The Wastrel*. Wakeman, who had never heard of the agent, had previously sold the rights to his book to an Italian producer.

The product that streams out of the 897 establishments engaged in the production, distribution and service of movies and television is put together by the collective imaginations of skilled producers, directors, writers and technicians. But the local con artists who have conjured up a limitless number of business-oriented scams rival the Hollywood professionals in the use of unfettered imagination.

A would-be financier operated out of an impressive Beverly Hills office and a Rolls Royce with a telephone for two years and bilked $425,000 from fourteen victims on fraudulent promises he could obtain large "no interest" bank loans. He pled himself guilty only to "naïveté" and "errors of judgment"—but the judge demurred. "You're not a little thief, you're a big thief," said his honor. "Every transaction you handled was saturated with fraud."

A forty-one-year-old operator oozed $1000 from a Camp Pendleton marine sergeant for the food and drink concessions on a 210-passenger ocean liner running between Oceanside and Catalina. There was no passenger liner.

A cowboy-booted six-footer got $1000 out of a retired rear

admiral by promising to repay him as soon as he sold one hundred tons of flagstone from his quarry in Arizona. There was no flagstone.

Nine counts of grand theft were lodged against a promoter who raised $30,000 from businessmen on promises he could deliver steel to them at a time when the mills were on strike. There was no steel.

One hustler made a decent living for years by selling for $500 "exclusive rights" to the receipts of a designated number of public telephone booths!

Embezzlements with a flair are a Los Angeles specialty. One of the top salesmen for a local business machines company kept himself in girls and gambling forays to Las Vegas by fleecing $20,000 to $25,000 a year for several years from his employers. He did it by chiseling the rivets off the plates holding the serial numbers of various machines and substituting fictitious ones. He wiped the record of the machines from his company's books, then sold the machines on his own and pocketed the money.

The investigator who handled the case said "he was as all-American-looking as Tom Sawyer." The case was especially memorable because the trial lasted for two weeks, but the jury was out for three, finally coming in with a hung verdict.

Quizzing the foreman, the investigator learned that the vote had been 10 to 2 for conviction. One of the jurors, the prototype of southern California's famed "little old lady from Pasadena," had declared at the outset of the voting, "I don't want to see any of the evidence or hear any of the testimony. That boy is just too nice-looking to do what they said he did." She was steadfast for three weeks and managed to get another juror to go along with her. At the second trial, the jury was out for only twenty minutes. It brought back a guilty verdict on all thirteen counts and "Tom Sawyer" was sentenced to maximum consecutive terms adding up to 113 years.

A clever embezzler, a $165-a-week assistant purchasing agent, mulcted $250,000 over two years by appointing himself "Western representative" of a reputable Eastern firm, writing orders on his employer's stationery and collecting the bills. When someone finally got around to asking why the company never received any of the ordered materials, the jig was up. Auditors uncovered

a long record of fictitious transactions and a booming affluence
on the part of the self-styled "Western representative." He had
bought an $80,000 Hollywood apartment building, had entered
escrow for the purchase of another valued at $250,000, and had
paid $15,000 down on a $35,000 Rolls Royce. Further investigation disclosed he had also served eighteen months on a previous
embezzlement conviction.

Though most embezzlers steal to cover gambling or business
losses, for money to spend on women or to raise their personal
standard of living, the motives of "The Saint of Spring Street" fell
into none of the conventional pigeonholes.

On a sweltering July afternoon in 1952, three men stood in an
automobile graveyard in downtown Los Angeles gazing with
fascinated attention at a pulverized wreck of a car, a worthless
heap of twisted metal and shattered glass that only a few days
before had been a factory-fresh Chevrolet.

The smallest of the three men asked, "What happened to it?"

"Smashed into a locomotive," said Percy M. Phillips, a big, flat-
footed ex-bookie who owned a half interest in an auto reposses-
sion business.

"Looks like it was hit by two locomotives," Phillips' partner, a
broad-shouldered two-hundred-pounder named Francis Henderson added with heavy humor.

The smaller man, trim in a cool, well-tailored dark blue summer
suit, was pleased. "She's a beauty," he said without batting an
embarrassed eyelash. "I can loan exactly $1,899.80 on her!"

The man in the well-tailored suit wasn't a fool or a philan-
thropist. He was John Charles Heilman, a sharp-eyed money
wizard who had spent his entire professional life in the finance
business. Currently, he was the respected senior loan officer at
the Spring Street branch of the Morris Plan, a small loan company
that had flourished throughout California for more than thirty-five
years under the slogan, "You may borrow from us for any worthwhile purpose."

Worthwhile or not, Heilman was now prepared to loan generously on the battered mountain of junk that glistened so de-
spairingly in the hot summer sun. Turning to leave, he told

Phillips, "Come down to the office tomorrow and we'll sign the papers."

At ten o'clock the next morning Phillips was at Heilman's desk. The little loan man shuffled the prepared sheaf of papers together, had Phillips sign in the appropriate places. Then the two men rose from their chairs and walked to the teller's cage. Phillips was handed $1899 in crisp currency and eighty cents in coin. The transaction completed, the two men said good-bye. Heilman stopped for a moment to have a word with a colleague. Phillips walked to a writing table, subtracted $100 from the money he was holding. The rest he placed in an envelope; then he sauntered over to Heilman's desk, opened a drawer and dropped it in.

A few moments later Heilman was back at his desk. He opened the drawer, fingered the envelope appreciatively and transferred it to his inside jacket pocket. The brazen swindle had been pulled off without a hitch!

Heilman now pushed his swivel chair back to a reclining position. He couldn't resist taking a moment to savor the triumph. He had a sudden impulse to plant his feet on the desk and bark out a couple of orders to passing subordinates. But he wasn't the type of man who would put his feet on the desk and he had never in his life raised his voice above its normal, almost timid pitch.

A little over five feet eight, he had the scrubbed, kindly oval face of the typical banker. Soaking wet, he weighed no more than 140 pounds. His only unusual feature was a rather theatrical streak of white that coursed through his dark brown hair. Otherwise, he was the living embodiment of Walter Mitty. But unlike James Thurber's harmless fictional hero, the loan officer had, for his own offbeat motives, suddenly decided to turn his dreams into reality. That the fulfillment of his dreams happened to be against the law was a circumstance that only added zest to his new-found identity.

It would be unthinkable to anyone who knew this Milquetoast to believe that he had daringly assumed the unlikely roles of cool con man, eager embezzler, fancy forger and suave swindler. Nevertheless, he was now in the process of becoming all those things, busily establishing himself at the hub of a complex three-spoke wheel of financial finagling that would bring him and his confederates more than $100,000—an especially remarkable accomplishment because they stole only a little at a time, as little as $396 and never more than $1995.

In all the annals of crime, there has never been an operation quite like the one that Heilman created and masterminded. He brought to the art of embezzlement unguessed imagination and improvisation, building not one, but three swindle rings, each of them totally independent of the others. None of his confederates was aware of the existence of the others.

Heilman skillfully juggled his three financial swindles for two years. So intricate were his money machinations that a final audit of what he stole was all but impossible. Ultimately, his case nearly plowed a virgin swath through the lawbooks. And in one memorable transaction, he was to establish what probably is still an unchallenged record—stealing the same money four times in the course of juggling one of his fraudulent loans!

Heilman came to this mighty threshold of accomplishment with the most doubtful of credentials. Taciturn, inconspicuous and hard-working, he was of frugal, hardy German stock. He had migrated to California with his wife and son in 1930 from Omaha, Nebraska, where he'd picked up two years of business college at night. Knowing the difference between a debit and a credit plus having an orderly, efficient mind smoothed his way up from a series of jobs with single-branch loan companies and a stint with the prestigious California Bank to his present well-paid eminence with the ubiquitous Morris Plan.

Twenty-two years in Los Angeles had been good to him. He owned a pleasant home free and clear. He had $16,500 in his own bank account, only $1150 in liabilities. He was happily married and, all in all, at forty-six, he had it made. If the road ahead wasn't exactly exciting, it was at least secure. Playing it cool, in the normal course of events he could expect a vice-presidency at Morris Plan and comfortable retirement.

The only thing wrong with that rosy picture was that it bored Heilman to death. The years loomed ahead like so many identical ice cubes, the time of his life melting inexorably away. Like Mitty, he had begun living inwardly. Unlike Mitty, the longing to translate fancy into fact became overpowering.

When Heilman made the decision to act out his fancies, he did

it by opening the one door of opportunity available to him—
boldly using his executive desk at the Morris Plan as a beachhead
to conquer the world.

Over the years, he had industriously built a large, loyal personal
following among widows, orphans, cleaning women, small mer-
chants, newspaper reporters and other non-members of the
affluent society who inhabited the downtown area of Los Angeles.
Most of his customers were what is known among loan men as
"second-grade risks." Banks on Spring Street, the roaring financial
quarter of the city, routinely sent Heilman this business, and at
his desk poor petitioners always found a sympathetic ear. Hundreds of times he bent the regulations to see clients through a
budget crisis.

An Irish scrubwoman had financed the birth of three children,
the acquisition of parlor furniture and her husband's insurance
with Heilman's help. She spoke for many when she said, "John
Heilman's a saint. Bless his immortal soul!"

It wasn't a saint, however, who had worked out the devilishly
clever scam with Phillips and Henderson. He'd done legitimate
business with them as free-lance auto repossessors a number of
times, calling on the burly pair to round-up cars on which unfortunate borrowers had failed to meet the payments.

Both Phillips and Henderson were flattered, awed and agree-
able when Heilman first approached them with his idea for the
swindle. He gave them the job of scouring the auto graveyards
for late-model cars that had been creamed in accidents and
could be bought cheap, thus allowing them to pick up a pink
ownership slip on a car of very recent vintage. Heilman would
come by and fill in an appraiser's report on the wreck, certifying
it as bona fide security. He naturally omitted to mention in his
report that it was now a vehicle that would be snubbed on Tobacco Road. The rest was easy. He attached that crucial pink
slip to the loan papers, filled out the other necessary documents
and had Phillips forge an assumed name. Then the money was
picked up and divided under a Fagin-like formula.

The normal expectation would be that the three conspirators
would divide the loot in thirds. But Heilman succeeded in con-
ning Phillips and Henderson into accepting only fifty dollars each.
For a couple of guys named Percy and Francis, they were still

pretty rough customers. Both had been in trouble with the law on and off most of their lives. Both were big men, and could have put Heilman into the hospital with a hard handshake. But both enjoyed the "prestige" of an association with "a big man on Spring Street," a doubtful bit of status, but important enough for them to go along with Heilman on the terms he dictated.

Now that he had the car swindle rolling, Heilman decided to diversify. All he needed was another scam and another scamp. Both began to take shape in August, 1952, barely a month after his first coup, with the appearance at his desk of Louis Ray, a nondescript, mildly alcoholic, middle-aged loser who came in off the street to borrow a couple of hundred dollars.

After a few moments of conversation, Heilman had Ray sized up as a failure with a weak will and a weaker bank account. He sensed there would be no problem in dominating him. He was absolutely right. Heilman felt completely safe in broaching the new scheme that was beginning to form in his mind.

As were Phillips and Henderson, Ray was flattered at the attention from Heilman. At Heilman's suggestion, they adjourned to a restaurant around the corner from the Morris Plan office. There they settled down to work out a workable swindle.

Ray listened with cheerful attention as Heilman showed him a sample loan application, which he had thoughtfully brought along. The loan officer patiently explained the form and the procedure at the Morris Plan.

"What we'll do is fill this out with somebody else's name," said Heilman.

"How about Ruth?" Ray volunteered. "I used to go with a girl named Ruth. And Freda. Used to go with her too. Ruth Freda! How's that?"

"No," Heilman said sharply. "You have to have a real name and a real phone number and employment verification. You have to have something to match with something when the girl in our credit department looks in the phone book. Let's take, for example John Brown or John Doe, there has to be a John Doe living at a certain street and working at a certain place when she calls."

"I got it," said Ray, brightening considerably. "How's it if I take a name from the phone book?"

Heilman brightened too. Ray was beginning to be a creative participant. "But that wouldn't work," he hedged, "unless you could be around to answer the phone when the girl calls to check."

Ray, who had a part-time job with a small real-estate firm, said he could easily arrange to be on hand to receive the calls.

It sounded good, so they tried it with a first small loan of $504.80, a sum carefully calculated by Heilman to allay undue notice or suspicion.

As agreed, Ray leafed through the white pages and picked a name and address at random, but on the loan documents he carefully assigned all mail and telephone calls to his own address and number.

Aside from the name and address culled from the phone book, all the other biographical information on the loan application was pure invention, including the nature of the security the Morris Plan demanded to back up the funds it loaned. Furniture was a standard, reliable item of security, so Heilman and Ray invented mythical rooms of beds, couches, chairs, dressers and dining-room tables. Heilman blandly listed these invisible rooms of furniture on his appraiser's report in the same unflinching spirit as he had listed the wrecked autos in the Phillips-Henderson transaction.

Ray then forged the names of the borrowers that he had so casually chosen, courtesy of the phone company. He then presented the phony application to Heilman, who in his position as senior loan officer had blanket authority to approve loans up to $3000. After putting his stamp of approval on the loan, it was turned over to the credit department for a routine check. When the call was made, Ray was at the other end of the line to verify every fictitious item that he and Heilman had invented.

It worked beautifully, and since the phone book held an unlimited supply of names, they decided to work the scheme on a regular basis. In dividing the spoils with Ray, Heilman again insisted on the lion's share. He was more generous than with Phillips and Henderson, allowing Ray 35 per cent of the take.

At first, Ray balked at his uneven share. "We should be splitting fifty-fifty," he said with some logic.

"You don't understand, Louis. I'm taking 65 per cent because

I have to make the payments on these loans as they come due each month."

There was truth to this. Heilman indeed had to keep up the payments or the scheme would have fallen apart. He thus was put in the position of having to constantly steal more to keep ahead.

But this was exactly the sort of challenge and excitement that he had craved when he launched his marvelous money merry-go-round. In the months since he had assumed his double life, his attitude had changed considerably. There was a spring to his step, and a boyish grin of satisfaction played impishly around the corners of his mouth. Each day was a new adventure, and things were going so well with confederates Phillips, Henderson and Ray that he decided to find still another conspirator.

Against the day of such need, he had already tentatively scouted a likely prospect. It had become his custom after a hard day of watching over the affairs of the Morris Plan and simultaneously watching over the even more intricate affairs of the Heilman Plan, to stop at a bar near the office for a little genteel drinking. There he'd developed a nodding acquaintance with a strapping 205-pound one-time sports promoter and truck driver named Eugene Buckner.

One evening Heilman invited Buckner for a couple of rounds on him. He learned that Buckner was currently living by his wits, and not doing too well. His last score, Buckner candidly related in the afterglow of a double Scotch, was a bunco scheme he'd worked against a pair of pigeons—promising them he could buy five Cadillacs in Detroit for $3000 apiece, the cars then to be re-sold at a 100 per cent profit. By the time the pigeons discovered the obvious fact that Detroit wasn't selling Caddies for $3000, he, naturally, had disappeared with the $7500 they had advanced him.

Heilman enjoyed the story, and found Buckner a bright, promising confederate. He was also good company with sense enough to defer to him—which in Heilman's mind made him an ideal conspirator for phase three of the Heilman Plan.

Without telling him about his two other sets of cronies, Heilman gave Buckner the highlights of the swindle he was working with Ray, including the avid scanning of the phone book.

"I got a better way," said Buckner, warming to the proposition. "On these applications, I'll use the names of my relatives! They'll never know, and that way I can add a lot of real personal details to make the whole thing look more genuine."

Heilman liked the new wrinkle. It was different and had one obvious advantage. It would enable them to secure loans with forged signatures of Buckner's relatives as both applicants and comakers instead of repeating the use of junk autos in the Phillips-Henderson loans or chattel mortgages on furniture in the Ray transactions. It opened up a whole new area.

"I suppose you have a large family?" Heilman wondered.

"Compared to my brood," Buckner beamed with pride, "the Hatfields and the McCoys were a bunch of birth control nuts."

Buckner said he would use his home address and telephone as a cover to take calls and correspondence from the Morris Plan. He also readily agreed to take only 35 per cent of the action.

In September, 1952, they put through a first loan of $1092 under the name of Buckner's brother-in-law. It was downhill all the way and when Buckner turned up at the teller's cage in Heilman's tow, the money was passed over without incident.

Heilman at this juncture was probably the busiest financial man on Spring Street. He was also the happiest, contentedly making honest loans to honest applicants interspersed with his dishonest loans to his lengthening list of dishonest pals.

Through the first nine months of 1953, his financial juggernaut rolled on. In a good month, he could expect to see each of his buddies trooping through the office to his desk. He all but wore a path in the floor as he escorted them to the bottomless money well at the teller's cage. A random sampling of his activity in this period shows that in March and April he, Phillips and Henderson worked two more thwacked autos into loans for $1575.70 and $1884. In April and August he and Ray bartered their mounting rooms of nonexistent furniture for scores of $993.80 and $504.80. In March and April he and Buckner bled in the name of unsuspecting relatives $1008 and $1178.85 from the Morris Plan treasury.

Incredibly, though Phillips, Henderson, Ray and Buckner appeared at the teller's cage almost often enough to be pickets, they were never challenged. None of them used disguises, the tellers assuming that anyone that their trusted senior loan officer vouched for was okay.

Though Heilman had changed his relationship considerably with his employers, he hadn't changed his personal life one jot. The extracurricular money he was stealing wasn't spent on gambling, women, a new home or a new car. He didn't so much as buy a new tie with his ill-gotten lucre. He kept his standard of living at precisely the same level. Some of the money he had to plow back in payments each month as the various loans came due, but he still had a bundle in unused profits.

For Heilman, it was the means, not the end, that was important. He was stealing more to prove he could do it than to get the money. He was stealing for the sheer thrill of the experience. And he kept right on stealing because his ego was considerably built up and flattered by the fawning attention of his confederates.

By now Heilman had consolidated his three money-making schemes. His word was law to all four of his underlings and, of course, Morris Plan officials had no inkling of the raids he was masterminding on the cashbox.

His only real problems were overseeing his massive bookkeeping and the fact that he had become a trifle bored with success. He craved more action and the more dangerous and sophisticated the action the better. He could, in theory, keep expanding the number of his confederates, developing perhaps a dozen little networks of accomplices. But he rejected that possibility on grounds of unwieldiness.

He pondered his next move and decided to step up his activity with the Phillips-Henderson wing of his operation. Of all his confederates, Percy and Francis had the toughest job. It was, after all, a little more complicated locating a decently wrecked automobile than a roomful of invisible furniture or a blissfully ignorant relative.

But it would be interesting, Heilman decided, to challenge Percy and Francis again with a tricky, brassy switch on the swindle he was already working with them. He called the boys together and explained that he wanted them to find somebody who was interested in obtaining an almost new car without a down payment. But it had to be somebody who had a respectable job, who could legitimately pass a rigid credit check and who was completely above suspicion.

Percy and Francis proved they were up to the challenge. In a few days they had run down a mark who met every one of Heilman's precise specifications. He was Charles Davis, a good-natured, easygoing acquaintance of theirs who, by any yardstick, had one of the most respectable jobs in town. He was a member of the Los Angeles Police Department!

Patrolman Davis' beat included the Western Avenue office of Phillips and Henderson, and in brief conversations as he made his appointed rounds, he had casually asked them to keep an eye peeled for a good, late-model car. Thus, when Percy and Francis informed him that he could buy a 1952 eight-cylinder Buick Riviera coupe for only $1800, Davis was interested.

There then ensued the somewhat incredible procedure of Phillips and Henderson qualifying the policeman for a loan, the proceeds of which they and Heilman planned to steal.

"I will have to take a credit rating from you," Phillips told Davis. The patrolman supplied the personal details of his life, his monthly earnings, his paydays, amount of pension and the estimated market value of his home. Without thought of irony, Phillips also asked the policeman to supply two personal references to vouch for his moral and financial character.

Phillips and Henderson turned all this information over to Heilman. He immediately ran a credit check on Davis, and the officer passed with flying colors. Heilman then ordered Phillips and Henderson to proceed as planned.

On the day he was scheduled to get his loan, Patrolman Davis met Phillips and Henderson at their office.

"We'll drive right over to the Morris Plan," said Phillips. "But we have to make a stop on the way."

The stop was at an auto graveyard. While Davis waited in the car, Percy and Francis went inside. They were back ten minutes later, faces wreathed in smiles. It had been a fruitful ten minutes. Phillips and Henderson had quickly closed a deal on a pile of junk, a '52 Buick Riviera all but unrecognizable as such since it had been telescoped in a head-on freeway collision. On that decimated vehicle, Phillips and Henderson had obtained a white and a pink slip.

With Davis none the wiser, the trio now continued on to the Morris Plan, pulling into a lot just north of Heilman's office. As they drove up, Davis waved to an off-duty buddy on the police force who was moonlighting as a parking attendant.

"Hello, Charlie, how long you and your friends going to be?" Davis looked at Phillips. "About half an hour," Percy said.

After they parked, Phillips handed Davis the pink and white slips on the battered Buick. He gave the cop careful instructions. "Take this into the Morris Plan. When you go through the door, halfway back you will see an enclosure. The first man sitting at the first desk will be Mr. John Heilman. He will have a streak of white hair in front. Just tell him that Percy sent you."

Officer Davis obeyed the instructions, easily locating Heilman. As he stood before the loan man, he said obediently, "Percy sent me." Soon Heilman was whipping through the paper work. Taking the white and pink slips from Davis, he stapled them to the completed loan application and credit forms. He had the patrolman sign his name a few times, then escorted him down the familiar path to the teller's cage. There, Patrolman Davis was handed eighteen $100 bills.

The deal completed, Heilman invited Davis downstairs for a cup of coffee. When they entered the restaurant, Percy and Francis were waiting.

"Did the loan go okay?" Phillips asked.

Davis pulled out the $1800 and laid it on the table.

For a long moment, the neat stack of hundreds held the transfixed, undivided attention of Heilman, Phillips and Henderson.

"Officer Davis, why don't you get yourself that cup of coffee," Heilman suggested, his eyes never leaving the money.

Davis turned his back and went to the counter. When he returned four minutes later, the money on the table had vanished.

The officer didn't ask for an explanation. "When do I get the car?" was all he wanted to know.

"In about a week," said Heilman, getting up to leave, his hand tapping the pocket which now held $1700. As soon as Davis had turned his back, Heilman had grabbed the cash, quickly peeled off one of the hundreds for Phillips and Henderson to split, then whisked the rest into his jeans.

And when Heilman had done that, he was on his way toward

accomplishing something that perhaps had never been done before—stealing the same money four times!

In strictly legal terms, under the doctrine of false pretenses he stole the money for the first time by knowingly misrepresenting the wrecked car to obtain the phony loan. He stole it for the second time, committing grand theft, when he snatched it off the table. Then by distributing to himself and his cohorts money entrusted to him for proper distribution, he stole it for the third time. Having obtained the money under false pretenses, then committing grand theft and embezzlement, he subsequently used some of the money to repay earlier phony loans for his own, not the company's purposes. And that, in the eyes of the law, was looting the loot for a fourth time.

Deputy District Attorney Fred N. Whichello, one of Los Angeles' crack fraud prosecutors, in pointing out the unique crime, says, "Though Heilman in fact stole the money four times, we didn't proceed on that theory in court. It's redundant and unnecessary. Once he steals it, he's stolen it!"

Then, with the reflective look of a man who loves the purity of the law, Whichello observes, "But wouldn't it have been something to take him into court on all those charges—besides the ones we did file."

Heilman, however, was not yet in the clutches of the law. He was still savoring the triumph over the hapless Officer Davis. When the duped policeman once again asked Heilman about his car, the loan man fended him off easily.

"Sorry," he said, "the deal's fallen through. But don't you worry about the payments on the loan. I'm canceling the whole thing."

Heilman, of course, was making the payments himself. More and more, as all of his scams leveled out, as he, Phillips, Henderson, Ray and Buckner pulled one slick deal after another, Heilman began to be fascinated by the bookkeeping of the financial monster he had created.

He had a huge file of papers to burrow through on each of the scores of fraudulent loans, and he began to get his kicks playing with financial fire. Long experience in the loan business had taught him that a small percentage of borrowers would default on repayment. Why then should he keep repaying on every one of his fraudulent loans? Such exactness might arouse more suspicion than a few delinquencies that even his superiors accepted as inevitable. Besides, it was against all laws of human behavior to expect scrupulous repayment from every borrower. He began to purposely miss payments on some of his own phony loans—and each payment he failed to make was a windfall of pure profit.

Despite this added risk, his various larcenies continued to go undetected. Heilman might have prolonged his successful operations indefinitely since he was in a position of trust and had the advantage of doing his own bookkeeping.

But what upset all his careful calculations and led to his downfall was a preposterous, unpredictable fluke that began on a leisurely Saturday in the suburban home of James and Vivian Sinclair. The morning mail had brought to the Sinclair hearth a delinquency notice from the Morris Plan and as soon as Mr. Sinclair returned from an early golf game Mrs. Sinclair confronted him with the communication.

"You didn't tell me you had borrowed money," she said.

"I haven't," her surprised husband answered.

At twenty-nine, James Sinclair was a careful, well-disciplined man who didn't panic easily. As he read the notice from Morris Plan, he was more confused than angry. It informed him that he had borrowed $1134. He hadn't. It said he was employed by the Hess Tire Co. He wasn't. It listed the names of two personal references. He had never heard of them. The name of his closest living relative was given as Arthur Sinclair. He had no relation by that name. He was also informed that his last payment was overdue. That made no sense at all. The only correct items were his name and address.

Sinclair put the paper aside. "It's obviously a mistake. I don't think"—he smiled at his wife—"that it's a case for the FBI."

He thought so little of the incident that he waited until his lunch hour the following Monday before strolling over to the Morris Plan, which happened to be only a few minutes' walk from his own office.

The polite receptionist would normally have referred Sinclair to Heilman. But Heilman also was on his lunch hour, a pity since an encounter between the two men would have been memorable.

Sinclair instead was referred to a vice-president in an inner office, and that tumbled Heilman's house of cards.

When Heilman came back from lunch he was confronted with the "irregularity" in the Sinclair loan. He was also confronted with the disturbing fact that his superior had begun an immediate inquiry into all his recent loan transactions. Additionally, he was confronted with the even more disturbing fact that the Mr. Sinclair, who had triggered all this sudden unhappiness, was not a man who could be ignored. Mr. Sinclair in fact was a quite unusual man. Mr. Sinclair, indeed, was a special agent of the Federal Bureau of Investigation!

Two weirdly unpredictable accidents had occurred. The Sinclair loan was one of those that Heilman, at random, had permitted to default. Then a busy secretary had glanced at the wrong line on the loan papers and mailed the delinquency notice to Sinclair's real home address instead of to Ray's cover address.

Since J. Edgar Hoover's agents are not in the habit of listing their professional affiliation in the phone book, Ray naturally never knew Sinclair was with the FBI. He had simply invented his job with the tire company as well as the other bogus information. But that he had picked Sinclair's name and address from a phone directory of 600,038 names was an incredible long shot.

As soon as he heard about the Sinclair disaster, Heilman turned on his heel, numb and shocked, and walked out the door of the Morris Plan forever. In a complete daze, unbelieving that the scheme had finally blown apart, he checked into a skid row hotel, and sat mute and wooden in a semialcoholic haze for seven days. Still in shock, he finally tumbled out of the flophouse, found his way to a police station and surrendered. Barely coherent, he named his fellow conspirators and gave a somewhat fuzzy account of all his intricate financial manipulations.

When the news broke along Spring Street, it had the impact of an exploding bomb. A high Morris Plan official said, "I've never been more surprised in my life. John was a perfect employee. He hadn't missed a day's work in four years." Heilman's clients were fanatic in their refusal to believe the "saint" was guilty of any wrongdoing. A couple of influential reporters from two major Los Angeles newspapers wrote glowing character tributes about him to the district attorney's office. He was liberally praised by all his former employers and associates.

But the facts of the embezzlements and the little matter of Heilman's four accomplices couldn't be ignored. Henderson and Buckner were arrested. Phillips, who had skipped to El Paso, Texas, was rousted by two officers out of a warm bed he was sharing with a female friend. Ray, after being trapped in a whole series of lies and contradictions in adroit questioning by Bureau of Investigation detectives, admitted his part in the swindle. He became the only one of Heilman's confederates who agreed to testify for the State.

The case was assigned to Whichello, and despite his long experience in fraud prosecutions, he was amazed by its complexity. After several months of patient digging and reconstruction, he narrowed the charges down to thirteen counts of criminal conspiracy, forgery and grand theft. Every count named Heilman, four named Phillips and Henderson, four involved Ray and five named Buckner.

In the preliminary hearing, Whichello also put before Municipal Court Judge Irvin Taplin a brilliantly reasoned argument that raised a unique point at law. In attempting to link all of Heilman's accomplices to each other, Whichello argued:

"Being common members of the conspiracy, even though they were not working jointly as to any one of their separate types of transactions, they are responsible for each other, just as where there are several conspirators without the complication of the three types of transactions; though not knowing each other all were working towards a common end, and each is the agent and responsible for the acts of each other. . . .

"In other words, Heilman being the common factor is responsible for all his conspirators in all three types of loans. Then that being true, then each of the other groups are responsible for the acts of each other, even though the evidence will not show that Ray aided and abetted Buckner on his specific type of transaction or that Buckner aided and abetted Phillips and Henderson, or in any combination of those things."

From the stupefied bevy of defense lawyers, Buckner's counsel was the only one to raise an objection. "This is the first time in the history of law," he declared, "that this theory is being used, that since there is one central figure, everybody else is connected with the conspiracy. I don't believe Mr. Buckner has any more to do with the counts naming the others than President Eisenhower had."

But the judge was ready for him. "I don't know," the bench observed with mock solemnity, "a conspiracy could involve a lot of people, and even though Mr. Eisenhower is President of the United States, it is possible he might be tied into something. The Democrats think so."

Intriguing as Whichello's legal theorizing was, in the end the judge disallowed it. But he ruled against the defendants on all the other charges. When the case was passed on to Superior Court, Phillips, Henderson and Buckner each pled guilty to one count of grand theft. Heilman confessed to three counts of grand theft, conspiracy and forgery. In exchange for his testimony for the state, the charges against Ray were dropped.

Pending sentence, all the defendants were released on bail. By now, Heilman had changed dramatically from the cool, confident mastermind to a broken shell of himself. In court, he had turned sullen and uncooperative, blaming his troubles on his code-fendants. "I tried to stop," he said, "but they wouldn't let me." He accused two of the D.A.'s investigators of being bought off by Ray. He complained that he was unable to find a new job.

He never really adjusted to the reality that he had been caught, and the prospect of going to jail terrified him.

As court convened at 10 A.M. on March 24, 1955, to mete out sentences to Heilman and his associates, the proceedings were interrupted by a stark announcement from Heilman's attorney.

"I am informed by the General Hospital that Mr. Heilman has expired!"

As the judge went on to sentence Phillips, Henderson and Buckner to one- to ten-year prison terms, the chamber was rocked again by the news that Heilman wasn't dead after all. He had been revived by frantically working doctors.

At the hospital, the last incredible chapter of Heilman's life was being written. In attempting death, the oddly tortured ex-loan man created the most bizarre episode of the case. At seven that morning, unable to face a jail term, he had taken an overdose of barbiturates. Rushed to emergency hospital, he had been pronounced dead, then revived. A few hours later, he was pronounced dead again, then revived for the second time.

It was as if Providence was giving him a chance to atone. What had happened to the money he had stolen? Did he repent?

John Charles Heilman passed to his reward with the questions unanswered. He died for the third and last time, the final sound from the lips of the ill-starred Walter Mitty a babbling curse against fate.

I I

SUBURBIA

"Who's That Knocking at My Door?"

Remember what you really wanted from California? To
make money in town, and to live on a hill by the sea.
—Advertisement for new Suburban Development

A pilot in a helicopter, churning through the steamy air over the
San Fernando and San Gabriel valleys in 1964, might have mistaken the terrain below for a battleground. The symmetry of the
rows of tracts was broken by 160 bowl-shaped craters, resembling
the aftermath of an enemy bombing.

But those who poured from the wounded homes weren't
refugees. They were well-heeled suburbanites. And they gathered, not in bomb shelters, but in the office of the Los Angeles
district attorney.

They all told the same story—of being stuck with the ungainly
back-yard holes in a giant fleecing by one of the largest pool
builders in Los Angeles.

The company had left all 160 unfinished, a disaster in southern
California's swimming-pool-oriented society equated with the
breaking of a commandment.

Charges of conspiracy and grand theft piled up like algae. The
suburbanites said oral and contractual promises by the builder
were not fulfilled. Subcontractors, who had dug the holes, claimed
the company had failed to pay for the work. The district attorney added a charge that company officers had offered a $6000
bribe to investigators of the State Contractors Board when its
license had been threatened.

One irate woman, a petite platinum blond housewife, complained that her $4400 pool was not completed to specifications and failed to meet code requirements. She had become so outraged that she launched a one-woman campaign against the builder, calling his suppliers and urging them not to do business with the firm.

The company had gone to court and obtained an injunction restraining her vendetta. But it was too late. "We had a business that was a gold mine," said the firm's president. "After her campaign got going," he sighed, "all of a sudden, there was no gold mine any more—just an empty office."

There were also those 160 empty pools, never completed. The officials were cleared of all charges, but the firm had its license revoked and its two top officers were barred from the pool business, small solace for the suburbanites facing another long hot summer and the loss of their investments.

In a state that already has one third of the nation's private swimming holes—about 130,000—banks are eager to float loans for the construction of new pools. Despite the availability of the Pacific, a pool in southern California is not considered a luxury, but an inevitable necessity for most families. It's part of the local image. And more than a hundred contractors are around to keep intact the shining image that a house in southern California is not a home without a pool.

In trying to overcome tricky advertising and leaky contracts, the Los Angeles Better Business Bureau declares that "the swimming pool industry has been the most difficult with which to deal and get results."

For several years after the postwar boom in pool construction, the industry was overrun by small, undercapitalized companies that swam into the business, made a fast buck, then disappeared.

An industry-wide agreement with the pool builders for "advertising and selling standards" was finally eked out in 1962. But violations were still so common that the BBB issued a public appeal for southern Californians considering the purchase of a pool "to assist us" in checking representations of salesmen. "The Bureau will supply recording equipment so that conversations with salesmen can be taped." Among other legal precautions, the bureau continues to urge prospective pool owners to obtain performance bonds and waivers of lien from suppliers of labor and materials. Otherwise, customers may sink before they swim.

As it has nowhere else on earth, suburbia has conquered in southern California. Despite the overheralded construction of a music center, art museum and the frantic building of high-rise office and apartment complexes in the downtown core, Los Angeles still is very much a collection of suburbs in search of a city. And the trend is accelerating—some 375 outlying acres per day are bulldozed for new homes.

As the new tracts are thrown up, the con man clips the street maps generously supplied in newspaper ads by the developers. The territory is staked off as new sucker land, and more often than not it is his hand that is the first to knock on the door. He's there usually before the Welcome Wagon.

Laid out like dominoes, the suburbs are a gleaming, irresistible, stationary target for the droves of door-to-door hustlers. In Palos Verdes, La Canada, Flintridge, Pacific Palisades, San Marino and eight other golden enclaves, half the families have annual incomes over $10,000. Beverly Hills, in a class by itself, boasts a yearly bonanza of $15,000 for 65 per cent of its residents. Families in twenty-one other suburbs rake in about $9000 a year, and twenty-seven communities have incomes of more than $7000 per household.

"Fifty years ago the snake oil salesmen hit the easily beguiled rural areas of our nation," says California's Attorney General Thomas C. Lynch. "They peddled rheumatism cures, wart removers, virility restoratives and cancer remedies. Today they are peddling patios, aluminum siding, water softeners, swimming pools or dancing courses. The con men found out that city folk can be sold as easily as the folks on the farms—and there are many more of them."

Con in the suburbs is big-business crime. The scams are planned with battlefield thoroughness by con-man generals who organize small, well-disciplined armies and run tough, resourceful, hard-hitting operations.

"They flock like birds from one product to another—from water softeners to patios to aluminum siding," says Lynch. "Whenever a particular community becomes too hot, they flee to another town or state. Whenever a particular product becomes too suspect, they choose another—leaving honest salesmen in that field to take the rap."

A classic campaign was marshaled in 1963 against one community by a con-man army selling a home freezer and food package. The town was first softened up by a flood of direct-mail advertising that promised the package would cut family food bills by more than 50 per cent. The follow-up was an attack by a task force of salesmen who made the door-to-door calls. In less than a week, over one thousand families (in a community with a population of twenty-seven thousand) had signed contracts for the $900 package—not including interest or carrying charges. Then the pitchmen moved on.

The community woke up a few weeks later when the $300 worth of "choice" food arrived—spoiled meat, limp vegetables and watery milk. Victims also discovered that the $600 they had paid for the freezer was exactly twice the price of a comparable model on sale in a local department store.

Before the gang was nailed, they had blitzed thousands of other families in fifteen counties. Their take was over $1,500,000 in cool, unfrozen assets.

But even that was topped by "the Great Aluminum Siding swindle." "The worst invasion California ever experienced at the hands of these floating bands of cheats came in this field," says Lynch. "These firms are generally owned and operated by a promoter, a pro in the fraud field. They obtain state approval as licensed contractors by employing a person with the required technical training as the 'responsible managing employee.' When the firm opens, the salesmen flock in. Like the firm's promoters, the salesmen are professional fraud artists. They also drift from product to product and state to state."

The siding scam was worked by a salesman falsely claiming he was a representative of a national company—Alcoa, Reynolds or Kaiser. The pitch was that a homeowner could have siding installed "free or at greatly reduced prices" if he agreed to permit "before and after" pictures of his home to be shown on television and if his wife would consent to act as "hostess" for the streams of visitors who would visit the house after the siding was installed and publicized. A bonus of $100, $200 or $300 was promised for every person who bought siding as a result of seeing the house. The salesman also explained he wasn't really interested in selling the siding, he was only involved in "advertising" or "testing the market" for the factory.

Householders were unaware that a rider to the contracts they signed gave the salesmen mortgages on their homes. Accompanying the phony sales pitches were many other fraudulent acts—forged contracts, forged trust deeds, concealed mechanics' liens and forged notarizations.

"More than three million dollars was taken from Los Angeles residents alone in an eight-month period," says Lynch.

Big bunco in California is bankrolled by finance companies which make the frauds possible.

Says the Attorney General: "These frauds cannot operate without cash. Finance companies supply the life-blood for these promoters. They buy the sales contracts from the various fly-by-night firms, often for full value. Licensed lending institutions normally do not handle this kind of paper. The finance companies dealing in these contracts change as often as the phony sales firms, but we find the same people involved over and over again. Whether they are innocent bystanders or knowing participants must still be determined."

Lynch is genuinely concerned about a possible link-up between the suburban con man and organized crime.

"The majority of these salesmen, firm owners and financial backers have no record of association with the older organized crime elements," he says. "But they are in their own way organized criminals. They flock together. They have a definite exchange of information on what is selling and where the hot territory is. They cooperate and they coordinate their activities.

"This loosely tied organization is dangerous enough in itself and is costing the consumer millions of dollars in California alone. If this organization is ever taken over by the older organized criminal elements, the ramifications are evident."

The National Better Business Bureau in Washington estimates that "home improvement" confidence men cheat the public of at least $500,000,000 each year. Some $5,000,000 of the total is swindled annually from southern Californians. Such cons are endless:

The chimney repair men who charge for getting rid of non-existent "mortar mice." The "inspectors" who tear down a furnace, claim it is dangerous and beyond repair and replace it with a new expensive off-brand model. The "experts" who run up large bills after ruefully reporting they've rid a house of termites when the alleged termites were nothing but ants. Peddlers and jobbers of inferior plants, shrubs, humus, and fertilizers; and traveling tree crews. The latter scam is worked by a "two-man" crew which quotes a $7.50 per man per hour price and ends up presenting a bill for $1800 to $2000. Horrified homeowners find twenty men suddenly working in their yards.

Roofing, painting, shingling, brickwork, room additions, etc., are all grist for the grifters. Most colorful of all the organized gangs who roam the southern California suburbs is a clan of gypsies, some two thousand strong and known by police departments from coast to coast.

Between 100 and 150 of the clan hit southern California each year between Thanksgiving and Christmas. They pose as roofing repair and blacktop driveway contractors. They use cheap roofing oils that wash off with the first rain, and inferior driveway coatings. The ladies of the clan work assorted rackets, usually selling imitation Irish lace.

Doorbell swindlers in southern California peddle phony antiques, substandard Oriental rugs, carpeting, electrical appliances, vacuum cleaners and sewing machines. Several organized gangs specialize in "knockout" sales. These con artists follow legitimate salesmen into an area, planting distrust in the minds of customers to generate cancellation orders, then sell them their own inferior, overpriced products.

Before many southern Californians can flock to the con men waiting to fleece them in phony churches, the missionary armies, selling Bibles, get first crack at them while they're still at home.

One self-styled missionary got one to ten for running a racket in which he had collected $106,000 for selling Bibles supposedly to be furnished to the needy blind. He claimed in court that he was broke. But moments after he was sentenced, he posted $7500 for an appeal bond. "The Lord has miraculously provided," he said.

These scam men dress in uniforms that resemble those of the

Salvation Army. A self-proclaimed reverend, a crew chief and a flock of salesmen make up each "army." They are carefully schooled in their pitch. "Tell them you're praying for them. That always gets you in the door," one of the slickers who worked the racket confessed. Each salesman was supplied with a card that read: "The bearer is hereby commissioned to minister the Gospel or perform religious activities in the capacity of missionary." Another "credential" carries the message: "We give Bibles to all faiths, regardless of race or color. Our Bibles are placed in prisons, alcoholic sanitariums, delinquent homes, homes for the poor and aged, hospitals of the sick, diseased and crippled, hotels, motels and waiting rooms in public places. . . . True happiness comes from making others happy."

The take is divided under a rigid formula: 30 per cent for the "reverend," 60 per cent for the salesman and 10 per cent for the crew chief.

Southern California morticians are world-famous for proving that death can be fun, flamboyant—and expensive. Tasteless billboards hawking the exclusive advantages of competing cemeteries are a long-standing hallmark of Los Angeles.

Since the widely publicized book, magazine and newspaper exposure of the "death vultures," private memorial and funeral societies have proliferated in California. They negotiate with mortuaries so members know exactly what the final charges will be. "I don't blame a guy who has $250,000 tied up for trying to promote his business," says the realistic president of one society. "But also I don't feel that people should have to pay for things they don't want."

The California Legislature, with Governor Edmund G. Brown's support, is writing a bill that will compel funeral directors to itemize their charges.

Trading off the southern California preoccupation with dying has been lucrative for the grim con men of death. They are the sleaziest of the doorbell swindlers, victimizing the bereaved by selling them Bibles, flowers, and other merchandise, falsely claiming the items were recently ordered by the deceased. Sometimes they render bills when nothing is owed, sometimes they claim part payment has been made by the deceased and try to collect an unowed balance.

The hearse chasers get leads from newspaper obituaries; some actually make a practice of attending funerals and noting automobile license numbers to compile a list of potential victims.

Authorities have also busted several well-organized "boiler room" operations that used telephone pitches to sell crypts in nonexistent mausoleums. One of them also sent out trading stamps as a lure for the purchase of a phony funeral plan.

Slowly, some relief appears to be in sight for southern California suburbanites. "We are strongly opposed to these operators who use the consumer's own home as the base for their bunco business," says Helen Nelson, of the State Consumer Counsel Office. Impatient for tighter laws with tougher penalties, some consumers and cities are acting on their own.

In Camarillo, door-to-door salesmen have been banned from doing business by the city council. The ordinance prohibits all solicitors and peddlers, including Welcome Wagon, cosmetics and brush companies, from ringing a bell or knocking on a door unless invited to do so. Charitable, religious and other nonprofit organizations are exempt. Other cities are flirting with the idea of enacting similar laws.

Some consumers want more imaginative solutions. There has been a proposal for establishment of a radio car–equipped flying squad for immediate investigation of complaints, before the scam men have milked an area and shifted their operation. Others urge adoption of a law similar to one in Britain which allows home-owners a four-day cooling-off period after a purchase from a door-to-door salesman. If during the four-day grace period a housewife decides she doesn't want to go through with the purchase of the item for which she signed a contract, she can return the goods and get her down payment back.

Of all the slick suburban swindles that have victimized southern Californians, one of the most imaginative—and successful—was worked by an elderly husband-and-wife team from the Midwest. They came, saw and "con"quered.

One of the smash hits of the 1957 Broadway season was *The Music Man*, Meredith Willson's nostalgic tale of a stylish con man who flimflams a whole town of trusting country folk.

Audiences were charmed by breezy, fast-talking Professor Harold Hill, a city slicker in a straw hat ("He's a music man, and he lives like a king.") But theatergoers scoffed at the idea that an entire town could be swindled with the crude pitch of a con man organizing a boys' band to sell musical instruments and uniforms.

The plot was preposterous. Perhaps in the vanished insularity of rural America before World War I, before the national magazines, movies, radio and television smartened everyone up, a town of corn-shucking Iowans might be gullible enough to fall for that sort of bunkum.

But as New York audiences were enjoying the presumed never-never land of Professor Hill among the River City rubes, one Willard Stacy Talbot was selling the same scam in southern California to some four thousand smartened-up magazine-reading, moviegoing, radio-listening, television-viewing suburban families.

As a real-life Professor Hill, Talbot merely substituted accordions for the famous "seventy-six trombones," and added a few modern flourishes. Otherwise, he followed the Broadway script almost page for page.

He became the most successful music man–con man in history, and it was no trick at all for him to live like a king. His scam racked up more than $1,500,000.

It was so carefully plotted and deftly executed that it was successfully worked, not in one isolated small town, but in nine booming suburban communities—Anaheim, El Monte, Long Beach, Pomona, Riverside, San Bernardino, San Gabriel, Torrance and Whittier.

Love and conscience, in the end, rescued River City from Professor Hill. He reformed. But the citizens who were gulled by Talbot weren't that fortunate.

There wasn't a reform-minded bone in Talbot's lanky body as he tooled his white Cadillac along Route 66, headed for Los Angeles, on a clear morning late in 1958. A one-time salesman of defective washing machines, he had conned his way through the better part of his sixty-four years. He'd had brief jolts in Joliet and Leavenworth for running bucket shops and peddling phony stocks, but the prison terms had not soured him on his fundamental belief in the gullibility of the average American.

Talbot had aged gracefully. He was a handsome six-footer with blue eyes and bushy, cloud-white hair. Well turned out in the neat pinstripes and conservative ties he favored, he had the mien of a contented Rotarian and the guile of a village horse trader.

Sitting beside him in the car was another of Talbot's considerable assets—his dumpy, friendly, grandmotherly wife, known affectionately as "Ma" to everyone, including the bunco squads of a dozen metropolitan police departments across the country.

Amelia Cranston Talbot had met Willard as a girl of twenty-two when he arrived at the front door of her home in Evanston, Illinois, selling his washing machine. She had seen through his phony pitch immediately. Willard, charmed and impressed by this wise and comely girl, proposed three nights later.

His bride showed an immediate talent for con, and was soon a thoroughgoing professional. In sickness and in health, for better and for worse, she and Willard had sailed through dozens of tricky, inventive schemes for over thirty years, winning a national police reputation as the "Ma and Pa Kettle of Bunco."

Managing to avoid a conviction herself, Ma had waited patiently for Willard while he did his time in Illinois and Kansas. When he was released, they picked up exactly where they had left off. A jolt was simply one of the risks of the trade.

"Radio too loud for you, Ma?" Willard asked as they reached the outskirts of Needles, California. The tune was bouncy, the sort of music Willard enjoyed. For a man soon to launch a high-volume music business, the fact that he was all but tone deaf would not prove an insuperable handicap.

"You might soften it a little," Ma said gently, gazing out at the rows of neatly stacked ranch homes.

To occupy his mind on the long dull drive as well as from force of habit, Willard sorted through a dozen possible scams that he and Ma might work to kill time in California. It had been two years since their daughter, Joan, had moved West with her husband, Chris Porter, an ex-musician who earned an uneasy living as the owner of two small accordion schools. Willard and Ma had decided on the trip West at this time to put as much distance between themselves and Chicago as possible. They had scored big there against a mark who inevitably would be visiting the police.

Posing as a vice-president of a Pittsburgh steel company, Willard had convinced a well-fixed widow that he was offering her a bargain on several thousand shares of his company's stock. He smoothly explained that he was retiring and needed cash, but if all his shares were suddenly dumped on the open market the price would tumble—thus angering his associates in the executive suite.

Ma, assuming the identity of another widow interested in the deal, had helped to convince the mark of the soundness of the proposition by bidding the price up.

The Chicago lady with the loot forked over $65,000. All she had bought was a packet of cleverly forged stock certificates on one of the nation's major steel companies.

It was a profitable scam, and Willard and Ma worked it from time to time. Usually, the suckers didn't bother to check with a broker until the dividend checks failed to arrive. The scheme thus had the added advantage of giving them at least several weeks' head start before the victim became aware of the loss and complained to the law.

By the time Willard wheeled the car into the driveway of his daughter's Los Angeles home, he had not yet made up his mind which scam he and Ma would work. This was his first trip to southern California and he had heard that it was a lotus land for bunk men. He decided there was no point in wasting thirty-five years of experience while he and Ma were on hand for a visit with the kids.

After a week of happy reunion, Willard began to show signs of restlessness. Ma and Joan kept themselves busy with endless shopping sprees, especially for costume jewelry, which Ma collected by the ton. But Willard was spoiling for action, and his opportunity came in unexpected form.

He was taken aside one afternoon by his son-in-law. Chris had accepted his wife's explanation that her father enjoyed his high standard of living because of his success as a salesman.

Chris told his father-in-law he was worried. Business at the music schools was falling off rapidly.

"People just don't seem interested in giving their kids the finer things in life," said Chris.

"It's a shame," Willard agreed, "every child should have music lessons."

"If I don't raise five thousand dollars, I can't keep the business going."

Willard realized it was a touch. "I might see my way clear to investing," he said, "but before I put my money into a deal I like to look it over carefully."

"I would have suggested that myself," said Chris, "but I didn't think a couple of little music schools would interest you."

"Let's see if they do not," said Willard.

With no thought as yet of using the pair of failing schools as a springboard to scam, Willard began to quietly nose around. He sat in on the lessons, carefully observing the children and their mothers. One thing his perceptive mind registered immediately was the unbounded parental pride in the faces of the mothers as they dropped their kids off for lessons. They had the self-satisfied look of women who thought they were buying their children a ticket to something very special with a few inexpensive accordion lessons.

Willard realized that if this vein of parental pride could be tapped with the right gimmick, the flow of gold might be endless. And he knew that anything—music lessons included—could be sold to a mass market if the trappings were right.

Willard talked his budding idea over with Ma. She approved and added a few embellishments. Next, Willard approached his son-in-law. He said he would loan him the $5000 on condition he be given a free hand to introduce several new ideas into the business. He outlined his plan.

Chris was disappointed. "I'm not sure it's honest, Dad."

"Son, it's honest as rain! You'll see."

"Even if it is, it won't work," said Chris unimaginatively.

"It could make a million dollars," Willard answered. "I've been looking for an opportunity like this all my life."

"Nobody ever made that kind of money out of music lessons," Chris argued.

Whether Willard Stacy Talbot at that moment thought of Professor Harold Hill is unrecorded.

"We partners or not?"

Chris shrugged. "I guess so."

Willard began orchestrating his scam symphony at once. He located a local accordion factory with an owner anxious to increase sales. He visited a number of finance companies and discussed certain business arrangements. He wrote and designed attractive brochures and had a fresh coat of paint and new false fronts slapped on the outsides of the two schools. He was ready now for the first trial run in the field. Willard also gave Ma the go-ahead to line up the marks. She had only to look as far as the telephone book.

Mrs. Joan Whalen had just finished the last of the breakfast dishes as the telephone rang in her modest two-bedroom tract home in Pomona.

"We are conducting a television survey," the cool, sweet, grand-motherly voice said. "Do you have any children between seven and sixteen?"

"I have a daughter, Susan. She's nine."

"What television programs does she watch?" Ma Talbot asked.

After describing her daughter's TV fare, Mrs. Whalen put the phone down and forgot about the call. Certainly she never re-lated that brief conversation with the appearance at her door a few hours later of a lanky, blue-eyed man with bushy, cloud-white hair.

"I'm from the Pomona Music Center," said Willard Stacy Talbot, handing Mrs. Whalen a business card. "It's a pleasure to inform you that your daughter's name was suggested at school for a youth band that the Center is going to sponsor."

Mrs. Whalen's eyes sparkled. Maternal pride oozed from every pore. "I'm not surprised," she said. "Susan's grandmother played the piano."

Willard, now settled comfortably in an armchair, said, "We can't be absolutely sure that Susan has as much musical ability as the school thinks."

A little knot of doubt momentarily creased Mrs. Whalen's face. "To tell the truth, I don't exactly remember any of Susan's teach-ers mentioning her talent for music."

"Those teachers," Willard explained, "can't afford to offend the parents of all the other children who wouldn't know a musical instrument from a plumber's wrench. But I have my own ways of finding out which kids have the talent."

To reassure her, Willard suggested an on-the-spot test of Susan's musical potential. It was a test that no child ever failed, and it was to win a considerable amount of local fame.

Mrs. Whalen called her daughter in from the back yard and Willard opened his case, extracting a small accordion.

"Try this on for size, darling," Willard said, helping Susan into the instrument.

He carefully explained the procedure. "Up here on the keyboard are the high notes and down here are the low notes. Let's hear you play one of the high notes and one of the low."

Without too much difficulty, Susan hit a high note and a low note.

Willard could barely contain his excitement. "The school's right, Mrs. Whalen. Your little girl has promise, definite promise!"

Susan's mother beamed.

"I suggest you enroll Susan at the Music Center for five weeks. After she completes the course, we'll know if she has the stuff to be a professional accordionist."

"I'm not sure if we can afford lessons right now. . . ."

"The Center isn't interested in your money. We are looking for talented children. We are doing this as a public service. There's only a nominal charge of ten dollars for the first five lessons and that includes the use of the accordion."

"I suppose we can manage that."

"What's more," Willard added, "if we find she isn't as gifted as you and I think she is, your money will be refunded."

Susan Whalen began her musical education the next day.

Using the same pitch, Willard soon had dozens of other youngsters enrolled. Business began to boom.

It would have been instructive for Mrs. Whalen and the other suburban mothers to observe the quality of the lessons at the Center.

Susan found the class abubble with a group of noisy, undisciplined youngsters about her own age. A bored, jowly man of forty-five, one of the new instructors Willard had hired, allowed the kids to run wild. He sat at the front of the room, impervious to the din, calmly reading a newspaper. Fifteen minutes of the hour was thus consumed. The next thirty minutes consisted of a desultory skimming of the scale. Instruction was uninspired, and the atmosphere precluded individual attention to a truly gifted child who had accidentally been enrolled. During the final fifteen minutes the kids were again allowed to run wild and ignore their instruments.

Though Susan was immediately bored with the accordion, she enjoyed the chance to mingle socially and cut up with the other youngsters. She began to look forward to the lessons with enthusiasm, an enthusiasm her mother assumed was a new-found dedication to music.

At the end of five weeks, Willard was back at the Whalen home. This time, John Whalen, Susan's father, was also on hand. By now he had been convinced by his wife that Susan was serious about the accordion.

"Your daughter has made exceptional progress," Willard announced. "We are accepting her as a member of the Pomona All-Accordion Band. Congratulations!"

"Susan in a band?" Mrs. Whalen exclaimed.

Professor Hill would have been proud of Willard. The whole elaborate charade he had invented was mere prelude to this crescendo.

"In a few months," Willard promised, "Susan will be marching and playing in the band. She'll be wearing a uniform of red trimmed with gold. We've contracted for our own float in the Rose Parade. And the band will play special performances at Disneyland, Knott's Berry Farm and at hospitals."

The Whalens listened, hypnotized.

"By special arrangement," Willard continued, "Myron Florin, the famous accordionist of the Lawrence Welk Band, will give Susan special instruction twice a week. Mr. Welk himself will attend our concerts and choose the most talented pupils for appearances on his television program. I don't mind confiding in you, that if Susan keeps up her current rate of progress, I am personally going to recommend her to Mr. Welk. Now all Susan needs is a professional accordion."

John Whalen said, "That's no problem. I've a friend who'll sell me one for almost nothing. His kid used to take lessons, too."

Willard Stacy Talbot was crestfallen. "I suppose that's all right," he said, "if you want Susan to be the only one of two hundred children in the band with an accordion that doesn't match."

"Doesn't match?" Mr. Whalen didn't quite understand. "Isn't one accordion pretty much the same as another?"

"A band depends for its effect on harmony," Willard said. "Harmony of color in the uniforms. Harmony of those four hundred small feet marching in perfect unison, the harmony of two hundred matched accordions as those youngsters swing down the parade route."

"I never looked at it that way," Mr. Whalen admitted.

From the large case he had carried into the house, Willard removed a gleaming white and gold instrument.

"The colors of *this* accordion have been designed to blend perfectly with the colors of the uniforms. Harmony, remember, is everything."

He showed the Whalens the "Cantino" name plate on the instrument.

"Mr. Dick Contino, one of the world's greatest accordion virtuosos, has exclusively authorized the Pomona Music Center to use his name on the instruments." (The Whalens failed to notice the small spelling difference between "Cantino" and Contino.)

"This accordion is made by the finest craftsmen in Italy," said Willard. "The parts are broken down, shipped over here, and reassembled. That's to avoid all those expensive duty charges."

He went on to explain that the price of the accordion was all that the Whalens would be expected to pay.

"How about the uniforms?" Mrs. Whalen asked.

"Those will be furnished at no charge by a generous widow, Mrs. Sue Martin, who loves children and music. She is sewing every one of them with her own hands." And transportation to the Rose Parade, Disneyland and all the other places where the band will perform will also be provided free of charge. As parents of one of our band members, you, naturally, will be given free tickets to all performances."

"How much for the accordion?" Mr. Whalen asked.

"I want you to remember that this instrument will last Susan for a lifetime. On the open market, it could not be bought for less than one thousand dollars. But because the Music Center is buying in volume, we can sell each instrument for only four hundred eighty-nine dollars."

Mr. Whalen whistled out loud. That was more than a month's

pay. Nevertheless, he signed the contract for the instrument.

In much the same fashion, other parents purchased accordions. Soon suburban telephones were buzzing with the news of the all-accordion band. Parents began calling the Center begging for a place in the band for their talented offspring. Willard always managed to find room "for just one more."

By now, the first big money was beginning to roll in. Willard and Ma were elated. They began an ambitious program of expansion into seven other communities, buying up cheap houses and quickly converting them into music schools. They also hired more salesmen, instructors and telephone girls.

Lessons learned by Willard in his bucket shop operations were adapted for selling more accordions. The scam, now shaken down, moved into high gear. Willard personally instructed each of his salesmen, taking them carefully through every step of the pitch. Ma ran the telephone network of two dozen girls who made the initial "television survey" contacts. The leads they rounded up were fed to the salesmen.

Then Willard sent his pitchmen out to beat a steady tattoo on the doors of suburbia. Their success was fantastic. All nine communities were soon engulfed in accordion madness. It was the new fad. At cocktail parties, the subject of the accordion bands replaced taxes, baby-sitters and infidelity as the major topics of conversation.

Proud housewives formed clubs of "accordion mothers" and made plans to attend the Rose Parade and the outings at Disneyland and Knott's Berry Farm. The Nielsen rating of the Lawrence Welk Show zoomed as parents tuned in to witness, with barely concealed resentment, the already successful accordionists featured in the Welk band.

Willard now was no longer in the field. He and Ma were far too busy overseeing their chain of schools. Enjoying the fruits of their labor, they became suburbanites themselves. They bought an $80,000 home in a swank, protected community where guards outside the walls fended off the door-to-door crowd (including Willard's accordion salesmen).

Chris had faded meekly into the background of the operation, awed by it all. He and his wife took to spending long vacations in Palm Springs and Las Vegas.

Willard and Ma managed to keep the scam rolling for eighteen months. Meantime, suburbia's initial accordion madness had spent itself. Hundreds of the young students dropped out of the schools. The Rose Parade came and went without representation from a single all-accordion band. Disneyland and Knott's Berry Farm continued to attract millions of tourists, none of them entertained by the young accordionists from Willard's schools. Lawrence Welk somehow managed to maintain his popularity without featuring any of Willard's pupils. Apparent paralysis had stilled the hands of Sue Martin at her sewing machine, a paralysis so complete that not a single uniform was spun off.

A flurry of complaints from the first disenchanted parents cascaded into the district attorney's office. The Bureau of Investigation began looking into Willard's operation. Announcement in the newspapers of the bureau's investigation triggered two immediate developments. It drove Willard and Ma from their suburban haven across the state line and it brought forth hundreds of fresh complaints from other parents, only now beginning to realize they too had been swindled.

Willard's nine schools were raided and closed. Chris Porter and two salesmen were arrested. An all-points bulletin was issued for Willard and Ma.

The magnitude of the scam slowly began to emerge. Authorities were thunderstruck. Parents were shamefaced. Not only had suburbia's mothers and fathers been sweet-talked into an unreasoning belief in the musical talents of their children, but they found the insult to their egos added to the injury of their pocketbooks.

The original charge of $489 paid by the Whalens and the other parents had bloated to a total of $626.50. The additional $136.50 was interest and carrying charges socked on by the finance company which now owned the contracts.

In pitching the deal to parents Willard and his salesmen had never mentioned an outside credit agency. The parents were assured that the local music center would carry the paper.

What Willard had done, once he had a signed contract, was to sell it immediately at a small discount to a finance company. And he didn't waste a moment doing it. David Murtagh, an Anaheim waiter, returning home from work about 11 P.M., discovered that his wife had signed the $489 deal without his permission. In a rage, he took off after Willard only minutes after he had left the house. Murtagh caught up with Willard at the school. He angrily declared he wanted out of the deal. "To hell with the damn accordion lessons," he shouted. Willard calmly informed him that a deal was a deal, a contract was a contract.

The outraged man demanded the cancellation of the contract and return of the check his wife had signed for the down payment.

"Impossible," Willard said. "It's all in the hands of the finance company."

"But she signed less than an hour ago. You couldn't possibly have made the deposit."

"The company has a night drop," Willard answered matter of factly. "Sorry, you'll have to deal with them."

Dealing with the finance company, one of several that Willard had lined up, proved a futile, frustrating experience for Murtagh.

Informing the company of Willard's misrepresentations and calling attention to the district attorney's action against the schools, he still received an implacable reply: "Our company paid $408.56 for your contract and we are interested in getting our money back with a profit. Sorry, but we expect payment!"

When Murtagh continued to protest, claiming he had been cheated and that the finance company was morally wrong in insisting on payment, the financial outfit wheeled up its big guns. The contract, the outfit said, conformed to the letter of the law. The finance company threatened Murtagh with a suit and a salary garnishee. The dun was ruthless, and in the end, to save trouble, Murtagh and all the other parents paid up. Additionally, some parents who had fought it out till the last moment were forced to pay "late" charges, interest on interest piled on during the time they were attempting to redress their grievances against the friendly finance company.

The role of the financial institutions in Willard's con was pivotal. Agreeing with Attorney General Lynch, Lieutenant White, one of the investigators on the case, says, "A scheme like this couldn't work unless the finance company went along. We suspected they knew what was going on, but couldn't prove it."

When parents tried to recoup something of their investment by selling the $1000 accordions, they discovered the instruments were a glut on the market. The accordions were objectively appraised at $100, but there wasn't a buyer interested at any price.

Many of the swindled parents decided to vent their frustration against state and county officials. In Torrance, several hundred of the victimized mothers and fathers called a protest meeting. They drafted an angry letter to Governor Brown. They also signed a petition to recall Los Angeles District Attorney William B. McKesson "unless some degree of justice is meted out to the swindlers."

McKesson, recalling the outcry, says, "When the promotional bubble burst, our office was flooded with demands that we simply arrest everybody involved and pack them away for as many years as the law would permit. However, the matter was just not that simple and it took months of painstaking investigation and work by our Bureau of Investigation and deputy district attorneys before the case was ready to be presented to the Grand Jury."

The grand jury issued a seventeen-count indictment against the Talbots, Chris Porter and the two salesmen.

Evidence at the trial brought out that Lawrence Welk and Myron Florin had never heard of the schools. Accordionist Dick Contino had not given permission for the slightly altered use of his name. A spokesman for the Rose Parade, the special events director at Disneyland and the public relations officer at Knott's Berry Farm all said they had never heard of the schools and had never been contacted about an all-accordion band appearing on their premises. An accordion expert testified that the instruments were student models of fair quality, but would not last anywhere near a lifetime.

Porter, shown by his attorney to be only a background figure in the scam, was acquitted. The two salesmen were given small fines.

Willard and Ma were traced to New Orleans, and Los Angeles authorities requested their extradition. But the Talbots had more than enough loot for a court fight. They won, and were never brought back to Los Angeles to face the music.

For Willard and Ma, the scheme had indeed been a gold mine. Authorities estimate they sold accordions to at least four thousand families. After allowing for the discount from the finance company, the arithmetic was still beautiful: $4000 \times \$408.56$ = $\$1,634,240!$

Moreover, Willard and Ma had got away clean. And though they didn't need the money, they stayed in action. When last heard from, they had bobbed up in Mesa, Arizona, where local bunco authorities were investigating a spate of complaints about a phony accordion school. But they were too late. Willard and Ma had skipped again.

In preparing the case against the Talbots, Lieutenant White had consulted *Grove's Dictionary of Music and Musicians* for background information about the accordion. According to Grove, ". . . the capabilities of the [accordion] are extremely limited, as it can only be played in one key, and even in that one imperfectly; it is, in fact, little more than a toy."

Lieutenant White thought of Willard and Ma and their million-dollar-plus accordion bonanza. "Some toy," he said.

So outrageous are the depredations of southern California con men, that the state attorney general was recently invited to give a series of radio broadcasts exposing the infinitely varied bunco schemes of The Golden Fleecers. *Intended to educate the public, the program was soon discontinued when a measurable increase developed in precisely those scams described and detailed by the attorney general.*

It is hoped that more potential victims than con men mark the lessons of this volume, and that it serves, as the attorney general's broadcasts unfortunately did not, as a road map for the prey rather than the pursuers.

INDEX